KU-770-367

NATIVES OF AUSTRALIA FE

AUSTRALIAN CHRISTIAN LIFE FROM 1788

AN INTRODUCTION AND AN ANTHOLOGY

Books in print by the same author

The Diary of Kenneth A. MacRae (*edited*)

The Forgotten Spurgeon

The Life of Arthur W. Pink

The Life of John Murray

The Puritan Hope: Revival and the Interpretation of Prophecy

Jonathan Edwards: A New Biography

The Reformation of the Church (*edited*)

D. Martyn Lloyd-Jones: the authorised biography
Volume 1 : The First Forty Years
Volume 2 : (in preparation)

Daniel J. Draper

AUSTRALIAN CHRISTIAN LIFE FROM 1788

AN INTRODUCTION AND AN ANTHOLOGY

Iain H. Murray

THE BANNER OF TRUTH TRUST

THE BANNER OF TRUTH TRUST
3 Murrayfield Road, Edinburgh EH12 6EL
PO Box 621, Carlisle, Pennsylvania 17013, USA

★

© Iain H. Murray 1988
First published 1988
ISBN 0 85151 524 x

★

Typeset in 10½/12 pt Linotron Plantin
at The Spartan Press Limited, Lymington, Hants
and printed and bound at The Camelot Press Ltd, Southampton

WITH THANKFULNESS TO GOD
FOR HIS PEOPLE IN AUSTRALIA
AND ESPECIALLY FOR THOSE
WHOSE CALL AND FRIENDSHIP
MADE THIS BOOK POSSIBLE

It will not be by individual aggrandisement, by the possession of numerous flocks and herds, or of costly acres, that we shall secure for the country enduring prosperity and happiness, but by the acquisition and maintenance of sound religious and moral institutions, without which no country can be truly successful.

Charles Joseph Latrobe, 1839
First Superintendent and
Governor of Victoria

The happiness and prosperity of the people is by Divine Providence placed within their power.

If they grasp at wealth to the neglect of their social and political duties,

if, for the sake of selfish ease, they resign to ignorant and violent men the business of legislation,

if they tolerate systematic debauchery, gambling and sharping,

if they countenance the press when sporting with religion, or rendering private reputation worthless,

if they neglect the education of the rising generation, and the instruction of the working classes,

if the rich attempt to secure the privileges of rank by restricting the franchises of the less powerful,

if worldly pleasure invade the seasons of devotion, and the worship of God be neglected by the masses of the people,

– then will they become unfit for liberty; base and sensual, they will be loathed and despised; the moral Governor of the world will assert his sovereignty, and will visit a worthless and ungrateful race with the yoke of bondage, the scourge of anarchy, or the besom of destruction.

John West, *The History of Tasmania*, 1852

CONTENTS

[vii]

Contents

CHAPTER 5

MEMORIES OF CHILDHOOD IN PIONEER DAYS

CHAPTER 6

THE NEW AND CHANGING POPULATION OF NEW
SOUTH WALES

CHAPTER 7

DEVELOPMENTS IN TASMANIA AND VICTORA

CHAPTER 8

PARRAMATTA AND NEW TESTAMENT
CHURCH GROWTH

CHAPTER 9

THE ABORIGINES, OUR BRETHREN

[viii]

Contents

ILLUSTRATIONS

[xi]

Illustrations

ACKNOWLEDGEMENTS

Of the original paintings and drawings reproduced in the insert of illustrations, numbers 7, 9, 12 and 18 are the property of the Mitchell and Dixson collections of the State Library of New South Wales; the miniatures, numbered 4 and 5, belong to Mr. John Campbell; and the photograph of Jane Barker belongs to St. Catherine's School, Sydney. To these sources our indebtedness is here acknowledged. The majority of the line drawings are taken from *Australian Pictures*, Howard Willoughby, 1886, and from *Victoria 1857 Illustrated*, S . T. Gill, 1857.

[xii]

PREFACE

A few years ago, while spending a weekend at the home of friends in Surrey, England, I stumbled on the vivid account of Australia given in *The Southern World* by Robert Young, 1855. Conscious of how little Australian Christian history seems to be known today – apart, perhaps, from the names of Richard Johnson and Samuel Marsden – Young's book prompted the thought, how many other such valuable volumes exist comparatively unknown and unread? This work is, in part, the result of that question. Australia does have a wealth of inspiring literature but most of it is in books long since unobtainable and some is still unpublished in original manuscripts.

In these pages I have made a selection from these old sources. My interest has not been in the development of the Churches as such but rather in the spread of what an older generation called 'vital Christianity' as seen in the lives of men and women of various denominations. The result is no more than an 'Introduction', for there are some subjects relevant to the history of Christianity in Australia which are not covered and little is said of the present century. The subject with which I have been principally concerned does, however, justify being treated in this way. Unlike the present era, the first century of the nation's history was a time of expanding Christian influence and of vigorous churches. That fact has been commonly recognized, even by those who have deplored it. F. B. Smith, for instance, writing of the 1880's, says that the churches of Victoria were 'the only units of popular opinion strong enough to exert power' and that Christians from these churches set the social standards:

The new men were pillars of the Presbyterian, Methodist and Independent Churches and they controlled the State. They had 'Chloe' banished from the Art Gallery, they passed a law banning Sunday newspapers and they kept the Library and Art Gallery closed on the Sabbath.[1]

[1]F. B. Smith, Religion and Free thought in Melbourne, 1870 to 1890, 1960, pp. 258-9, quoted in *The Young Man from Home, James Balfour 1830-1913*, Andrew Lemon, p. 2.

Smith attributes the influence of these 'narrow, austere Dissenters' to their money. The true explanation of their lives lies too far beyond his interest or sympathy. The fact is that what made these Christians what they were deserves far more attention than it has yet received and it deserves attention for more than mere historical reasons. Today the assumption is often made that the main hindrance to Christian influence lies in the uncongenial and indifferent spirit of our age. This book, in showing how Christianity became a living force by the quality of its life – often amidst great opposition – challenges that assumption. It indicates rather that the main reason why our witness today does not attain to equal influence lies *within* the church.

This conviction grew upon me as I prepared these pages. It was only after I had finished that I came across the last work of William George Taylor, his book, *Pathfinders of the Great South Land*.

Writing in the mid-1920's, after fifty years in his adopted country, and shortly before his death in 1934, Taylor's final testimony was to the truth that the Christian Church herself must be revived before there can be any advance of her influence in the world. He writes:

The other day I was chatting with one of our most popular preachers on the distressing problem of the empty down-town church. I ventured upon an old man's argument, and referred to the full churches of a quarter of a century ago. The answer came swiftly and fiery: 'The world has all altered since then. We are breathing an entirely different atmosphere. Men are not to be reached to-day as they were reached two or three decades ago.' I don't believe a word of it. It is the changed atmosphere within, and not outside of the Church, that explains our failure. It does not require that a man should be a very keen student of Church history to be set at rest upon that point. . . . Try as I may, I cannot rid myself of the feeling that it is the Church of God that is largely to blame for much of the present neglect of religion, the forgetfulness of God, the ignoring of His laws, everywhere so patent to us all.

The Church of God is absolutely powerless to meet the dreadful unrest of these days, the enervating materialism everywhere in evidence, until it gets back to its original programme; and, ceasing to pare down eternal truth to the level of present-day maxims and fashions, really girds itself to seek to conquer the world by a definite return to 'the faith once delivered unto the saints'.

At times I am tempted of the devil, tempted to think, 'I have

Preface

laboured in vain and spent my strength for nought', but I am thinking of Martin Luther, and that story of his flinging the ink-bottle at the devil's head. I know all about how he was feeling, and so, when the enemy of my soul comes at me with his 'well-circumstanced' temptation, and reminds me of the Prophet's wail, 'Who hath believed our report? and to whom is the arm of the Lord revealed?' I just throw at his head the glorious facts of bygone days, and with confidence say to him: 'Now, devil, what do you make of them?'[1]

It is time that we all learned again how to 'throw facts' at the devil.

It has only been through the help of many people that this book was possible. Very special thanks belong to Les M. McKinnon without whose enthusiasm and advice on sources the whole project would have been quite impossible for me to attempt. To Mr. McKinnon also I am indebted for assistance with the illustrations. A number of friends have helped me in the search for books. They include Rex Burns, Julian Bull, Rex Dale, Garry Howard, David Ide, Beverley Reynolds and David Schulz. In the same connection, special thanks are due to Eric Clancy, Librarian of the Historical Society of the Uniting Church, and to Sir Marcus Loane whose own writings have often helped me. Barbara Wilson, now serving as a missionary in Pakistan with her husband, Mike, may not recall the first lesson in Australian history which she gave me in April 1980, but her effort is now remembered with appreciation.

For permission to quote from copyright material I am grateful to the following: Dr. Philip L. Brown, whose monumental volumes, *Clyde Company Papers*, provide the source for the testimony of Jane Reid; Dr. Arnold Hunt and the Lutheran Publishing House, Adelaide, for the quotation from *This Side of Heaven*; and the Trustees of the Mitchell Library, Sydney, for use of the manuscript journal of Jane Barker. A typed copy of the latter was kindly loaned to me by Professor K. J. Cable.

Finally I must record that I have had more than usual family aid in the preparation of this title. In addition to my wife's customary assistance and encouragement, our youngest son, James, has found time in a busy period at school to undertake some of the photographic work necessary to the printing of a number of the illustrations.

[1] *Pathfinders of the Great South Land*, n.d. (1927?), pp 67–69, 139–40.

[xv]

AUSTRALIA

A Word of Introduction

First vaguely described as *Terra Australis* ('Land of the South') and then, by 17th-century Dutch seafarers, as 'New Holland', Australia remained remote and virtually unknown until two hundred years ago. Only when Captain James Cook discovered its more fertile eastern shores in 1770, followed by the first British settlement in 1788 and the annexation of over one third of the land area, did it begin to enter modern history. From 1817 the title 'Australia' came into use and, with the settlement of Perth, Western Australia, in 1829, the whole continent was declared British.

Australia had unique difficulties in its development. They included: the ethos created by the transportation of 160,000 convicts during its first eighty years; the nature of the virgin terrain; the irregularity of the rainfall; and the 'tyranny' of the distance not only from the rest of the English-speaking world but between the few towns scattered on 12,000 miles of coastline, in an island nearly 2,000 miles from its northern to southern extremities and 2,400 from east to west. From these far-flung towns, led by Sydney and Hobart, came the separate British Colonies: New South Wales, the mother Colony; Van Diemen's Land (Tasmania); *et cetera*. The end-paper map shows the four Colonies as they were in the late 1840's. New South Wales at that time included Queensland and Victoria ('Australia Felix'), and the original settlement, in a radius of some 200 miles around Sydney, is shown divided into the nineteen counties defined in 1829. In 1901 the former Colonies, as States, were federated into a national government and Australia became an independent nation while retaining the British monarch as its head.

Best known in the last century as a country of farmers and gold-miners, Australia's industrialization began in the 1920's and, with accelerating immigration, it has become one of the most urbanized countries in the world. In 1830, 70,000 white settlers were still a minority in a land of, perhaps, 200,000 Aborigines. But

[xvii]

Aborigine numbers steadily declined in a population which reached 7.5 million in 1947, 12.5 million in 1969 and 15.5 million today.

Estimates in the year 1979 showed the population as being 86% British in origin. The figure did not indicate the widespread change already occurring. Popular culture was being Americanised, new trading patterns indicated more exports to Japan than to Britain by 1966–67 and there were increasing numbers of European and other non-British immigrants.

Australia is a different land in much more than its southern hemisphere seasons, its short June–August winters and its hot summers. Harsh in its droughts, bush-fires and deserts ('like the entrance into Hell', the explorer Charles Sturt said of one of them in 1845), the sun-drenched landscape has often a compelling beauty, with shimmering colours, unique gum trees, fragrant 'wattles' and bird-life greater in variety than exists in Europe.

Australians today are not generally familiar with their country's history, which is one reason for the too-ready acceptance of the popular media caricature of the average Australian as an easy-going individual, of irreverent speech, who looks up to no one. Earlier this century a Chancellor of Sydney University, Sir William Cullen, thought very differently when he spoke of the pioneers as 'men who blazed the track, and who had left behind them descendants who had shown that, in physique, in spirituality, and in intellectual power Australia need not fear the future in competition with other parts of the world'. Such pioneers were men and women who did not believe the 20th-century view that Australia's first needs are for 'men, money and markets'. Rather, they took their priorities from the Bible and, trusting in the God whom they knew in Jesus Christ, they believed that the best way to build a nation is to serve God and live for eternity.

With the rest of the English-speaking world, Australia today has serious moral problems. The nation's soul is starved yet many do not look to Christianity for the answer, too often because they have confused a weak and frequently faithless modern religion with the real thing.

This book sets out to show that true Christianity was once a vital power in this land and that it can be so again.

THE FIRST YEARS

Richard Johnson

OMICRON TO JOHNSON,

GOING TO BOTANY BAY.

The Lord, who sends thee hence, will be thine aid;
   In vain at thee the lion, Danger, roars;
His arm and love shall keep thee undismayed
   On tempest-tossed seas, and savage shores.

Go, bear the Saviour's name to lands unknown,
   Tell to the Southern world His wondrous grace;
An energy Divine thy words shall own,
   And draw their untaught hearts to seek His face.

Many in quest of gold or empty fame
   Would compass earth, or venture near the poles;
But how much nobler thy reward and aim –
   To spread His praise, and win immortal souls!

Verses written by John Newton ('Omicron') for Richard Johnson in
1787 – the first poetry to be prompted by Australia.

John Newton, An Autobiography and Narrative,
JOSIAH BULL, 1868, p. 287

I

Richard Johnson

The spiritual duties of the thirty-two-year old Yorkshireman and Cambridge graduate, the Rev. Richard Johnson, who arrived in New South Wales with the First Fleet in January 1788, were never precisely defined by those who appointed him.[1] He was certainly chaplain to the convicts (568 males, 191 females with 13 children) who survived the eight-month voyage, but he clearly also felt a responsibility for the four companies of Marines and the Governor, Captain Arthur Phillip with his staff, who made the total initial number in his 'parish' just over one thousand people. As the first and, for a while, the only, Christian preacher in Australia ('New Holland' as it was then commonly known), Johnson could say of the infant white population, 'It is my duty to preach to all, to pray for all, and to admonish every one'. Few men ever faced a more demanding responsibility.

Johnson shared fully, with his wife Mary, in all the initial sufferings of the colony. They had probably only just moved into their first home at Sydney Cove – a hut made from cabbage tree palms and rushes – when their first child was born dead in October 1788. Here they lived until a brick house was built for them in 1791. But their spiritual trials were more severe than the temporal ones. Governor Phillip, an Anglican 'churchman' who was evidently untouched by the influence of the evangelical revival, was not pleased to find that his chaplain was a 'Methodist'. Phillip ordered a first service of public worship in Australia at 10 a.m. on Sunday, February 3, 1788 – 'No man to be absent on any account whatever'. The meeting place was 'a great tree' close to the harbour and here Johnson preached from Psalm 116:12: 'What

[1]Johnson is one of the few of the first Christians in Australia to have a dependable modern biographer, Neil K. Macintosh, *Richard Johnson, Chaplain to the Colony of New South Wales*, 1978.

shall I render unto the Lord for all his benefits toward me? I will take the cup of salvation and call upon the name of the Lord'. In the words of a Lieutenant Ralph Clark, reporting this historic moment, 'We had a very good sermon . . . the behaviour of the convicts was regular and attentive'. If Governor Phillip approved the sermon it was not long before he was directing Johnson 'to begin with moral subjects'. There is no indication that the chaplain complied. He believed that saving faith in Christ had to precede Christian practice. In the first piece of Christian literature written in Australia (to be edited by John Newton and published in England), Johnson gives us a clear idea of how he approached his hearers:

I do not address you as Churchmen or Dissenters, Roman Catholics or Protestants, as Jews or Gentiles. . . . But I speak to you as mortals and yet immortals. . . .
The gospel . . . proposes a free and gracious pardon to the guilty, cleansing to the polluted, healing to the sick, happiness to the miserable and even life for the dead.

In November 1788 the boundaries of Johnson's 'parish' were extended by the settlement of Parramatta or 'Rose Hill' as the district was originally called. At first he made monthly visits on Sundays by boat, then fortnightly. In the 1790's when he obtained a horse, he would ride the fourteen miles to Parramatta and include a sermon to the convicts at Toongabbie. (In 1792 there were only 11 horses in the colony. By 1800 the figure had risen to 203.)

Richard Johnson's difficulties were much increased after the departure of Governor Phillip in December 1792. The so-called Second Fleet had arrived in June 1790, a quarter of the 1017 convicts which it carried having died at sea. That Fleet had also brought new gaolers, the New South Wales Corps, a regiment for the most part poorly officered which had been raised for service in the colony. In the view of a later arrival, John Dunmore Lang, 'the formation of the New South Wales Corps was, both in a moral and political sense, the most ill-advised and unfortunate measure that the British Government could possibly have adopted'. By the endeavours of some of its officers, the importation of rum and other spirits (from Bengal) began in 1792 and soon led both to liquor shops in Sydney and to the practice of paying those convicts who worked outside the stipulated government hours in rum. Before it was ordered home in 1809 the influence of low-principled officers in the New South Wales Corps had done great harm both to Europeans and to the native population of Aborigines.

After Governor Phillip's departure, and until a new Governor arrived over two-and-a-half years later, the commanding officers of the New South Wales Corps ruled the colony, and the first of these, Major Grose, was in constant opposition to Johnson's ministry. He positively discouraged attendance at Johnson's services so that at both Sydney and Parramatta (both now possessing populations of between twelve to fifteen hundred people) the chaplain often preached to 'twenty and seldom above a hundred'. No building was provided for a church in either place and it was to Grose's annoyance that Johnson, with helpers, built one himself in Sydney in 1793.[1] When the chaplain sought compensation for the cost, Grose, referring the matter to London, represented the chaplain as 'one of the people called Methodists' and 'a very troublesome, discontented character'. When Johnson introduced a second service, on the alternate Sundays when he was in Sydney, Grose forbade it. As Lieutenant-Governor he ordered the first service (which he never attended) for 6 am and, on occasion, he even had the soldiers marched out in the middle of the sermon. It was at this low point, when, in Johnson's words, 'almost all common morality and even decency was banished from the Colony', that he had the encouragement of the arrival in March 1794 of a like-minded assistant, fellow-Yorkshireman Samuel Marsden, who took over the work in Parramatta.

Equally significant, in terms of immediate influence, was the settlement of the second Governor, Captain John Hunter, in September 1795. Hunter, a Scots Presbyterian, was sympathetic with Johnson's evangelical principles and J. D. Lang believed that if his influence had not been counteracted by the established power of officers of the New South Wales Corps, 'the colony would have prospered greatly under his administration and profligacy would have hidden its head and been ashamed'. The principal opponent of both Hunter and Marsden was Captain John Macarthur who Grose had made commanding officer, in charge of public works

[1]Built of strong posts, wattle and plaster, with thatched roof, it was burned down maliciously on October 1, 1798. Not until 1809 was another church building in Sydney (St. Phillip's) ready for use.

and convict labour, in the Parramatta area. It is impossible to avoid the conclusion that it was the Governor's Christian principles which aroused the evident antagonism. Macarthur scorned Hunter as 'a self-declared evangelist for goodness, for religion and morality'. For his part, Hunter came to believe that 'the sacred character of our Saviour, were he to appear in this colony in its present state, would not be secure from the dark attack of those whose private views he might oppose in favour of the public interest'.[1]

Worn out in health, Johnson was not able to take full advantage of 'the happy change' brought about by Hunter's administration. In 1798 he determined to return to England and, at length, departed in September 1800. By that time John Hunter had been replaced by the government in London on the representations of his enemies, and the two men sailed together. For the remainder of his days Hunter was to live 'universally esteemed' in Leith, Scotland.

On grounds of health Richard Johnson remained in England, serving curacies in Norfolk and Essex before being presented to the united parish of St. Antholin and St. John the Baptist in the city of London. Here he continued his evangelical ministry until his last illness. A few minutes before his death he said, 'Christ is precious', and to his wife – who survived him by nearly four years –'God bless you'. It is clear that the Johnsons never lost their interest in Australia. To an official who had influence in the appointment of chaplains he wrote in 1815: 'I have, Sir, from the beginning, been uniformly of opinion that the morals of the inhabitants [of the colony in New South Wales] should be one of the prime objects attended to . . . those clergymen will be found more likely to be useful in promoting the most important objects of morality, and religion, who are of plain habits, and who humbly yet zealously devote their time and talents in the discharge of their clerical duties . . .'

A plaque erected in St. Antholin's bore the inscription:

[1]An illustration of Hunter's values occurred in the early 1790's when he was court-martialled for running his ship ashore in Torbay. A sailor having fallen overboard, Hunter had turned the vessel round while in a very difficult position to manoeuvre. His explanation to the court was 'he considered the life of a British seaman of more value than any ship in His Majesty's navy'.

[6]

To the memory of the Rev. Richard Johnson, B.A. who died March 13th, 1827, aged 74 years. He was the first, and for many years the only, chaplain appointed to the extensive Colony of New South Wales, and afterwards 17 years Rector of these parishes, where he faithfully preached Christ and him crucified.

2

Letters and Journal of Richard Johnson

A FIELD-PREACHER IN SYDNEY

Letter to Henry Fricker, from Sydney Cove, Port Jackson, New South Wales, November 15, 1788

It is now near ten months since we first arrived at this part of the world. I travel about hours; with much labour and no small cost we have got into our little cabbage tree cottage – no small curiosity it is, I assure you. Am happy, however, that it in some measure answers our purpose though now and then in excessive rains, we are all in a swim within doors. My little garden also begins to flourish and supplies us daily with either one kind of vegetables or other. As to the country in general, I confess I have no very great opinion of nor expectation from it. The greatest part of it is poor and barren and rocky and requires a great deal of labour to clear it of trees, roots, etc, and to cultivate it; and, after all, the corn that has been sown hitherto looks very poor and unpromising. I think I can say none have given it a fairer trial than myself. Have been at work in my little farm for a day together, burning wood, digging, sowing, etc, but do not expect to reap anything nearly adequate to my labour. Others seem to be in the same predicament and all almost, at least with but few exceptions, are heartily sick of the expedition, and wish themselves back safe in old England. I hope I have said enough to dissuade you from ever emigrating to this part of the world. One thing excepted, I should be most heartily glad again to see you on that side of Southern and Atlantic Seas – and what without? Why the pity and concern I feel for these poor people with whom I am connected. Happy would I be were I to live upon bread and water . . .[1] severe hardship, did I

[1]Two words illegible.

but see some of those poor souls begin to think about their latter end. Am sorry to see so little good yet done amongst them. They seem to be destitute both of eyes and ears. They neither see nor will be persuaded to seek the Lord of mercy and compassion of God. They prefer their lust before their souls, yea, most of them will sell their souls for a glass of grog, so blind, so foolish, so hardened are they.

The Colony begins already to be a good deal dispersed. About seventy or eighty are gone to settle in New Norfolk.[1] This took place soon after our arrival. Ships have been backward and forward, and the last particularly brings us a flattering promising account of that island as to wood, garden stuff, etc. Others have been lately sent to the top of this harbour to cultivate the ground. Understand that I am sometimes to go thither to perform Divine Services. The distance is 12 or 14 miles by water, which will make it very inconvenient and unpleasant.[2]

Mrs. Johnson was delivered on the . . .[3] ult. of a man child, but my babe was stillborn and my dear partner, for some time, was in the utmost danger. Through mercy, however, she was at length safely delivered and continues to recover though but very slowly.

I am yet obliged to be a field preacher. No church is yet begun of, and I am afraid scarcely thought of. Other things seem to be of greater notice and concern and most would rather see a tavern, a play house, a brothel – anything sooner than a place for public worship.

HARDSHIPS: PHYSICAL AND SPIRITUAL

Journal[4]

Sunday, December 28th, 1788. Rose about four o'clock. At five took

[1]The fertile Norfolk Island was the first settlement after Sydney. Its population (almost entirely convict) was 1,200 in 1803, while that of NSW was 7,134.

[2]The reference is to the future Rose Hill or Parramatta.

[3]Original Blank. This letter and those that follow are given in *Some Letters of Rev. Richard Johnson*, George Mackaness, Australian Historical Monographs, vols XX and XXI (new series), 1954.

[4]Nothing has survived of Johnson's 'Copious Journal' apart from the few extracts given in these pages. They form an appendix to Johnson's funeral sermon by the Rev. H. G. Watkins.

boat; went to Rose Hill; arrived about eight o'clock; between nine and ten began public service. Preached from 2d chap. Eph. 17. After sermon I distributed some books among the convicts; to several that could not read, I gave spelling books, recommending them to learn to read; assuring them that nothing I could do to further this desirable end should ever be wanting on my part. May the Lord bless this desirable plan, dispose them to be instructed, and by coming to read the Scriptures, may they be convinced of the sinfulness and folly of their past conduct. Returned about three o'clock, and arrived at Sydney about eight. Bless God, O my soul, for this day's mercies and protection.

1789. This morning I got up at four o'clock. Took boat at five for Rose Hill; arrived there about half-past nine. Preached from 1 Cor. 1.7. Am more and more convinced of the total insufficiency of all human efforts to change the heart without the grace of God. Have been now nearly two years preaching, as well as privately admonishing these people; but after all, they seem to grow more and more abandoned. Have distributed many books among them; but this I fear has done little good. One sold his Bible for a glass of liquor; others tear them up for waste paper; – this discourages me greatly. I have no heart to go amongst them; my spirit is sorely grieved to see the misery and blindness of this people. Oh that they were wise!

December 6th. Rose at three o'clock. At four took boat for Rose Hill; arrived there about eight; performed divine service in the hospital. Preached from Matt. 3.12. The weather very hot; my spirits much depressed; and the more so on seeing such inattention among the people. After service, I visited some of their huts; found great murmuring amongst them. Several sick, owing to the shortness of provisions, the heat of the weather, and the hardness of their labour! Oh, that these hardships may bring them to think and repent of their past folly. Returned home to Sydney, much fatigued, about seven o'clock in the evening.

April 2d, 1790. Set off for Rose Hill this morning about five o'clock; arrived there at nine. Performed divine service. Returned home to Sydney about eight o'clock in the evening. A very unpleasant day altogether. And though I have been to Rose Hill from time to time for now two years, I have no place provided for myself, neither a room, a table, nor a stool, and no place of worship. In short, no attention seems to be paid to these things, though I have so frequently desired it. God help me to bear with such treatment in a becoming manner.

On account of coming to short allowance we were brought into a state of starvation; our allowance of provision, 2½ lb. of flour, 2 lb. of salt pork, and often no pork at all, but a little fish. At this unpleasant juncture, the Governor called a council, to know what was to be done; and it was ordered that every gentleman in the colony should take his turn to superintend every night the fishery, to see that none of it was purloined by the convicts, for all had the same allowance granted.

On the *15th of April, 1790*, rose at one o'clock in the morning. At two took boat to go a fishing; had five boats under my charge; returned about nine in the morning. In the first part of the morning it was fair and fine, but soon began to blow very hard, which caused our speedy return.

AMONG DEAD AND LIVING

Letter, c. July, 1790[1]

The *Lady Juliana* brought out from England two hundred and twenty-six women convicts, out of which she had only buried five, though they had been on board for about fifteen months. The case was much otherwise with the other three ships. There were on board –

		Died on board.	Sick landed.
The *Neptune*,	520	163	269
The *Scarborough*,	252	68	96
The *Surprise*,	211	42	121

The short calculation or account given me will account for what I am going to relate.

Have been on board these different ships. Was first on board the *Surprise*. Went down amongst the convicts, where I beheld a sight

[1]The date and name of addressee are missing from this letter. Whoever received it passed it on to Mr. S. Thornton of the Eclectic Society. Johnson's kindness received comment from a number of convicts. One reported that his 'assistance out of his own stores makes him the physician both of soul and body'.

truly shocking to the feelings of humanity, a great number of them laying, some half and others nearly quite naked, without either bed or bedding, unable to turn or help themselves. Spoke to them as I passed along, but the smell was so offensive that I could scarcely bear it. I then went on board the *Scarborough*; proposed to go down amongst them, but was dissuaded from it by the captain. The *Neptune* was still more wretched and intolerable, and therefore never attempted it. Some of these unhappy people died after the ships came into the harbour, before they could be taken on shore – part of these had been thrown into the harbour, and their dead bodies cast upon the shore, and were seen laying naked upon the rocks. Took an occasion to represent this to his Excellency, in consequence of which immediate orders were sent on board that those who died on board should be carried to the opposite north shore and be buried. The landing of these people was truly affecting and shocking; great numbers were not able to walk, nor to move hand or foot; such were slung over the ship side in the same manner as they would sling a cask, a box, or anything of that nature. Upon their being brought up to the open air some fainted, some died upon deck, and others in the boat before they reached the shore. When come on shore, many were not able to walk, to stand, or to stir themselves in the least, hence some were led by others. Some creeped upon their hands and knees, and some were carried upon the backs of others. The next thing to be considered was what was to be done with all these miserable objects. Besides the sick that were in the hospital previous to the arrival of the fleet, there were now landed not less than four hundred and eighty-six sick; but the hospital erected here is not sufficient to hold above sixty or eighty at most; what then must be done with the rest? It was fortunate that a new hospital was brought out in the *Justinian*. This was set up with all speed; a great number of tents, in all ninety or a hundred, were pitched. In each of these tents there were about four sick people; here they lay in a most deplorable situation. At first they had nothing to lay upon but the damp ground, many scarcely a rag to cover them. Grass was got for them to lay upon, and a blanket given amongst four of them. Have been amongst them for hours, may say days together, going from one tent to another, from one person to another, and you may imagine that what I here beheld was not a little affecting. The number landed sick were near five hundred, most at the hospital and some few dispersed here and there throughout the camp. The misery I saw amongst them is inexpressible; many were not able to turn, or even to stir themselves, and in this situation were covered over almost with their own nastiness, their heads, bodies, cloths, blanket, all full of filth and lice. . . . The usage they met with on board, according to their own story, was truly shocking; sometimes for days, nay, for a considerable time together, they have been to the middle in water chained together, hand and leg, even the sick not exempted, – nay, many died with the chains upon them. Promises, entreaties were all in vain, and it was not till a very few days before they made the harbour that they were released out of irons. The greatest complaints by far were from those persons who had come in the *Neptune.* No wonder that they should be so afflicted; no wonder to hear them groaning and crying and making the most bitter lamentations. Endeavoured to commiserate them under their afflictions, pitied them, encouraged them to hope many of them would soon recover; that every indulgence, every attention would be paid to them; prayed with them, and gave some books amongst those of them that were able to read.

You will, perhaps, be astonished when I tell you a little of the villany of these wretched people. Some would complain that they had no jackets, shirts, or trousers, and begged that I would intercede for them. Some by this means have had two, three, four –nay, one man not less than six different slops given him, which he would take an opportunity to sell to some others, and then make the same complaints and entreaties. When any of them were near dying and had something given to them as bread or lillipie (flour and water boiled together), or any other necessaries, the person next to him or others would catch the bread, &c., out of his hand, and, with an oath, say that he was going to die, and therefore that it would be of no service to him. No sooner would the breath be out of any of their bodies than others would watch them and strip them entirely naked. Instead of alleviating the distresses of each other, the weakest were sure to go to the wall. . . .

Journal

Oct. 2, 1790. Oh, how my mind is daily tossed about, wandering hither and thither, and will not come to any thing settled and stable. I am yet in a most miserable hut, and at times find it difficult where to read, pray, or write; cannot but think myself exceedingly injured and slighted. While the Governor has one grand mansion at Sydney, and another at Rose Hill, I am forced to live in a miserable hut, and that built at my own cost; and as for any place of worship, that is the last thing thought of. Oh for more Christian patience and fortitude.

PREACHING CHRIST

To Henry Fricker, from Port Jackson, October 4, 1791

I have received your very kind and affectionate letters, the last dated Feb 21st, 91, for which I thank you.

I observe what you say as to the doctrine preached in St. Peter's, Portsmouth Common, and cannot but lament that any, ah! that many, very many of my brother clergymen go aside so much from the principles and fundamental doctrines held in our established church, and so flatly contradict those very articles which they have subscribed to. But, blessed be God, I trust I see things in a different light, however stigmatized by the name of Methodist, Enthusiast, etc., I am not ashamed of the precious gospel of Jesus, have long since come to the Apostle's resolution, 1 Cor. 2:2, well knowing that, whatever doctrine does not tend to humble the sinner, and to exalt the Saviour, is anti-christ.

But I rejoice to hear at the same time, that while some are thus pulling down (or rather are attempting to do so) this spiritual building, others there are in different parts of England as elsewhere, who are building up the Church of God, and I hope and trust their numbers will increase still more and more, and finally that God will still smile upon our establishment to the bringing of many from darkness to light and from the power of Satan to God.

But I beg your pardon, I had almost forgotten I was writing to a Baptist. I must therefore draw in a little, or perhaps I may be carrying things too far. But I know my good friend too well, and however we may differ about circumstantials, I am persuaded we most cordially and fully agree on the essentials of Christianity, and I am persuaded, that, let but sinners be wrought upon and be turned from the error of their ways to God, whether it is in a Church or Meeting, a store house or barn, a Cathedral or a Chapel, my friend so will rejoice.

There is one part of your letter, astonished or surprised me a little, and that is the ideas which you and others have formed of my returning home to England so early as in a year or two. I may probably have expressed in my letters to you and others that I am sick of my situation and in many respects I am sorry that I am compelled to be in the same mind still, (for never surely was a man, a minister, more exercised and tried with the crooked and ungodly ways of sinners; and few I believe have met with more or greater trials in worldly matters considering my station and office). – But after all, I assure you I have no immediate intentions of returning to Europe. I am persuaded that I am where God aims and intends me to be, and till I see my way home more clearly than I do at present, I think it my duty to abide where I am.

I still have cause to lament and complain with Isaiah 59:1. But I hope and trust I have not laboured wholly in vain, and I trust in time, in spite of all opposition and obstacles, God will make bare his holy arm in the conversion and salvation of the souls of men.

Our Colony begins to increase gently. Last Sunday I preached I suppose to not less than six or eight hundred, and I have since heard that one at least went away sorrowful and heavy-hearted, and some others rejoicing in the Son of God manifested towards them. I endeavour always to adapt my discourses to the state and capacities of my people generally. My sermons are upon the awful strain, as was the case last Sunday. Texts: Prov. 19:21, first part; 1 Pet. 4:18. But I know that this is not the only way of working conviction upon the conscience and see it necessary and find it precious work at times I trust, to speak of the great and inestimable love of Jesus in dying for sinners, and in inviting them to come to him, to believe in and to rest upon him for life and salvation.

After being here for nearly four years you may reasonably suppose that by this time we have become more settled; in some respects I am happy to inform you we are so, as we have lately removed out of our old little cottage and are now in a house as comfortable and convenient as I can wish. My garden, too, is in a flourishing state; but yet in some other respects and especially in my public line, I am little better off than ever. No Church is yet built or even begun of, and the only place that we can procure for the purpose of public worship, is an old store-house or Barrack etc. I have frequent promises and assurances made me however, that in a little time a Church shall be built, both here at Sydney and at Parramatta or Rose Hill.

Rose Hill lies at the head of this harbour, distant from this Cove, about 12 or 14 miles. At first I used to go up, perform public duty, and return on the same day. This I found more than I could well go through; and after some time obtained a room (a miserable one it is indeed, but trust I have at times found it a spiritual Bethel) where I sleep on the Saturday and Sunday evening, which gives me an opportunity of visiting the convicts in their huts, and I declare to you that I have found more pleasure at times in doing this than in preaching.

Another clergyman came out in the *Gordon*, who is Chaplain to the New S. Wales Corps. His name is Bain,[1] who informs me that he saw you at Portsmouth. He has preached on shore two Sundays, but I have never heard him, being elsewhere employed at the same time. I wish rather than hope that he may prove a fellow labourer in the same blessed Cause. As yet he seems to be greatly caressed by our great ones and I fancy is not suspected as being a Methodist. I have need of wisdom and I hope my good friends will not cease daily to pray for me. . . .

STANDING ALONE

From Port Jackson, March 23, 1792[2]

. . . As to my habitation, I am very well satisfied; it is pretty commodious – few better provided for in this respect in the Colony than myself. My principal family complaint is, that I cannot better provide for them. We are now eight in number,[3] and Mrs. J. at this time far gone with child. Our allowance [rations] at present is scanty, and is likely to be still less. 'Tis seldom we can get any fresh meat, and then in general it is at a dear rate, fresh pork one shilling per lb. . . .

[1] The Rev. James Bain, a shadowy figure described by one army lieutenant as 'a peevish old bachelor', returned to England in 1795.
[2] The addressee of this letter is unknown.
[3] i.e. his daughter, Milbah Marie (born 1790), two Aboriginal girls, three servants and themselves. Their son Henry Martin was born the following August.

I did not come here as an overseer or a farmer. I have other things more, much more, important to attend to. My duty as a clergyman fully takes up all my time, neither will my constitution admit to it. This is much impaired since I came into this country, and at this very time I feel such rheumatic pains and weakness that I can scarcely go through the duties of my office.

This brings me to mention another circumstance. I have to perform Divine Service at three different places, viz., at Sydney, Parramatta, and at a Settlement about three miles to the westward of Parramatta,[1] and at never a one of these places is there to this day any place of worship erected, or as much as talked of. The last time I preached at Sydney was in the open air. On the 11th inst. we could not have any service at all because of the rain. Next Sunday, if the weather will permit, we shall assemble in an old boat-house, close by the river side; the sides and ends quite open. I declare to you it is a place not fit or safe for a stable or a cowhouse, and I declare further, owing to the violent pain I this moment, and have all this day felt in my temples, etc., I dread Sunday coming, aware of the danger, and the consequences I have to expect. By the grace of God, however, I am resolved to go on in the discharge of my duty till I can hold out no longer, and then I must give up and leave this miserable people to spend their Sabbaths wholly like heathens.

Last Spring there was the foundation of a Church laid at Parramatta. Before it was finished, it was converted into a jail, or a lock-up house, and now it is converted into a granary. Have had this place to perform Divine Service in for several Sundays, but now and again turned out, and must again turn field preacher there also. I go up to Parramatta, as usual, once a fortnight – the distance by water about fourteen miles. Generally go up on the Saturday, sometimes four, five, six hours upon the water. On Sunday morning early, I now ride up to the new Settlement, preach in the open air about seven o'clock to about 600 convicts. At ten, and four in the afternoon, I preach at Parramatta. I fear, however, I shall not be able to continue this much longer, especially as the winter is now approaching, unless some places be erected for the purpose.

Besides my public duty, I have to visit the sick, which at

[1]Toongabbie.

present, both at Sydney and Parramatta, are a great many – numbers dying every day. Last month about sixty died, and I fear before this expires, there will again be near the same number. . . .

Journal

In *1793*, began to build my church; and for this purpose had to work with my own hands. Went out early this morning with my boat to cut grass; returned late in the evening greatly fatigued, not a convict in the colony having laboured harder than myself. – My feelings almost overwhelmed to think of the hardships I meet with; at other times I rejoice in the reflection that what I was doing, I was doing for the honour of God and for the good of my fellow creatures. Hold out faith and patience!

CHRISTIAN LEADERSHIP

To Henry Fricker, from Sydney, August 15, 1797

. . . With pleasure I can likewise inform you that Mrs. J. and my two young ones are well, myself but middling, but I bless God, I am still able to go on in the discharge of my duty, and trust I still feel the gospel of Christ very precious to my soul.

The path I have for many years had to tread, has been rough and thorny, and have often had to wonder how I have got on at all and hence am led to adore the wisdom, power, faithfulness etc. of God, whose promises I trust I can say have been verified 'when thou passest through waters I am with thee', etc.

'Tis now more than ten years since we left England, a long time to be banished from my friends and what is still more painful, from the enjoyment of the means of grace which I once enjoyed. This consideration often leads me to reflect upon David's case in the 42 Psalm. Should God spare my life, I still hope, however, once more to enjoy with you those inestimable privileges, intending, should God be pleased in his providence, to open a way for me to return home.

Since the arrival of Governor Hunter, which is near two years, my situation has been much more comfortable than for some time before. His Excellency sets a becoming example in regularly attending public worship, and wishes as much as he can, to promote and establish the principles of morality and religion, but I am sorry to add few seem to be influenced by his example. Our congregations, however, are much larger than before his arrival, and bad as things yet are, I still hope that out of all this confusion, God will bring some order.

Have just now been up with the Governor, and found him alone and reading a sermon. He showed me the book, and believe the subjects were very important. I only mention this to show you that his Excellency is disposed to promote virtue and morality in the Colony.

It gives me pleasure to hear that all friends with you are well, and I beg you will present our Christian respects to all that inquire after us. I would have wrote to some of them, but I could not find opportunity. Besides the duty of my particular office I have for some time had to perform the duty of a Magistrate, a most unthankful, troublesome office, from morning to night am I more or less pestered with one complaint or another; should wish much to give up this duty, as it is almost too much for my health and spirits, but in my present situation, I consider it my indispensible duty. . . .

THE FIRST SCHOOL[1]

Sydney, New S. Wales, August 29, 1798

It is from a long and ardent wish that the minds of the rising generation of this Colony may be duly thus impressed with such moral and religious sentiment, that the following plan has been adopted and rules and regulations have been made, which I hope every parent as well as others concerned in bringing up children will see it to be their duty and interest to promote. . . .

[1]Johnson had, it seems, first employed a school master in 1793. By August 1798, when the school began to meet in his church (shortly to be burned down) there were three masters. An official return for 1799 listed 526 children in Sydney with 239 at Parramatta and 166 at the Hawkesbury. In a letter of the same date to the Society for the Propagation of the Gospel in London (which supported the school) Johnson spoke of the rising generation as his only hope: 'Immorality prevails too much among the others'.

1. That this School is to be considered for the benefit of children of all descriptions of persons, whether soldiers, settlers or convicts, provided they comply with the rules here laid down.
2. Any parent, etc., as intends to send a child to School is to give a week's notice to the Revd. Mr. Johnson, that the child's name together with that of its parents may be registered in a book, which Mr. Johnson will keep for that purpose.
3. No child is to be admitted, till he or she shall arrive at the age of three years.
4. The School hours to be from nine to twelve o'clock in the morning and from two to five in the afternoon. No School on Saturday afternoon.
5. Every fresh scholar to pay sixpence at first entrance. – Such children as are learning to read, to pay four pence pr week; those learning to write, or arithmetic, six pence. . . .
8. Persons incapable of paying for their children will not be required to do so.
9. Any child or children guilty of swearing, lying, stealing, or any other idle or wicked habit at School are to undergo such punishment as the Masters (first acquainting Mr. Johnson with the Crime and having his concurrence) shall think proper to inflict; if after frequent correction no reformation be effected, that child to be turned from school.
10. All children belonging to this School, are regularly to attend public worship on the Sabbath Day, (except upon necessary and proper occasions they may be prevented) and to appear clean and decent.
11. The children to be catechized, and to sing one of Dr. Watts's Hymns for Children every Saturday forenoon, and to be catechized at Church at such times as Mr. Johnson or the clergyman officiating may find convenient. Such parents as neglect or refuse to send their children to be thus instructed, to be deprived of the privilege of the School.
12. A Form of Prayer to be read by one of the School Masters, and one of Dr. Watts's Hymns to be sung morning and evening. And it is strongly recommended that parents will send their children early to School to pray, as they are able, for a blessing to attend the instruction given them.
13. The Church Bell to ring a quarter before Nine in the morning, as a warning for the children to prepare immediately to School. . .

15. As books of learning are at present very scarce in the Colony, the children are to give up their books to the Master every noon and evening, except on Saturday, when they may be allowed to take them home that the parents on Sundays, during the interval of Divine Service may hear their lessons, and thereby see the improvement they have made during the week. But such children as either tear, lose, or do not bring back their books, must not expect other books to be given them.
16. The pecuniary benefits derived from teaching school from the time these Rules and Regulations were made to be divided equally amongst the Schoolmasters appointed for that purpose.

A CHRISTIAN MURDERED

To Joseph Hardcastle, from Sydney, August 26, 1799[1]

By this time, I suppose you have heard that part of the Missionaries sent first to Otaheite have left that Island, and have come to Port Jackson. These gentlemen arrived here on the 14th of May, 1798, at a time when I was confined to my room through a long and severe sickness. Upon their first arrival, Messrs. Cover and Henry, with their families, spent a few days with us, after which they removed up to Parramatta, about fifteen miles from Sydney, where they still reside.

During the time of my illness, Mr. Samuel Clode frequently called upon me, and I believe was pretty well acquainted with the nature of my indisposition; and after I recovered a friendly intimacy was formed between us, and I confess the more I came to know of him, the more I esteemed him. But it has pleased God to remove my friend away from me, to meet him no more till it pleases Him to remove me likewise from this vale of sin and misery. I will now, Sir, give you a short account of this painful melancholy event.

[1]Hardcastle (1752–1819) was Treasurer of 'the Missionary Society' (later 'the London Missionary Society') whose first missionaries had reached Tahiti (Otaheite) in 1797 on the *Duff*. Their lives imperilled, 11 men, 4 women and 4 children from this missionary party had fled to Sydney from Tahiti on a trading ship. Samuel Clode, who practised medicine, was one of them, as were James Cover, William Henry and Rowland Hassall.

Mr. Clode had signified to me his intentions of returning to England, and at that time was preparing things necessary for the voyage. A soldier, of the name of Jones, had for some time owed Mr. Clode a sum of money, Mr. Clode now thought it necessary to ask for it, and after some altercation Jones desired him to call on Tuesday, the 2d of July, in the afternoon, and he would settle with him.

My friend had dined with me on the Sunday and Monday preceding, and was likewise in the camp of the Tuesday. About four o'clock he called upon us, sat a few minutes, and then took his leave for the night, promising to call the next morning, and to bring with him something for my little boy, who at that time was indisposed. But truly it may be said, we know not what a day may bring forth; for the next morning, instead of seeing my friend, tidings were brought me that he was murdered – was found in a saw-pit under water – his scull was fractured in different parts, and his throat cut from ear to ear.

It pleased God, however, that this horrid murder did not lie long concealed; divine justice and vengeance soon pursued and over-took his cruel and blood-thirsty murderers. News of this shocking event soon spread in all directions. Numbers of all descriptions of persons ran to the spot; Jones the man above-mentioned among the rest, and was the first to lay the murder upon an innocent person who found my friend in this melancholy state. But this wretch's crime in the murder, and his no less wicked intention in throwing it upon another, were both soon discovered. Suspicions falling upon Jones, the path leading from the pit to his house was closely examined and blood traced to the very door, and making further search in the house, blood was discovered in different parts, particularly in a small skilling, where, as afterwards appeared, my friend was dragged after this horrid butcher had knocked him down. An axe was found with blood and brains upon it, though it had been previously washed; a knife and blanket were discovered in the same state; and, upon examining the person of Jones, blood was found upon one of his fingers. These and other circumstances, fully confirmed the suspicion of his guilt. . . .[1]

---

[1]Jones, with the aid of an accomplice, Trotman (whom he bribed with drink), and his wife, had arranged to kill Clode with an axe when he came to receive payment of the money owed him. In addition to circumstantial evidence, Trotman and Mrs Jones were to confess the truth.

The providence of God appears singularly in bringing this horrid murder to light. A man had been at work hoeing for several days upon the ground round this pit, and in the evening used to leave his hoe in the pit; going to work the next morning, and looking for his hoe, he was surprised to see so many green boughs laid over the pit; suspecting something was there *planted*:[i.e.] some property that had been stolen was concealed, he put in his hoe and removed the boughs, when he immediately saw the hand of a dead man. He then called out to another man cutting firewood at a small distance; three or four others came at the same time, Jones among the rest, and immediately charged the man that first discovered Mr. Clode in this woeful plight, with the murder, and wanted to tie his hands with an handkerchief, and take him into the camp a prisoner. Jones came into the camp with others to bring tidings of the murder, expressed his concern for the murder of a man he so much loved, and to whom he was indebted for his attention to him and family, in times of sickness, and again endeavoured to throw the murder upon the man that first discovered Mr. Clode in the pit. From the tale he told, and other circumstances concurring, the man was committed to prison; but at the very time Jones was thus speaking, another man came up (myself and the Governor and other gentlemen present) and said to Jones – 'Jones, you are the murderer; blood is traced from the pit directly to your house. . . .'

That this unfeeling wretch had reason to love Mr. Clode, you may easily perceive by his wife's declaration to me whilst under sentence. Speaking to her of this horrid business, and lamenting the unhappy end of a friend I so much esteemed, she replied, 'Oh, Sir, that dear man was the saving both of my life, and the life of my husband. His attention to Trotman was such as I never saw in any other person in my life: three times a day he came to visit him, washing and cleaning his sores, and had it not been for his attention, he would have surely lost his hand. Who, my dear Sir, can hear such a declaration as this, but must shudder, to think that such horrid monsters can exist?'

By an order from the Governor, the house in which the murder was committed was on the Saturday pulled down, and burnt to ashes; a temporary gallows was erected upon the same spot, and at twelve o'clock, these three inhuman wretches were taken out, and conveyed in a cart to the place, where, having discharged my duty as chaplain, they were launched into eternity, to appear at the tribunal of a righteous sin-avenging God, and rather execrated than pitied by a numerous multitude of spectators.

In the interim, I gave directions to have the body of my deceased friend brought into the town to a small hut of my own, and ordered a decent coffin and shroud, &c., to be made. Numbers came to see him, and many with tears, lamenting his untimely end. On Friday, his body was committed to the silent grave. The pall was borne by five surgeons and Captain Wilkinson. His Excellency the Governor walked with me before the corpse; and Messrs. Cover, Henry, Hassall, Smith, Oakes, and the Puckey's behind the corpse,[1] and after them several officers and others. After having read the burial service, a hymn was sung, given out by Mr. Cover. I then spoke a little upon the melancholy occasion; many being in tears, and myself so much affected, that I could indeed say but little, but gave notice that I purposed to preach a discourse on the Sunday but one next following.

The ensuing week I composed two discourses, and on the 14th of July preached in the morning from 2d of Samuel 16:17, middle clause, 'Is this thy kindness to thy friend?' Spoke to the general character of the deceased, the aggravating circumstances attending his death (and what these were you will easily judge, Sir, from what I have above related) and concluded my sermon with an exhortation to different descriptions of persons. In the afternoon, I preached from Jeremiah 6:10, 'To whom shall I speak and give warning, that they may hear?' which was intended as a solemn warning and exhortation to the living, and particularly to those guilty of drunkeness, Sabbath-breaking, &c., the reigning vices committed in the Colony; the fatal consequences attending which, my dear Sir, I have long seen and lamented, but alas! I fear all to little or no purpose. . . .

And I cannot conclude my letter, without saying, that Mr. Clode's conduct, as a Christian, was both humble and exemplary; as a surgeon, humane and attentive; and as a Missionary, he spent much of his time among the natives, by whom, as well as by persons of every description belonging to the Colony, he lived beloved, and died lamented.

My friend Henry appears anxious to return to Otaheite. He is a studious, serious young man and appears well adapted for the

[1] All former members of the mission to Tahiti.

work, upon which he was sent out, and, I hope ere long, a door in providence may open for his return.[1]

Mr Cover does not appear too anxious to return, unless a stronger body of people were upon the island, to defeat any evil intentions of the natives. He is, I trust, a person of solid piety, and possessed of good ministerial abilities, and he, together with Messrs. Henry and Hassall, have almost from their first arrival at Port Jackson, gone to the Settlements, established at different parts of the Colony, to preach, and to exhort the settlers, I sincerely wish them every success in their attempts and endeavours.

[1]William Henry did return to the islands. Later he was to become the first minister of Ryde where he died in 1859 at the age of 89.

A SPIRITUAL CONFLICT

Samuel Marsden

I

Samuel Marsden

After a difficult voyage on the *William*, Samuel Marsden, aged 28, and his wife Elizabeth, arrived in Sydney on March 10, 1794. Their first child, Anne, had been born during a storm at sea seven days earlier. 'The child,' Marsden wrote, 'was no sooner born than a great wave washed over the Quarter Deck and forced its way into our little cabin through the port hole'. With no fire, he had to air the damp linen needed for the baby 'as well as I could by putting it between my shirt and skin'. Among the trials which had accompanied the voyage was the one which so many future Christian immigrants were to experience:

Sunday, 29 September, 1793: How different is this Sabbath from those I have formerly known, when I could meet with the great congregation! I long for those means and privileges again. 'Oh, when shall I come and appear before God?' Yet it is a great consolation to me to believe that I am in the way of my duty.

There was certainly little attractive about the 'town' of Sydney which the Marsdens first viewed from the deck of the *William* in Sydney Cove. Around the crescent-shaped inner harbour lay 'an untidy semicircle of brick and stone storehouses, official dwellings, huts and hovels', with the wattle-and-daub church on the eastern side one of the few buildings which they might identify. After for months here, sharing the Johnsons' home beside the Tank Stream on Bridge Street, they were not sorry to move to Parramatta which, at this date, easily rivalled Sydney as the cradle of the future nation. It was ahead of the first settlement in wheat growing, in its formally laid-out 'George Street' (leading from a wharf to Government House) and even, for a time, in the size of its population. For many Parramatta was more attractive than Sydney, and for the Marsdens it was to be their home for the rest of their lives.

Towards the end of their first year in New South Wales, Elizabeth wrote to Britain (December, 1794):

I have met with nothing so bad as I might have expected before we sailed from England. Since we arrived in this colony we have been very well provided with all the common necessaries of life. The climate is fine and healthy and agrees very well with my constitution. I have not suffered one single day of sickness since we came here.

The country is very romantic, beautifully formed by nature and will be most delightful when it becomes a little more opened. It abounds with beautiful shrubs and ferns of various kinds.

But sorrows lay ahead and they included the death of their two elder sons as infants. One was thrown from his mother's arms by a sudden jerk in the gig in which they were driving, another, left in the care of a servant, fell into a pan of boiling water.

As well as his duties in Parramatta, where Governor Hunter laid the foundation of what was to be the first permanent church building in Australia (St. John's, opened 1803), Marsden was also to be responsible for Sydney itself after the departure of the Johnsons in 1800 and until the arrival of a colleague, William Cowper, in 1809. It is said that Marsden's horses came to know the road to Sydney so well that he used 'to throw the reins behind the dashboard, take up his book, and leave them to themselves'. The actual Christian fellowship in both places was certainly small, with a large majority of his Sunday hearers being soldiers and convicts who were present from compulsion rather than by their personal choice. 'I cannot describe our situation,' he wrote home in the year of his arrival. 'All the higher ranks are lost to God and Religion, and you may so form an idea of the characters of the lower orders'. At a later date he wrote of his personal loss in this situation: 'Living where iniquity abounds so much, our civil connection with the worst of men renders our soul dry and barren. We feel little of that vital spirit of life which is essential to the happiness of the real Christian.'

But there were exceptions amidst the prevailing paganism. Men such as Commissary John Palmer, who had carried baby Anne ashore in a silk handkerchief on the Marsdens' arrival, and Surgeon Thomas Arndell were committed Christians. Both men owned land at Parramatta as well as at Sydney Cove. Palmer's wife, Susan, was the first American known to have settled in Australia.[1]

[1]Palmer (1760–1833) who joined the navy at the age of nine, had met his wife during the American War of Independence.

This nucleus of future Christian leadership in the community was strengthened at the end of the country by the coming of Robert Campbell who, obtaining valuable land on the west side of Sydney Cove – soon to be known as 'Campbell's wharves' – became Australia's first merchant. By 1804 the stores at his wharf were worth £50,000. Campbell married John Palmer's sister, Sophia, and, like his brother-in-law, he became a life-long friend of Samuel Marsden. The youngest of the Campbell sons was to be named Frederick Marsden Campbell.

The arrival of the fugitive missionaries from Tahiti in 1798 was also a major help to Marsden. Three of these missionaries – Rowland Hassall, Francis Oakes and James Main – were to settle permanently in the Parramatta area, and, with growing families, they soon swelled the numbers at St. John's. Oakes was appointed Chief Constable of Parramatta in 1805. Hassall, in particular, became a close friend of Marsden's and his son, Thomas, in due course, opened the colony's first Sunday school at Parramatta. In this endeavour Thomas Hassall was specially helped by a former convict, now an earnest Christian, by the name of Smith. It was Smith who also had the expertise to build the two towers of St. John's which stand today as the only surviving parts of the church once described as 'the best public building in the colony'.

Marsden's duties stretched to the mudflats of the upper Hawkesbury river and to the convicts stationed there. Here, forty miles from Sydney at Portland Head, Thomas Arndell acquired land and began to hold services in his home prior to a thatched building of wood being built as a meeting-place in 1803. Services were supported by free settlers who, six years later, put up a permanent church building, 'Ebenezer', the first in Australia to be erected by voluntary subscriptions.

The few signs of increasing Christian influence which Marsden saw stretched over a long period and in his early years he saw very little indeed. Rowland Hassall spoke of him in 1802 as experiencing 'little else but trouble and grief in his striving to do good to the souls of men'. The absence of spiritual response was probably a factor in leading Marsden to take on too much other work. In the course of time, he supervised two schools for orphans and was closely involved in the supervision of the government clothing factory worked by female convicts at Parramatta. To the spiritual care of these degraded women, says his daughter, 'he devoted a good deal of his time'. The magistrate's bench also occupied him. Desperate for men of principle as magistrates, Governor Hunter appointed Marsden to that office. For his subsequent exercise of magistrate duties, and especially for his share in the common sentences of flogging, Marsden has received much criticism. Certainly he was a man of his age in his acceptance of standards of punishment which were sometimes inhuman, but to accuse him of being personally inclined to cruelty is an entire misrepresentation of his life.[1] The fact is that the censure from which his reputation has suffered goes back to men of his own era – men equally supportive of a harsh penal system – and it is hard to avoid the impression that this hostility to Marsden originated chiefly from a hatred of his spiritual convictions. 'To strive against sin and immorality,' he wrote on one occasion, 'brings upon me the hatred of some men in power. We have some Herods here who would take off the head of the man who dared to tell them that adultery was a crime.' Nor was it only the higher ranks of society he offended as the following record reveals:

He was one day walking by the banks of the river, when a convict as he passed plunged into the water. Mr. Marsden threw off his coat, and in an instant plunged in after him and endeavoured to bring the man to land. He contrived however to get Mr. Marsden's head under the water, and a desperate struggle for life ensued between them; till Mr. Marsden, being the stronger of the two, not only succeeded in getting safe to shore but in dragging the man with him. The poor fellow, struck with remorse confessed his intention. He had resolved to have his revenge on the senior chaplain, whose offence was that he had preached a sermon which had stung him to the quick; and he believed, as a sinner exasperated by the reflection of his own vices does frequently believe, that the preacher had meant to hold him up to the scorn of the congregation. He knew too that the sight of a drowning fellow-creature would draw out the instant help of one who never knew what fear was in the discharge of duty; and he threw himself into the stream confident of drowning Mr Marsden, and then of making good his own escape. He became very penitent, was a useful member of society, and greatly attached to his deliverer, who afterwards took

[1]An extreme version of such misrepresentation is currently offered in a set book for the Australian Higher School Certificate, Kenneth Slessor, *Selected Poems*, 1977, 'Vesper-Song of the Reverend Samuel Marsden'. In the 1850's Jane Barker met one of Marsden's former servants who declared that he had been the best master in New South Wales.

him into his own service, where he remained for some years. We cannot give a more painful illustration of the malignity with which he was pursued, than to state that the current version of this story in the colony was, that the convict had been unjustly punished by Mr. Marsden as a magistrate, and took this method of revenge.[1]

While Marsden believed in stern measures to uphold order in brutal times, it must be added that he did not view legal action as anything more than a restraint upon sin. As he writes to a friend, something much more was needed:

The importation of convicts from Europe is very great every year; hundreds have just landed on our shores from various parts of the British empire, hundreds are now in the harbour ready to be disembarked, and hundreds more on the bosom of the great deep are hourly expected. These exiles come to us laden with the chains of their sins, and reduced to the lowest state of human wretchedness and depravity. We must not expect that magistrates and politicians can find a remedy for the dreadful moral diseases with which the convicts are infected. The plague of sin, when it has been permitted to operate on the human mind with all its violence and poison, can never be cured, and seldom restrained by the wisest human laws and regulations. Heaven itself has provided the only remedy for sin – the blessed balm of Gilead; to apply any other remedy is lost labour.

The limits of Marsden's multiplied labours did not end with his duties as a magistrate. The great need for home-grown food in the colony led to a government policy of generous grants of land to free settlers for farming and in this he also participated, augmenting these grants with purchases of his own. Tough and country-bred, he was to become, in the words of one Governor, 'the best practical farmer in the country'. As well as developing agriculture, he and his Parramatta neighbour and enemy, John Macarthur were the first to see the value of wool for the colony's future. For the extent and the financial success of this farming, in which Rowland Hassall acted as his manager, Marsden has also been criticized. Employment which may have been necessary in the hardships of

[1]Here, as elsewhere, we are quoting from the *Memoirs of the Life and Labours of the Rev. Samuel Marsden*, J. B. Marsden, n.d. (1858). The two men were unrelated. A. T. Yarwood's biography, *Samuel Marsden, The Great Survivor*, 1977, is fuller but less sympathetic.

the colony's early years was harder to justify with the passage of time.

Marsden's extensive acquisitions of land for farming did not befit his calling as a Christian preacher yet there is good evidence that it was this latter calling which remained uppermost among his concerns. It was the need to recruit more clergy and Christian teachers which took him back to England in 1807, and this home visit accounts for his absence from New South Wales the following year when the influence of Christian principles led to a major confrontation within the colony. Until Robert Campbell's arrival at Sydney Cove in 1798, officers of the New South Wales Corps led by John Macarthur, had maintained a monopoly of trade, purchasing all incoming cargos and reselling at inflated prices. Campbell's honesty soon contrasted with their greed.[1] The trade in rum became central to the whole issue, and two successive Governors, Hunter and King, were finally beaten in their attempts to curb the power of these merchant soldiers. Captain William Bligh, appointed Governor in 1806 with clear instructions to stop the trade in liquor, was a man unaccustomed to defeat, and in January 1808 Macarthur and other officers came to the conclusion that there was no alternative to the destruction of their profits save in the overthrow of 'the tyrant'. Taking authority into their own hands, they thus deposed and arrested Governor Bligh. On the night that this occurred it was, significantly, the Campbells and the Palmers who were dining at Government House. John Palmer and Campbell's business colleague, Charles Hook,[2] were arrested, while – as Rowland Hassall reported in a letter to England – Campbell's house beside his wharves was virtually under siege in the months which followed.

In this rebellion against Bligh, the officers evidently viewed

[1]When Campbell became the leading member of Sydney's Chamber of Commerce in 1825 and one of the three private members of the newly constituted Legislative Council, *The Sydney Gazette* wrote, 'It would have been impossible to select a man of more unblemished reputation'. In contrast, John Macarthur made the huge profit margin of £557.53 on one sale of 447 gallons of liquor in 1807. For many years after 1808 Campbell's circumstances were greatly reduced 'due largely to his support for Governor Bligh's fight against extortion and profiteering' both in Australia and Britain (*From Sydney Cove to Duntroon*, a Family Album of Early Life in Australia, Joan Kerr and Hugh Falkus, 1982, p. 12).

[2]A window in St. John's, Parramatta, commemorates Hook.

Christians as his main supporters.[1] Accordingly a detachment of troops was even sent to Ebenezer church at Portland Head, arriving during the hour of Sunday morning worship. What instructions were given to the officer in charge of this detachment is not on record, but tradition has it that, having heard out the service, he shook hands with the congregation and declared that he would neither disperse nor interfere with them.

Marsden, who was regarded by the insurgent officers of the NSW Corps as 'a proper incendiary in the Colony', wisely decided to wait in Britain until 'the rum rebellion' was settled. A new Governor (Lachlan Macquarie) was appointed; the New South Wales Corps was shipped home and eight years were to pass before its chief trouble-maker, John Macarthur, was given leave to return to Australia. The whole incident shows the contrast between the two types of society which were in conflict. Yet Bligh's stand was only partially vindicated. In the words of the early Tasmanian historian, John West, the ministers of the British crown, after re-establishing legal government by the appointment of Macquarie: 'fell back into long slumber. Thenceforth, and for many years, rum was a great agent in the working of government, and the source of private opulence. . . . The influence of this interest cannot be overstated.'

★　　★　　★

Marsden returned to New South Wales in 1809 having had some success in finding new clergy as well as two workers for New Zealand, where, as yet, Christian influence was non-existent. He had always entered deeply into the initial evangelical vision for a Christian Australia as a base for missions in the Pacific, and it was

[1]Both in Britain and Australia Bligh was associated with evangelicals. In the words of one of his biographers, George Mackaness (*The Life of Vice-Admiral William Bligh*, 1951), 'Though he lived at a time when profligacy was the rule rather than the exception, and when drunkenness was often considered the vice of a gentleman, no one among his many detractors has ever dared to attack the moral character of Bligh'. Macarthur sought to attack him on the grounds of 'tyranny' – an attack subsequently made more famous by another unprincipled man, Lord Byron, in connection with Bligh's earlier service on the *Bounty*. The propaganda against Bligh in 1808 even included an artist's fictitious cartoon of the Governor being dragged from a hiding place beneath a bed at the time of his arrest.

on this visit home that he secured the approval of the Church Missionary Society for plans to begin in New Zealand. These plans came to fruition in 1814 when, at his own expense, Marsden purchased a schooner and took three English missionaries and their families across the Tasman Sea. Eight Maoris came with them in support and on arrival one of them interpreted after Marsden had preached from, 'Behold, I bring you glad tidings of great joy'. The date was December 25, 1814 – 'The first Sunday on which the one true God was worshipped in New Zealand since the creation'. Surveying the need of his vast audience, says Marsden, 'I felt my very soul melt within me'.

New Zealand was to be the scene of Marsden's greatest spiritual encouragement in the southern hemisphere. The response among the Maoris, both now and later, was to him a matter of supreme joy, contrasting as it did to the indifference in New South Wales and the many failures experienced in attempts to help the Australian Aborigines. Not long after Marsden's return from his first of seven visits to New Zealand he wrote in June 1815:

It is wonderful how Divine Providence opens a way for me to accomplish my desire for the promotion of the Gospel. For many years I had ardently wished to visit New Zealand, but I had neither pecuniary means, nor could I obtain permission from the Government here. . . .

My own life has been checkered with various scenes. I have seen much of the kind providence of God in times of danger and trouble. Had I known the warfare I should have had to maintain in the beginning of the Christian life, I should have chosen strangling and death rather than enter upon it. However, one contest over and another comes; by and bye they will all have an end. . . .

Such was the spiritual opposition in New South Wales that more than twenty years after his first arrival Marsden was sometimes still almost ready to give up. As he confessed to his people at Parramatta: 'My soul has been so vexed within me for the wickedness of some of this Colony that I have been strongly tempted to leave it altogether. I have wished myself in any corner of the world, only let me get away from this present society!'

On one occasion at this date Marsden raised the possibility of returning to Britain with his wife. At which, as he related to a friend, she demanded, 'What will New Zealand do?' and 'What will the missionaries in Otaheite do?'. Confessing in the same letter, 'My burden is sometimes more than I can bear', he went on:

We have need of patience in this miserable world and to look for our reward in the next. We are not to have it here. I have seen much of men and human things. Few have had to contend for twenty years as I have done with men of all kinds and spotted with all crimes. I have seen human nature in all its various colours, and I am led to think that the miseries of hell will be greatly increased by all restraints being removed from the minds of the wicked. . . .

Marsden did play a key role in the era of missions in the South Pacific which was now beginning. 'His unwearied diligence calls for the highest praise,' wrote one Tahiti missionary in 1817. Others saw the New Zealand mission as 'the great work' of his life.[1]

In missionary endeavour Marsden made generous use of his own money. Many benefited from the help which his success in farming enabled him to provide. The following letter to the Rev. Josiah Pratt, Secretary of the Church Missionary Society in London, gives some interesting personal details and an idea of how Marsden viewed the measure of prosperity which he had received:

I believe in the year 1786 I first turned my attention to the ministry, and from the year 1787 to 1793 I received pecuniary assistance, more or less, from the Elland Society, but to what amount I never knew.[2] First I studied under the Rev. S. Stores, near Leeds. In 1788, I went to the late Rev. Joseph Milner, and remained two years with him. From Hull I went to Cambridge, and in 1793 I left Cambridge, was ordained, and came out to New South Wales. I shall be much obliged to you to learn, if you can, the amount of my expenses to the Elland Society. I have always considered *that* a just debt, which I ought to pay. If you can send me the amount I shall be much obliged to you. I purpose to pay the amount from time to time, in sums not less than 50*l*. per annum. When I close the Society's accounts on the 31st of December next, I will give your Society credit for 50*l*., and will thank you to pay the same to the Elland Society on my account. When I know the whole amount, I will then inform you how I purpose to

[1]On this subject see *Marsden and the Missions, Prelude to Waitangi*, Eric Ramsden, 1936.
[2]The Elland Society was a group of evangelicals in the North of England who gave financial help for the training of suitable men for the ministry of the Church of England.

liquidate it. Should the Elland Society not be in existence, I have to request that the Church Missionary Society will assist some pious young man with a loan, per annum, of not less than 50*l*., to get into the church as a missionary. In the midst of all my difficulties God has always blessed my basket and my store, and prospered me in all that I have set my hand unto. The greatest part of my property is in the charge of common felons, more than a hundred miles from my house, in the woods, and much of it I never saw, yet it has been taken care of, and will be. A kind providence has watched over all that I have had, and I can truly say I feel no more concern about my sheep and cattle than if they were under my own eye. I have never once visited the place where many of them are, having no time to do this. We may trust God with all we have. I wish to be thankful to him who has poured out his benefits upon me and mine.

In his latter years in New South Wales Marsden had an increasing number of Anglican colleagues but their principles were not always the same as those of the first two chaplains. It seems that other appointments were deliberately made to reduce the offence given to nominal Christians by a resolute evangelicalism. In 1825 the Rev. Thomas Hobbes Scott was appointed to the new office of Archdeacon of New South Wales. In Lang's opinion Scott viewed religion 'as a mere matter of state policy. . . . Of the doctrines and practice which constitute what is styled by the Christian world *evangelical religion*, Mr. Scott had no idea'. In 1829 Scott was succeeded by William Grant Broughton who, in 1836, was consecrated as the first Bishop of Australia. Marsden remained 'Senior Chaplain', being still at this date in sole charge of St. John's, Parramatta. In the words of his biographer: 'He had never sought either honours, wealth, or preferment for himself'. When a person once expressed surprise to him that he had been slighted by the appointment of Broughton, he replied, 'It is better as it is; I am an old man; my work is almost done'.

In Marsden's last years his thoughts often turned to the old friends he had once known in England and who were now among 'the good men I expect soon to meet in heaven'. The list, which he would sometimes count on his fingers, included such men as William Romaine, John Newton, Rowland Hill and Charles Simeon.

An incident which occurred late in his life is a fine illustration of the kind of man that he was. As Bishop Broughton was to visit his

[38]

home on a particular day, Marsden rode to the barracks at Parramatta to invite one of the officers and his wife to dinner with them. The lady, noticing that his face had none of its usual cheerfulness, asked what was distressing him. The reason was that down the road he had found a man lying drunk in the road. He was long accustomed to the sight of depravity but it had not ceased to move him. Speaking of the answer which Marsden gave to the officer's wife, his biographer records her memories of that event:

He gave us the unhappy cause, and turning his horse's head round to leave us, he uttered with deep emotion –

Why was I made to hear thy voice
And enter while there's room?

Throughout the day the subject dwelt upon his mind; after dinner the conversation turned to it, and he was casually asked who was the author of the hymn he had quoted in the morning. He shook his head and said, 'I cannot tell, perhaps it was Watts, or Wesley,' and several hymn books were produced in which the bishop and others instituted a fruitless search, the bishop at length saying, 'I can't find the hymn, Mr. Marsden.'[1] 'Can't you, sir,' was the reply, 'that is a pity, for it is a good hymn, sir – says what the Bible says, free sovereign grace for poor sinners. No self-righteous man can get into heaven, sir, he would rather starve than take the free gift.' In the course of the day the conversation turning upon New Zealand, the bishop expressed the opinion, once almost universal though now happily exploded, an opinion, too, which Mr. Marsden himself had regarded with some favour in his younger days, that civilization must precede the introduction of the gospel; and his lordship argued, as Mr. Marsden himself had argued thirty years before, in favour of expanding the mind of savages by the introduction of arts and sciences, being impressed with the idea that it was impossible to present the gospel with success to minds wholly unenlightened. Mr. Marsden's answer is thus recorded – 'Civilization is not necessary before Christianity, sir; do both together if you will, but you will find civilization follow Christianity, easier than Christianity to follow civilization. Tell a poor heathen of his true God and Saviour, point him to the works he can see with his own eyes, for these heathen are no fools, sir – great mistake to send illiterate men to them – they don't want men learned after the fashion of this world, but men taught in the spirit and letter of the Scripture. I shan't live to see it, sir, but I may hear of it in heaven, that

[1]The verse is part of Watts' hymn, 'How sweet and awful is the place . . .'.

New Zealand with all its cannibalism and idolatry will yet set an example of Christianity to some of the nations now before her in civilization.'

Marsden died while on a visit to the home of a friend who was rector at Windsor. In the words of Bishop Broughton, he was 'a truly honest man'. The preacher at his funeral service spoke of him as 'raised up in this southern hemisphere and admirably fitted for the work, and made the instrument of diffusing the light of . . . [the] gospel'. In his sermon he reminded the mourners that for nearly forty-five years Australia's second preacher had taught 'justification by faith, the necessity of regeneration and holiness as indispensable'. The message which Samuel Marsden had lived to see established was, in brief, that 'Christ is all in all to the sinner'.

Parramatta in 1824, Joseph Lycett

2

Letters of Samuel Marsden

HOPES OF THE FUTURE

To John Terry, Esq.

Parramatta, October 26, 1810.

DEAR SIR. – I received your kind and affectionate letter, also a bottle of wheat, with the Hull papers, from your brother; for all of which I feel much indebted. We had a very fine passage, and I found my affairs much better than I had any reason to expect. The revolution had caused much distress to many families, and the settlement has been thrown much back by this event.[1] My wishes for the general welfare of the colony have been more successful than I expected they would be. The rising generation are now under education in almost all parts of the country. The Catholic priests have all left us, so that we have now the whole field to ourselves. I trust much good will be done; some amongst us are turning to the Lord. Our churches are well attended, which is promising and encouraging to us. My colleagues are men of piety and four of the schoolmasters. This will become a great country in time, it is much favoured in its soil and climate. I am very anxious for the instruction of the New Zealanders; they are a noble race, vastly superior in understanding to anything you can imagine a savage nation could attain. Mr. Hall, who was in Hull, and came out with us with an intention to proceed to New Zealand as a missionary, has not yet proceeded, in consequence of a melancholy difference between the natives of that island and the crew of a ship called the *Boyd*. The ship was burnt, and all the crew murdered;

[1]A reference to the deposition of Governor Bligh by officers of the New South Wales Corps in 1808.

our people, it appears, were the first aggressors, and dearly paid for their conduct towards the natives by the loss of their lives and ship. I do not think that this awful event will prevent the establishment of a mission at New Zealand. Time must be allowed for the difference to be made up, and for confidence to be restored. I wrote a letter to Mr. Hardcastle, and another to Rev. J. Pratt, Secretary to the Society for Missions to Africa and the East, and have pointed out to them the necessity of having a ship constantly employed in visiting the islands in the South Seas, for the convenience, safety, and protection of the missionaries, either at Otaheite and New Zealand, or at any other island upon which they may reside.

THE CHRISTIAN'S NEEDS IN AUSTRALIA

Parramatta, December 26, 1824.

DEAR MRS. F., – I received your kind letter by Mr. Franklane, and was happy to learn that you and your little boy were well. The circumstance to which you allude is not worthy to be had in recollection for a single moment, and I hope you will blot it out of your remembrance for ever; we are so weak and foolish, and I may add sinful, that we allow real or imaginary trifles to vex and tease our minds, while subjects of eternal moment make little impression upon us. It is a matter of no moment to our great adversary, if he can only divert our minds from attending to the best things. He wishes at all times 'a root of bitterness' should 'spring up' in our minds, as this will eat like a canker every pious feeling, every Christian disposition. 'Learn of me,' says our blessed Lord, 'for I am meek and lowly in heart, and ye shall find rest unto your souls.' 'The meek will he guide in judgment, and the meek will he teach his way.' It is for want of this meekness, this humility of mind, that we are soon angry. The apostle exhorts us 'to be kindly affectioned one towards another,' and live in unity and godly love, and 'bear ye one another's burdens, and so fulfil the law of Christ.' Situated as you are, remote from all Christian society, and from the public ordinances of religion, you will want, in a very especial manner, the consolations which can only be derived from the Holy Scriptures. You are in a barren and thirsty land where no water is; you have none to give you to drink the waters of Bethlehem, and you must not be surprised if you grow weary and faint in your mind. Though God is everywhere, and his presence fills heaven and earth, yet all places are not equally favourable for the growth of religion in our souls. We want Christian society; we want the public ordinances; we want social worship. All these are needful to keep up the life of God in our souls. Without communion and fellowship with God, without our souls are going forth after him, we cannot be easy, we cannot be happy; we are dissatisfied with ourselves, and with all around us. A little matter puts us out of humour, Satan easily gains an advantage over us, we become a prey to discontent, to murmuring, and are prone to overlook all the great things the Lord hath done for us. Under your peculiar circumstances you will require much prayer, and much watchfulness; religion is a very tender plant, it is soon injured, it requires much nourishing in the most favourable situations, but it calls for more attention where it is more exposed to blights and storms. A plant removed from a rich cultivated soil, into a barren uncultivated spot soon droops and pines away. I hope this will not be the case with you, though you must expect to feel some change in your feelings of a religious nature. Without much care the sabbaths will be a weariness; instead of your soul being nourished and fed upon this day, it will sicken, languish, and pine. I most sincerely wish you had the gospel preached unto you; this would be the greatest blessing, but it cannot be at present. There is no man to care for your souls, you have no shepherd to watch over you, and must consider yourselves as sheep without a shepherd. You know how easily sheep are scattered, how they wander when left to themselves, how soon the wolves destroy them. It is impossible to calculate the loss you must suffer, for want of the public ordinances of religion. My people, says God, perish for lack of knowledge. You know it is true that there is a Saviour, you have your Bible to instruct you, and you have gained much knowledge of Divine things, but still you will want feeding on the bread of life, you will want Jesus to be set before your eyes continually as crucified. You will want eternal things to be impressed upon your minds from time to time. Though you know these things, yet you will require to have your minds stirred up by being put in remembrance of these things. As you cannot enjoy the public ordinances, I would have you to have stated times for reading the Scriptures and private prayer; these means God may bless to your soul. Isaac lived in a retired situation, he had no public ordinances to attend, but we are told he planted a grove, and built an altar, and called upon the name of the Lord. This you have within your power to do. Imitate his example, labour to possess his precious faith, and then it will be a matter of little importance where you dwell. With the Saviour you will be happy, without him you never can be. When you once believe on him, when he becomes precious to your soul, then you will seek all your happiness in him. May the Father of mercies give you a right judgement in all things, lead you to build your hopes of a blessed immortality upon that chief corner stone, which he hath laid in Zion; then you will never be ashamed through the countless ages of eternity.

Mrs. M. and my family unite in kind regards to you, wishing you every blessing that the upper and nether springs can afford.

TESTIMONY IN OLD-AGE

Parramatta, August 27, 1833.

MY DEAR MRS. GOOD,[1] – We received Miss Good's letter, which gave us much concern to learn that you had met with such severe trials. . . . How mysterious are the ways of God! We cannot comprehend them now, but we are assured, that what we know not at present we shall know hereafter. Our heavenly Father has promised that all things shall work together for good to them that love God, and the Scriptures cannot be broken. He willingly suffers none of his children to be afflicted. In the end we shall find that he hath done all things well. At present our trials may bear heavy upon us, but St. Paul tells us they are but for a moment, and eventually will work for us a far more exceeding weight of eternal glory. Job, when he had lost all his children and property exclaimed, 'Naked came I out of my mother's womb, and naked shall I return; the Lord gave and the Lord hath taken away; blessed be the name of the Lord.' We know Infinite Wisdom cannot err in any of his dispensations towards us, and he will never leave or forsake them that trust in him. I pray that the Father of mercies may support you under all your trials and afflictions. The

[1]The wife of John Mason Good, a medical practitioner and active Christian in London with whom Marsden had maintained a long friendship.

very remembrance of the pleasure I experienced in the society of your ever-to-be-revered husband is very refreshing to my mind. We often speak of you all, and humbly pray that we may meet again in another and a better world. I am now almost seventy years old, and I cannot but be thankful when I look back and consider how the Lord hath led me all my life long. I have gone through many dangers by land, by water, amongst the heathen and amongst my own countrymen, robbers and murderers, by night and by day; but though I have been robbed, no personal injury have I ever received, not so much as a bone broken. I have also had to contend with many wicked and unreasonable men in power, but the Lord in his providence ordered all for good. Most of them are now in the silent grave, and I have much peace and comfort in the discharge of my public duty, and I bless God for it. I have visited New Zealand six times.[1] The mission prospers very much; the Lord has blessed the missionaries in their labours, and made their work to prosper.

I am happy to say my family are all pretty well. . . . Mrs. M. enjoys her health well at her age, so that we have everything to be thankful for.[2] The colony increases very fast in population; 599 women arrived from Europe a few days ago. Provisions are very cheap and in great plenty. Our number increases some thousands every year, so that there is a prospect of this country becoming great and populous. Your daughter mentions the sheep; she will be astonished to hear that one million eight hundred thousand pounds of wool, were exported last year from New South Wales to England, and we may expect a very great annual increase from the fineness of the climate, and the extent of pasturage. . . . Wool will prove the natural wealth of these colonies and of vast importance to the mother country also. We are very much in want of pious ministers . . . None but pious men will be of any service in such a society as ours . . . I should wish to go to England again to select some ministers, if I were not so very old; but this I cannot do, and therefore I must pray to the great Head of the church, to provide for those sheep who are without a shepherd.

May I request you to remember us affectionately to Mrs. Neale

[1] His last visit to New Zealand was to be in 1837. By that time there were 11 mission stations, 35 missionaries, 51 schools, 178 communicants and 2176 worshippers.
[2] Elizabeth Marsden died in 1835.

and Dr. Gregory.[1] I pray that you and yours may be supported under every trial, and that they may be all sanctified to your eternal good.

[1]Olinthus Gregory, professor of mathematics at the Royal Military Academy, Woolwich. In his biography of John Mason Good, Gregory speaks of meeting Marsden first in January 1808, 'he had just returned from Hull, and had travelled nearly the whole journey, on the outside of the coach in a heavy fall of snow, being unable to procure an inside place'.

3

TRAIL-BLAZING

Samuel Leigh

I

Samuel Leigh and the First Methodists

The arrival of Samuel Leigh in New South Wales in 1816 was to open a new chapter in Australian history. Hitherto the spread of the Christian faith had depended largely upon the fixed ministries of the Anglican chaplains whose many commitments restricted the extent of their preaching. By establishing a wide preaching circuit, and by the wise use of lay agency in the Wesleyan tradition, Leigh introduced a new missionary era. For the first time steps were now taken which made 'the diffusion of vital Christianity' a credible possibility. When he finally left the southern hemisphere in 1831 there was established in Australia, and in the islands of the South Pacific, nine circuits of the Wesleyan Methodists, fourteen missionaries, 736 communicants, and 1000 children in schools. As the Methodists, at this period, exercised care over who was admitted to sit at the Lord's Table, the number in church attendance was a higher figure.

The spiritual success in New South Wales under Leigh's ministry was not, however, achieved by a mere development in organization. It was much more than that. Leigh was a trail-blazer because he believed, with the Apostles, that Christian witness requires men 'full of faith and of the Holy Ghost'. To a marked degree he was possessed with that missionary spirit which cannot rest satisfied with anything less than the prospect of conversions and the reaping of a harvest. Born near Hanley, Staffordshire, England, on September 1, 1785, Leigh trained for overseas work at David Bogue's Academy in Gosport. While there he joined the Wesleyan Methodist Society at Portsmouth, and at their annual Conference in London in 1814 he was appointed to North America. When on the verge of crossing the Atlantic, a letter from Montreal, reporting the disturbed conditions there, stopped his sailing, and it was while he was unexpectedly delayed that an appeal came from New South Wales to which he responded. Leigh thus became the first Wesleyan minister to go to the Antipodes. Leigh's years in Australia were comparatively few. He was there (with a brief visit to New Zealand) from 1815 to 1820 when he returned to England. Then he married and once more sailed for Australia in 1821, this time entering upon pioneer missionary endeavour in New Zealand until illness brought him back to Sydney in 1823. Further ministry in Australia continued until the decease of his wife and his own breakdown in health in 1831 led to a permanent return to Britain where he was able to continue in the regular duties of the Christian ministry until 1845. It was while he was addressing a missionary meeting on Australia that Leigh suffered a stroke in November 1851 and died the following year on May 2 at the age of sixty-six.

There can be little doubt that Samuel Leigh might have served for longer than thirteen years in Australia if his spirit had been less ardent. Letters from England warned him of 'killing himself', but when Walter Lawry, a first helper from home, arrived in May 1818 he was too much of a kindred spirit to be able to effect any change. 'Mr. Leigh,' Lawry wrote, 'is every thing I could wish in a colleague. I need not dwell upon his wanderings in these forests without food, having no shelter by day, and frequently no bed by night. His patient soul endures all in quietness; and the effects of his labours will be seen in after days. By his exemplary conduct he has established himself in the good opinion of almost every one here, from His Excellency the Governor to the fisherman at the stall. We are agreed to live upon two meals a day, if we may have another missionary and a printing-press.'

Leigh could not be other than what he was and, under God, it was his burning testimony and his simplicity of life which, more than anything else, was to make his example so permanent and significant. His joyful self-denial and missionary zeal lit the path for others. Speaking in praise of his character, the Anglican chaplain, Robert Cartwright, wrote in 1820: 'None of us have escaped, like yourself, the tongue of slander. All classes have united in the opinion, and considered Mr. Leigh a faithful servant of Jesus Christ.' Samuel Leigh set a pattern, and Methodism was to be pre-eminent in sending out preachers of his spirit to Australia – men who had no concern to become comfortable settlers, but whose ambition it was to seek the salvation of souls. Many of

Trail-Blazing

Leigh's successors – Walter Lawry, Benjamin Carvosso and Joseph Orton[1] – were, like him, to treat both the colony and the islands of the Southern Seas as *one* field of labour, serving happily in either location as opportunities occurred. Their business was the same in every place. They were wise for eternity, and their forgotten journals and memoirs show that they belong to that number who 'turn many to righteousness' and who will shine 'as the stars for ever and ever' (Daniel 12:3).

Our extract from the biography of Leigh is restricted to the years 1815–20.

[1]Of these three men only Carvosso has a biography: *The Faithful Pastor: A Memoir of the Revd. Benjamin Carvosso*, George Blencowe, *c*. 1858. J. Russell Orton has written a short account of Joseph Orton in Methodist Historical Society of Victoria Publications, No. 17, October 1965, and Lawry's wife has recently been made the subject of a good historical novel, *Currency Lass*, Margaret Reeson, 1985.

2

Sydney and a 150-mile Circuit

'SEND US THE GOSPEL'[1]

Just at this time,[2] a voice from another quarter of the globe reached the committee, saying, 'Come over, and help us.' As the communication is full of interest, not only as it marks the commencement of a new era in the history of the country whence it came, but also as it led to results far more extensive and glorious than could have been anticipated, we subjoin the substance of it:

There are probably twenty thousand souls in this colony of New South Wales, natives of the British Isles, with their descendants. From the description of people sent hither, much good cannot be expected. The higher ranks of those who were formerly convicts, are, in general, either entirely occupied in amassing wealth, or rioting in sensuality. The lower orders are, indeed, the filth and offscouring of the earth, in point of wickedness. Long accustomed to idleness and iniquity of every kind, here they indulge their vicious inclinations without a blush. Drunkenness, adultery, sabbath-breaking, and blasphemy, are no longer considered even as indecencies. All those ties of moral order, and feelings of propriety, which bind society together, are not only relaxed, but almost extinct. This is the general character of the convicts, high and low; and, excepting the civil and military departments of the Government, there is no other difference than that which wealth naturally creates in the means which it affords for greater indulgence in vice. The policy of the present Government is just, mild, humane, and encouraging. The climate is uncommonly fine and healthy, and peculiarly favourable to an English constitution.

[1]From *Remarkable Incidents in the Life of the Rev. Samuel Leigh, Missionary to the Settlers and Savages of Australia and New Zealand*, Alexander Strachan, 2nd edition, 1855.
[2]1814, when the way was unexpectedly closed for Leigh's voyage to North America.

The country is beautiful and exceedingly fertile, and intersected with roads. The necessaries and luxuries of life are abundant, and easily to be obtained; and the mode of living and social habits of the people are nearly the same as in England.

Sydney, the principal town and seat of Government, is populous and extensive. Nearly one-half of the colonists live there, and there a preacher would find much to do. Parramatta, a populous village, is situated sixteen miles up the country, nearly in the centre of the colony. Within from five to ten miles of Parramatta, on every side, are the following settlements; namely, Liverpool, Prospect, Concord, Baulkham-Hills, Castle-Hill, and Kissing-Point. Twenty miles in-land from Parramatta lies the village of Windsor, on the banks of the Hawkesbury River. At first there was but one family of Wesleyans, now we have nineteen persons meeting in class.

We call upon you in our own behalf: leave us not forsaken in this benighted land. We call upon you in behalf of our children: let them not be left to perish for lack of knowledge. We call upon you in behalf of those who have neither opportunity nor inclination to speak for themselves: leave them not in their blood. We call upon you in the name of the outcasts of society, landing daily upon our shores: administer to them that word of life which may make their exile a blessing. Send *us* that gospel which you have received from the Lord to preach to every creature. Send amongst us one of yourselves, and many shall rise up and bless you.

Messrs. Bowden and Hoskins, by whom this document was signed, were formerly Wesleyan schoolmasters in London. They were recommended to the colonial chaplain[1] by Joseph Butterworth, Esq., MP, and appointed to take charge of the charity-schools of Sydney. They agreed to meet in class on March 6th, 1812, and held the first class-meeting on the evening of that day. There were present the schoolmasters and their wives, three of the senior girls from the school, two soldiers, and Mrs. I., and J. F.; making, in all, twelve individuals.

A class of six members was formed at Windsor by Mr. E. He was a native of Ireland, and had been educated for the bar. In a moment of severe temptation, he committed forgery, was convicted, and sentenced to death. While preparing for the day of execution, his heart was changed, and he obtained peace with God. Several extenuating circumstances having come to the knowledge of the Government, his sentence was commuted to transportation

[1]Samuel Marsden.

[53]

for life. He carried into banishment the sacred scriptures, and the fear of God. He was much and deservedly respected, being intelligent, consistent, zealous, and humble. On the week-days he taught a school; and on the Lord's day went into the neighbouring villages, where he read the Liturgy and explained the word of God.

The committee regarded the appeal from Australia as the call of God, and proceeded at once to make arrangements for the departure of Mr. Leigh to that country. [Leigh sailed from Portsmouth on the *Hebe*, February 28, 1815, and arrived at Sydney, August 10, 1815.]

CONDITIONS IN SYDNEY

On landing in Sydney Harbour, Mr. Leigh inquired for Mr. —— and, on approaching the residence of that gentleman, found him standing in the door. Expecting a hearty reception, he walked up to him, and, taking him frankly by the hand, said, 'I am a Wesleyan missionary, just arrived from England by the ship *Hebe*.' 'Indeed!' said Mr. E., 'I am sorry to inform you, that it is now doubtful whether the governor will allow you to remain in the country in that capacity. You had better, however, walk in, and remain in my house until that question can be settled.' The manner and observation of Mr. E. gave a severe shock to a mind naturally sanguine and ardent. Next day, at eleven o'clock, he called at the government-house, and sent in his name and designation. After waiting some time, he was ushered into the presence of His Excellency[1] by his aide-de-camp, and received with much formality. Addressing himself to Mr. Leigh, he inquired, 'Who sent you here in the capacity of a Wesleyan missionary?' 'The committee of the Society,' said Mr. Leigh, 'at the request of several British emigrants, and, as I understand, with the concurrence of His Majesty's Government.' The governor replied, 'I regret you have come here as a missionary, and feel sorry that I cannot give you any encouragement in that capacity. . . . If you will take office under government, I will find you a situation in which you may become rich, and one in which you will be much more comfortable than in going about preaching in such a colony

[1]Lachlan Macquarie.

[54]

as this.' After thanking His Excellency for his generous offer, Mr. Leigh informed him, that having come to New South Wales as a Wesleyan missionary, he could not act in any other capacity while he remained in the country. He then briefly stated the objects of his mission, and the means he intended to employ for the attainment of those objects. The governor, who had listened with marked attention to his statement, observed, 'If those be your objects, they are certainly of the first importance; and, if you will endeavour to compass them by the means you have now specified, I cannot but wish you all the success you can reasonably expect or desire'.

★   ★   ★

Few scenes could have been more discouraging than that which presented itself to the newly-arrived missionary. Beyond the frontiers of the colony, there lay a nation of savages, covering a territory extending, in a direct line, two thousand miles and numbering nearly two hundred thousand souls. In the colony itself was a vast community of convicts, who – 'being filled with all unrighteousness, fornication, wickedness, covetousness, maliciousness; full of envy, murder, debate, deceit, malignity; whisperers, backbiters, haters of God, despiteful, proud, boasters, inventors of evil things, disobedient to parents, without understanding, covenant-breakers, without natural affection, implacable, unmerciful' – were suffering the 'due reward of their deeds', and living 'without God in the world'. The free settlers and squatters were thinly spread over a large section of the country, and removed but a few degrees from the preceding classes in ignorance and vice.

In the mean time, what had the legislature done to stem the tide of ungodliness that was undermining the foundations of the social edifice, and threatening to sweep every vestige of truth, honour, and honesty from the country? It had provided military establishments, jails, and gibbets! It is true that the colonial government, as administered by Major-General Macquarie, was conciliatory in a high degree; but the criminal laws were still sanguinary. Such indeed were, at that period, the laws of the mother-country and of the other states of Europe.

Governor Macquarie evinced a deep and humane interest in

every expedient that seemed calculated to reclaim the convict, or promote his personal well-being. 'His maxim,' says Montgomery Martin, 'was to make every convict consider his European life as a past existence, and his Australian one a new era, where he would find honesty to be the best policy, and good conduct its own unfailing reward. He raised to the Commission of the Peace a few who had been convicts; patronized the thoroughly-reformed; gave others colonial situations; and distributed among them large quantities of land. But noble, generous, and philanthropic as were the motives which dictated such conduct, it has been regretted that he was not more discriminating in the exercise of his patronage.' He suggested and executed several new and comprehensive plans for the general improvement of the country, and the extension of the colonial trade and commerce. He erected many public buildings, constructed hundreds of miles of public roads, and established several model-farms. Without depreciating the talents of the able statesmen by whom he has been succeeded, we have no doubt, looking at the difficulties which he had to overcome, the few facilities which the colony supplied for aiding him in his arduous undertakings, and the bold and equitable principles of government which he permanently established, that the historians of other times will accord to him the honour of having laid the foundations of what must become, in the course of years, a great, populous, and wealthy state.

The changes which he introduced into the capital itself were as judicious and extensive, as they were necessary and beneficial. Each proprietor had been allowed to build on his land when and how his caprice dictated; so that, no attention having been paid to the laying-out of the streets, the town of Sydney was exceedingly rude and irregular. It did not contain one thousand houses; and, with the exception of a few private residences, these were generally small and of mean appearance. After much opposition and many efforts, His Excellency at last succeeded in establishing a perfect regularity in most of the streets; and even reduced to a degree of uniformity that confused mass of buildings known by the name of the 'Rocks', which for many years was 'more like the abode of savages than the residence of a civilized people'. From the earliest times of the colony there had congregated, in this part of the town, the worst characters in the country – the felon, whose ill-directed punishment had only rendered him more obdurate, cunning, and slothful; the prostitute who, if such a thing be possible, had sunk yet lower; the *fence*, watching for a livelihood, by plundering the plunder; – and many who, without great positive vices, were drawn, through ignorance or the want of energetic resolution, into the vortex of ruin.

The runaway convicts were generally concealed in the 'Rocks'. They were in strict hiding during the day-time, and only showed out at night, creeping through the darkness, up and down those intricate streets, to the place of assignation for concocting some desperate deed, or thence to the place of perpetration. Almost every house of the lower orders in this district partook, at this period, more or less of the same lawless character. It was astonishing what numbers kept illegal spirit-shops; what numbers, again, of those were receivers of stolen property; and what numbers either harboured bush-rangers on their premises, or received them and purchased their plunder at night. Many of the constables themselves were no better than the rest. As might be expected, the police courts presented, from week to week, melancholy proof of the demoralized condition of the people. On a Monday forenoon, scores of men, women, and children might be seen, who had been dragged off the streets on the preceding night for drunkenness, fighting, and similar offences, standing before the magistrate to receive their sentences. 'Six hours to the stocks' –'Ten days to the cells' – 'Twenty days to the treadmill' – or, 'Fifty lashes', were generally the awards of the bench. Among the motley group of culprits thus convicted of drunkenness, riot, and theft, might be seen elderly and young women dressed in silks.

In the vicinity of Sydney, and on all the principal roads leading to the interior of the colony, the most serious depredations were frequently committed by the bush-rangers. They were generally well-mounted and armed, and travelled in bodies of from two or three to half-a-dozen. Their main object being plunder, they seldom committed murder, unless resisted in their attempts at the commission of robbery. The numerous receivers of their stolen property, in Sydney, and especially amongst the inhabitants of the 'Rocks', provided them from time to time with supplies of ammunition, food, and clothing; and informed them when valuable stores were about to leave Sydney, and by what roads; also, what gentlemen were supposed to keep money in their houses, and how they might be most easily robbed.

Does the reader inquire what had been done by the established Church to meet the spiritual necessities of her expatriated children, now perishing for lack of knowledge in a strange land? In the exuberance of her zeal she had sent out four colonial chaplains, at the expense of the state. These were indeed excellent men but their attention was chiefly confined to the military and the convicts and, besides, what were these among so many? To attempt the establishment of a Christian mission amongst such a population as has just been described, was surely one of the loftiest exercises of Christian benevolence! It was like entering the charnel-house, and 'preaching Christ, as the resurrection and the life' to the dead. Never was the efficacy of the gospel more severely tested!

A FEW PRAYING HELPERS

Being alone, with limited means and no patronage, Mr. Leigh felt it necessary to form his establishment in Sydney upon very economical principles. The few Wesleyans, who had sent to England for a missionary, had rented a house in the 'Rocks' in which they assembled from sabbath to sabbath for exhortation and prayer. The partition-walls of this building were removed, and the interior fitted up as a place of religious worship. Here Divine service was celebrated on the Lord's day, at six o'clock in the morning, and again at the same hour in the evening. The congregations soon presented a singular variety. Persons attended who belonged to nearly all the great divisions of the human race and of almost every shade of complexion; with European emigrants, soldiers, and convicts.

The missionary soon became known to the inhabitants of the 'Rocks', and well acquainted with their true character. Finding the adults generally deaf to reason, and impervious to conviction, he resolved to make a determined effort to rescue, at least, some of their children from impending ruin. With this object in view, he re-organized the Sunday-school, which just existed, and placed it upon a new and improved basis. Having obtained the assistance of a few pious soldiers and reformed convicts, he soon collected a considerable number of scholars. The blessing of God was upon the institution in a remarkable degree. While the children were obtaining a knowledge of the first principles of revealed religion,

Mr. Leigh was brought into a constant and profitable intercourse with their families.

One of the most valuable auxiliaries in this and in every other good work, was Sergeant James Scott. Mr. Scott was converted and joined the Wesleyan church in the West Indies. The detachment to which he belonged was ordered to New South Wales, where he distinguished himself by the able and conscientious discharge of his duty as a non-commissioned officer. Having seen much service, and being now considerably advanced in life, he was anxious to retire from the army. On an application being made for a discharge to the officer in command, the case was referred to the Governor. On looking at the Regulations of the Army, the Governor informed him, that he could not retire upon a pension without returning to England. His Excellency had a high opinion of Mr. Scott, and, being wishful to retain him in the colony, offered him a clerkship in the commissariat department. He had not been long in the offices before one of the magistrates, between whom and the Governor there existed some misunderstanding, applied to him for permission to inspect some of his books. Mr. Scott would neither give up the books, nor allow him to examine them in the office. When His Excellency was informed of the circumstances, he was so impressed with the integrity of Scott that he at once promoted him and gave him an official appointment. Those gracious interpositions of Providence were regarded by Mr. Scott as being intended to draw him into closer communion with God and His church, and seemed only to quicken his zeal and expand his benevolence. He opened his own dwelling-house for religious worship on the week-nights; and there Mr. Leigh had the pleasure of preaching to his family and neighbours, from week to week, 'the unsearchable riches of Christ'. Mr. Scott himself began to exhort and subsequently became a preacher.

The Lord having raised up two or three lay-helpers, Mr. Leigh purchased a horse, and began to make excursions into the country. A gentleman in Sydney expressed a wish that he would visit a friend of his at the settlement of Castlereagh. 'I will give you,' said he, 'a letter of introduction to him: he will be glad to see you; for, like yourself, he is a Staffordshire man.' Mr. Leigh mounted his horse, and reached Castlereagh late in the evening. On riding up to the fence enclosing the premises, he observed the gentleman standing in the door. 'Sir,' said Mr. Leigh, 'I have a letter from your friend, Mr. M. of Sydney. He wishes you to allow me, as a Wesleyan missionary, to preach to your people.' The haughty settler replied, peremptorily, 'I shall do nothing of the kind.' 'Perhaps,' said Mr. Leigh, 'you will be so kind as to allow my horse to remain in your yard all night, and permit me to sleep in your barn? I shall pay you whatever you may demand for our accommodation.' The gentleman repeated, in a tone and with a vehemence that settled the question, 'I will do nothing of the kind.' 'Do you think,' inquired Mr. Leigh, 'that anyone in the settlement will take me in for the night?' 'I think John Lees will,' said the farmer: 'he lives about two miles off, in that direction,' – pointing with his finger.

Mr. Leigh turned his horse, and rode, as fast as the entangling nature of the underwood would admit, in search of the homestead of John Lees. On arriving at his wood-hut, he knocked with the end of his whip at the door and called out, 'Will you receive a Wesleyan missionary?' The door opened and out came a little, stiff, ruddy lad, who laid hold of the bridle with one hand, and the stirrup with the other, and said, 'Get off, sir! My father will be glad to see you.' Mr. Leigh dismounted, and entered the hut. His astonishment may well be conceived, when he observed a number of persons sitting round a three-legged table in the most orderly manner. Directing the attention of the stranger to some books that lay on the table, old Lees said, 'We were just going to have family worship. Perhaps you will have no objection to take that duty off my hands.' 'Not at all,' said Mr. Leigh; and, taking up the Bible, opened it on Isaiah 35: 'The wilderness and the solitary place shall be glad for them; and the desert shall rejoice and blossom as the rose.' Here he was obliged to pause, and allow the tears to flow, until he could again command the power of utterance. He then proceeded with the second verse: 'It shall blossom abundantly, and rejoice even with joy and singing: the glory of Lebanon shall be given unto it, the excellency of Carmel and Sharon, they shall see the glory of the Lord, and the excellency of our God'; but he could proceed no further. Five minutes before, he had felt himself to be a stranger in a strange land, enclosed in the woods of Australia at a late hour and without a home: now he was in Bethel; while the verses which he had read opened to his view the moral renovation of the world. He was quite overcome. The emotion interrupted the harmonious flow of their evening song, while their prayers, offered in broken sentences, were the simple expression of humble and adoring gratitude. When they rose from their knees, the farmer crossed the floor, and, seizing Mr. Leigh's hand, squeezed it until he felt as if the blood were dropping from the points of his fingers. 'We have been praying for three years,' said Lees, 'that God would send us a missionary: now that you are come, we are right glad to see you. We had not even heard of your arrival in the colony.' After supper they retired to rest, exclaiming, 'We have seen strange things to-day.'

Next day Lees gave the missionary an account of the circumstances under which he became serious. He was formerly a soldier, belonging to the New South Wales corps. After the corps was disbanded, the government granted him a small allotment of land, with some other aid, to commence the 'settler's life'. He married, and soon had a rising family. After hard work, several acres of tall trees were felled by his own axe, and the timber burnt off. His live stock increased, and he began to thrive. But his former propensity for strong drink, checked for a while by industry, again developed itself, and grew on him, till he bore all the marks of a reckless, confirmed drunkard. It happened in his case, as in a thousand others, that one useful article after another went, till part of his land and all his live stock were gone, *except one pig*, now fat, and ready for the knife. The unhappy man was contemplating the sale of this *last pig*, to pay off a debt which he had contracted for spiritous liquors, when a circumstance occurred which changed the whole course of his future life, and, we believe, his final destiny. While in bed one night, and in a sound sleep, his mind wandered to the usual place of conviviality: he was in the act of grasping the spirit-bottle to fill another glass, when, to his terror, he observed a snake rising out of the bottle with expanded jaws, and striking its fangs in all directions. Its deadly eye, flashing fire, was fixed upon him, and occasioned a convulsive horror, which awoke him. He thanked God that it was but a dream; yet the impression then made upon his mind could never be obliterated. He regarded the whole scene as indicating the inseparable connection between intemperance, suffering, and death. The more he reflected upon it the more deeply was he convinced of his guilt and danger. His distress of mind so increased, that he resolved to go over to Windsor, a distance of twelve miles, to consult the assistant colonial chaplain, the Rev. R. Cartwright.

That gentleman spoke earnestly and kindly to him, recommending the reading of the scriptures, much prayer, and a believing appropriation of the promised mercy of God in Christ Jesus. 'Having obtained help of God', he continued in the diligent use of these means up to the time of Mr. Leigh's arrival.

TO PARRAMATTA AND THE HAWKESBURY

Mr Leigh's next visit of observation was to Parramatta.[1] This town was situated at the distance of fifteen miles by land, and eighteen by water, from Sydney. The town consisted principally of one street about a mile in length. The population, which was chiefly composed of small traders, publicans, artisans and labourers, did not exceed, at that period, twelve hundred persons. The situation of the town was exceedingly delightful. It lay in a spacious hollow, covered with the richest verdure, and surrounded by hills of a moderate elevation. Nothing could exceed the beauty of the scenery which presented itself on all sides as the voyager proceeded from the capital to this provincial town by water.

This was the second place in the colony into which Christianity was introduced. Divine service was first celebrated here in 1791, just three years from the first landing of the English. Mr. Shepherd, of Kissing Point, was present on that occasion, and gave Mr. Leigh the account we here subjoin:

The first assembly of people for the worship of God I ever witnessed in this country, was at Parramatta. We assembled in a carpenter's shop near the house of Governor Phillip. The military chaplain, the Rev. Richard Johnson, officiated. He subsequently divided his labours between the barracks and prisons of Sydney and Parramatta. I soon became acquainted with several persons who, I had reason to believe, enjoyed the favour of God. We agreed to meet privately for religious conversation and prayer. The place selected for our meetings was the banks of the little river which flows into the quarry. Here, under the open canopy of heaven, we read the word of God, prayed for Divine grace and the guidance of Divine Providence, and sang a hymn before we parted. Those meetings were continued for seven years. In 1798, the missionaries of the London Missionary Society, who had been driven from Otaheite, landed in New South Wales, and took up their

[1]This visit to Parramatta and travel which followed was evidently undertaken in August 1817.

residence at Parramatta. One of them, the Rev. James Cover, preached on the sabbath afternoon from, 'Behold, I stand at the door, and knock: if any man hear my voice, and open the door, I will come in to him, and will sup with him, and he with me.' At the close of the service, two men from Kissing Point, who had been deeply impressed by the sermon, informed the preacher that many in their settlement were living like heathens; that, if he would come over and preach to them, they would give him a hearty reception, and get a good congregation. Next sabbath, Mr. Cover and a few Christian friends walked to Kissing Point, and held a meeting for the exposition of scripture and the worship of God. Much interest was excited. Perceiving a number of fine children running about, 'like the wild ass's colt', Mr. Cover advised the people to build a school and get them educated. They entered heartily into the undertaking; and, as I was appointed to raise subscriptions, I witnessed the frankness with which all contributed. The house was soon finished, and the colonial chaplain opened it by celebrating Divine worship. We had no bishop; but the presence of the Lord consecrated the place. The missionaries preached on the Lord's day and, after the arrival of the Rev. Samuel Marsden, he came out, and conducted a service on the week-night. Most of the young people in the district were educated at this school and several of them are now honourably employed in preaching Christ in the islands of the sea.

There was only one church in Parramatta in which the Rev. Samuel Marsden, senior chaplain, officiated. This distinguished man was a native of Leeds. He was in early life a member of the Wesleyan society in that town; and several branches of his family still remain in connection with that body. By a peculiar train of providential events he was led to connect himself with the Church of England, and had assigned to him the chaplaincy of New South Wales. Characterized by a sound judgment, fervent piety and enlightened zeal, he acquired great influence with the public, and long commanded the confidence and respect of the civil and military authorities in the colony.

We are aware of the severe strictures of Dr. Lang upon what he regarded as being the secular character of Mr. Marsden, and the incongruity of his combining the office of minister and magistrate. But though we admit, as a general principle, that to associate the ministerial office with the secular offices of state is, under ordinary circumstances, a degradation of the clerical character, yet it must not be overlooked that Marsden was put into the commission of the peace at a time when the government required the most vigorous co-operation of all the loyalty and intelligence in the country. We have no hesitation in saying, that the characteristic prejudices of this writer led him to form and to publish an erroneous estimate of Mr. Marsden's principles and conduct.

The religion of the senior chaplain was not an occasional emotion awakened by some new development of the justice or mercy of God, but a vital and spiritual warmth, shedding its influence over his whole soul, and drawing out its sympathies and charities towards all men. He received Mr. Leigh at Parramatta with great cordiality, and wished him 'God speed!' The missionary commenced preaching in a private house, but some time afterwards obtained the government school-room, and formed a small class of invalided soldiers. One of his first converts was John W——[1]: he was a native of Brighton, and a convict. He was deeply convinced of sin and, after many distressing conflicts, entered the fold of Christ. As he had a small family entirely dependent upon his own industry, he was advised to get a little horse and cart. It was suggested that by putting a board across the cart, he might carry a few passengers and light parcels to Sydney. With the assistance of a few friends, he commenced, and soon became known in the town. The integrity and punctuality with which he executed the orders confided to him, his obliging manner, and unwearied diligence, gained him the confidence and patronage of the public. His business increased so much, that he was obliged to get a larger horse and a covered conveyance. He became a great favourite; another horse was added to his establishment, and a stage-coach substituted for the covered cart. He would not be bound to carry any passenger who either swore or became quarrelsome on the coach. When any thing of the kind occurred, he would pull up and inform the party, no matter who he might be, that he was acting contrary to his regulations, and that he must desist, or quit the coach. He gained more than he lost by his firmness and consistency. The gentlemen settlers entered into a subscription, sent to London for four superb sets of harness, and set him up with a coach and four horses. John's was the first public conveyance in Australia.[2] He had an affecting recollection of his

---

[1] James Watsford. Strachan mistook the Christian name. He was the father of John Watsford, see below, p. 141.

[2] This appears to be doubtful. In 1826 James Watsford was advertising a pair-horse light coach between Parramatta and Sydney. John Raine, in Sydney, had introduced the stage-coach a few years earlier.

early life, and of the distress and disgrace in which he had involved his parents. After the death of his father, he kept up a filial correspondence with his mother; and, as the Lord prospered him, he settled £20 *per annum* upon her for life. His children were also made partakers of the grace of God; and his son, the Rev. J. W., is now preaching that gospel, which, as a moral lever, raised his family to comfort and respectability.

After preaching at Parramatta on the Sunday, Mr. Leigh went to Seven Hills, a distance of only three miles, and preached at a settler's house on Monday evening. A journey of twenty miles brought him to Windsor on Tuesday night.

This town is built upon a hill, close by the river Hawkesbury, which now forms the boundary of the county, and which, after flowing one hundred and forty miles, pours its waters into Broken Bay. The buildings were weather-boarded without, and lathed and plastered within. There was a government house, military and convict barracks, a court-house, and a jail. The population did not exceed three hundred; composed chiefly of farmers and their servants, with a few small traders, mechanics, and general labourers. They were mostly English, Welsh, Scotch, and Irish. They were rude and intemperate; while many of them had completely outlived all respect for even the 'form of godliness'. A sermon on the Lord's day was the only religious agency which the state supplied to check the turbulence and profligacy of the people. The lands in the neighbourhood of the town were exceedingly fertile; but this advantage was more than counterbalanced by their extreme liability to inundations from the Hawkesbury.[1]

Mr. Leigh employed the whole of Wednesday and Thursday in visiting the settlers, in Windsor and its vicinity, from house to house.

On Friday morning he rode to Portland Head. There was no religious teacher in that settlement. On Saturday forenoon he went around the neighbourhood, and published that he would preach that evening in the corn-shed of T. B., at seven o'clock. The attendance was so encouraging, that, at the close of the service, he told them that he would preach again, in the same place, on the

---

[1]In time of flood the river was frequently known to rise by seventy or eighty feet. The Rev. R. Cartwright on one occasion speaks of stepping out of church into a boat in 'one of the streets of Windsor'. A flood in June 1867 covered very nearly the highest parts of the town.

following morning, which was Sunday, at the same hour. A few Presbyterians had erected a small house in the wood, in which they had assembled on the Lord's day for reading the scriptures and prayer. They earnestly requested the missionary to give them a sermon in this lonely sanctuary at eleven o'clock. The news of his arrival had spread with surprising rapidity, considering how thinly this part of the country was populated at that time. When he reached the meeting house, he found several persons who had come thirty miles to hear the word of God. They had crossed two rivers, and travelled along roads scarcely passable. 'It was truly animating,' he observed, 'to see those distant settlers approaching this retired spot, in their one-horse carts, and arranging their vehicles round the house of prayer.' The service brought the land of their fathers and early times to their recollection; and many a tear fell that day.

From thence Mr. Leigh travelled five miles to Wilberforce, and preached at a farmer's house, at two o'clock in the afternoon. When he came within sight of the house, the good woman began to prepare his dinner; and when he arrived he found the damper and tea upon the table. Surrounded by his earnest congregation, he partook of her hospitality, then all of them united joyfully in the worship of God.

On concluding the service he mounted his horse, and rode five miles further to Windsor, where he preached again in the evening at seven o'clock. Having travelled twenty miles, and conducted four public services, he retired to rest, at a late hour, wearied, but happy.

On the following day he rode to Richmond, a distance of only three miles, where he preached in a private house. It was then a rising town, and contained a considerable population. 'The scenery around the town,' said Mr. Leigh, 'is varied and beautiful in a high degree. I was astonished when I crossed the main street, and, for the first time, looked down on the celebrated Australian river, the Hawkesbury, as it flowed, smooth and deep, at the other side of the eminence on which the settlement stands.' There was nothing, however, in the moral or religious condition of the people in harmony with the beautiful arrangements of nature or the fruitfulness of the soil. Yet, notwithstanding the ignorance and licentiousness which every where abounded, the commencement of the labours of the missionary was regarded as forming a new era in the history of their township.

On Tuesday morning he set out for Castlereagh. His road lay parallel with the Blue Mountains. He held several religious services at the huts of the settlers on his way, and concluded the day with a sermon at the house of John Lees in the evening.

On the day following he left Mr. Lees at an early hour, for Macquarie Grove, the residence of Mr. Hassall, where he arrived in time to hold an evening service.[1] This was a dangerous and fatiguing journey. He had to find his way through one unbroken forest, without road or path of any kind, for thirty miles. He had to force his horse between the trees and through the entangled brushwood, frequently using his axe, and directing his course by the sun, whose rays were so condensed in the wood that the brass mountings of the saddle burned the hand on being touched.

He rode to Liverpool on Thursday, a distance of twenty miles. The town was then in its infancy, having been founded by Governor Macquarie about the time that Mr. Leigh received his appointment to New South Wales. On his arrival, he found the usual accompaniments of a town in that colony – barracks for soldiers and convicts, several settlers, a few traders, artisans, publicans, and labourers. There was no place of worship. A small weather-boarded school-room had been built, a short time before, by subscription. Here Mr. Leigh preached his first sermon, and promised to visit them again as soon as possible. On the following day, Friday, he returned to Sydney. He had now traversed the most important and populous districts in the colony, and made arrangements for supplying them with regular services at convenient intervals.

FIRST REPORTS HOME

So soon as the sphere of his labours had assumed a definite shape, he made the following communication to the committee:

I have just returned from my eighth tour through the different colonial settlements. My circuit extends one hundred and fifty miles, which distance I travel in ten days. I have fourteen preaching-stations, and have formed six classes – three in Sydney, one at Parramatta, one at

[1] Macquarie Grove was the farm of Rowland Hassall.

Windsor, and one at Castlereagh. We have established four Sunday-schools which are in a satisfactory state. When I go into the country on the Sunday, I preach at ten o'clock in the morning; dine, ride seven miles, and preach at two; ride six miles, and preach at five, from thence I ride six miles more, and preach at seven in the evening. My constitution, I fear, will not long stand so much exertion in the heat of the day. But what can I do? The sight of the people flocking to the house of God, some with chairs and others with stools on their shoulders to sit upon, urges me to persevere; and, while I am praying and weeping for their salvation, I forget my fatigue. A poor man walked fourteen miles the other day to converse with me about his soul. We want chapels at several places and more missionaries. The state of society here is awful. With regard to myself, I desire to live every moment to God, and to die in the missionary field.

To a correspondent in India he writes: 'Our place of worship in Sydney will hold about two hundred people, and it is generally crowded. I can only supply the country places once in three weeks. The clergy give me every encouragement. I have fifty-eight communicants.'

At this period Mr. Leigh was peculiarly buoyant, and confident of ultimate success. In writing to his mother, he said:

I am truly happy in my work; and, although I cannot boast of any great things done, as yet, in this mission, I believe that those who come after me will have the pleasure of making known, to the friends of missions, great and glorious results. God has promised it. The Saviour has sealed the promise with His blood. The Holy Spirit has given the earnest; and the end is sure: 'My word shall not return unto me void,' saith the Lord. Yes; when you and I shall be in heaven, thousands upon earth will praise God and the Lamb for this mission. We want more missionaries. The harvest truly is great: multitudes are perishing, and I am here alone. You are saving something for me : here is a call : give it now : after your death I shall be provided for. O God, thou who hast the hearts of all men in thy hands, send us faithful labourers into this vineyard!

To another correspondent he writes:

You say, 'Return to England.' Were I to attempt it, I should expect to be engulfed by the waves before I could get clear of the shores of New South Wales. Let no man despise the day of small things. God has promised that 'all the ends of the earth shall see His salvation'. In the prosecution of my mission, I am as happy with a crust of bread and a draught from the brook, as when I used to dine on your roast beef. But I am sometimes without even a crust. Travelling in the woods one day lately, I became quite confused, and lost all idea of the direction in which the settlement lay where I was going. After riding until I was exhausted, I threw the reins upon the neck of my horse, and allowed him shape his own course. He brought me, at last, to a stockman's hut. I alighted, and begged that he would give me something to eat. He said that his master had just left, and that he was not allowed to give anything away in his absence. He had thrown some Indian corn to the fowls, who were picking it up in the back yard. I cheerfully joined the fowls, to which he offered no objection; and felt refreshed and strengthened by this providential repast.

What can one missionary do in such a country as this? Yet I have seen many penitential tears.[1] I sometimes travel twenty miles, preach to twenty persons, retire to rest with twenty thousand blessings, and go off again in the morning, singing for joy. Pray that I may be filled with faith in Christ, and with a burning zeal for the spread of His gospel.

★   ★   ★

The church at Newcastle, with a congregation of eight hundred hearers, being without a clergyman, the governor applied to Mr. Leigh for assistance. The spirit was willing, though the flesh was weak, and he consented to go. He sailed in one of the government ships, and resumed his labours amongst the thieves and murderers of that settlement; but increasing indisposition rendered his speedy return to Sydney indispensable. He was now incapacitated for all public duty and, for some time his friends despaired of his life.

The physicians of Sydney were of opinion that nothing but a long voyage could justify the slightest hope of Mr. Leigh's ultimate recovery. The stewards apprized the committee in

---

[1]Increasing numbers required larger buildings. In 1819 new chapels were opened at Windsor and at Sydney (Princes Street). On the opening of the latter building, which was able to hold 400 people, Leigh wrote: 'The congregations were large and attentive. I cannot express what I felt during the evening service as I looked round upon the audience, and reflected on the wonderful change that had taken place since I first preached in Sydney "Rocks". I was "lost in wonder, love, and praise!"' It was in these years that a magistrate once complained to the Governor that 'unless some restraint were laid upon Leigh, they would soon become a colony of Methodists'.

London of this opinion in an official note, dated February 24th, 1820. In it they observe:

Mr. Leigh has fairly worn himself out in this mission. For three years he has travelled through this uncultivated and extensive colony alone and without help, during the burning heat of summer, and the cold and wet of winter. We all perceived what would be the result of such incessant labour, and only wonder that he sustained it so long. It is the unanimous opinion of all the medical men here that the only chance of recovery is a voyage to England. After much persuasion, he has consented to return home. He is exceedingly respected in this country. Should his health be restored, the committee cannot send any man who will be so acceptable to the people as Mr. Leigh. In the name of the friends of the mission, we request that, so soon as it may be considered safe, Mr. Leigh may be sent out to us again in preference to any other person.

4

TASMANIA AND THE TESTIMONY OF JANE REID (MRS. WILLIAMS)

Views in Tasmania

Tasmania and the Testimony
of Jane Reid (Mrs. Williams)

THE GOSPEL IN VAN DIEMEN'S LAND

Tasmania, a mountainous island of similar size to Ireland, was discovered by the Dutch navigator Tasman in 1642 and named Van Diemen's Land after his fellow-countryman, Anthony Van Diemen. It was colonized by the British in 1803–4, with the chief settlement at Hobart Town. As British shipping to eastern Australia approached from the Indian Ocean around the south of Australia rather than the north, Hobart was strategically placed as a port. By 1810 the white population of Van Diemen's Land, largely convict, had risen to 1,277, and by 1817 to 3,114, yet the territory at this time appears to have been wholly without an evangelical ministry. Robert Knopwood (1763–1838), for long the sole chaplain with the settlers, was a Cambridge graduate who had squandered an inherited fortune by gambling. Patronage rather than suitability for the work seems to explain Knopwood's appointment. In the opinion of John West, the first historian of Tasmania: 'He had not much time to care for the spiritual interests of his flock, and of his success in their reformation nothing is recorded: his convivial friends are the chief eulogists of his character'. A first interruption of the prevailing indifference in the north of the island came with the appointment of a former missionary to Tahiti (John Youl) as an assistant chaplain in 1819, and in the south when a Methodist minister, Benjamin Carvosso, landed in April 1820 while *en route* to Sydney. Greatly moved by the spiritual ignorance of those 'whose ears had for a long period been unaccustomed to listen to the name of Jesus as the Saviour of sinful men', Carvosso turned the steps of the building used as a

[73]

Court-House in Hobart into a pulpit, and preached to a surprised gathering in the street from the text, 'Awake thou that sleepest!' As he reported to a friend:

The people here are literally as sheep without a shepherd. Considering the former character of these colonists, and their destitution of the means of grace, what can be expected but the greatest profligacy? The lieutenant-governor was quite agreeable to my preaching in the street, and ordered the chief constable to attend, and prevent interruption. I preached frequently to numerous, attentive, and increasing congregations. Animated by the example of the apostle of the Gentiles, I felt a strong desire to have the honour of laying the foundation of a church on this island, whose light should be seen from afar. Here is a fine opening for a 'man full of faith and of the Holy Ghost'.

Not long after Carvosso's departure a few soldiers of the 48th Regiment, who had become Christians in Sydney, were drafted to Hobart. Seeing the evil around them, their first action was to secure a place where they could meet to pray. 'In this they at length succeeded, but were ere long called to endure persecution for righteousness' sake. The meeting of the praying soldiers soon began to excite attention; many of the town's-people found their way to the humble sanctuary, and some were convinced of sin and brought to a knowledge of the truth. At this Satan began to rage. Many of the people "of the baser sort" assembled around the cottage at the hour of prayer; and by loud and boisterous shouting, throwing stones at the door, and breaking the windows, attempted to daunt the humble worshippers, and destroy the infant-cause of the Redeemer. In this they were mistaken; for the more they opposed the more mightily grew the word of God and prevailed. Tidings of these wicked proceedings soon reached the ears of the Lieutenant-Governor: the persecutors were silenced, peace restored, and from that time to the present no attempt at open opposition has ever been made in Hobart-Town.'[1]

Led by a Corporal Waddy, and assisted by an ex-convict carpenter who was a descendant of the family of Archbishop Cranmer, this band of men had established a church and a Sunday school before the next Methodist minister, Ralph Mansfield, arrived in August 1821. From this period the prospects of a Christian colony began to dawn. In December 1822 the first

[1] *The Southern World*, Robert Young, 2nd edition, 1855, pp. 389-90.

Presbyterian preacher in Australia settled in Hobart. He was Archibald Macarthur, a minister of the Scottish Secession Church who became 'a burning and shining light to all'. Knopwood was succeeded as principal chaplain by the evangelical William Bedford in 1823. The Methodists also followed up their first successes, and Carvosso came back to serve in Van Diemen's Land from 1825 to 1830. In their labours they were to be helped considerably by the sympathy of the new Lt. Governor, Sir George Arthur, appointed in 1824. Arthur's official reports were to favour their work ('they have rendered the most essential service to morals . . . the outward conduct of many of the convicts has been reformed') and his personal commitment on the side of evangelical Christianity had its own influence. In the words of J. G. Turner, 'The abettors of social laxity were reproved, if not restrained, by the example of family piety at Government House'.

★   ★   ★

As in New South Wales, the change in Van Diemen's Land was to be brought about, in part, by the character of the new immigrants, and it is in this connection that the records of Jane Reid, and her family provide a valuable illustration. Unintended for publication, these documents, now carefully gathered in the *Clyde Company Papers*,[1] give a vivid impression of the convictions and the Christian living to be found among a number of Tasmania's early free settlers. Speaking of the correspondence of the Reid family, Dr. P. L. Brown has written:

Comedy, tragedy, all the essential elements of drama, are to be found in it. There is a besieging sense of distance and isolation – as though the earth were divided into fragments, Australia, India, Britain, each a separate world; and, a shield against that and other frightening things, a profound belief in the watchfulness of God. This belief was a cardinal fact.

THE REIDS COME TO RATHO

Alexander Reid (of Ratho, six miles west of Edinburgh) emigrated from Scotland to Van Diemen's Land with his wife, Mary, in

---

[1] Published by Oxford University Press in 7 vols, 1941–71, and the whole edited by Dr. P. L. Brown.

1821. He was partner of a business in Leith which went bankrupt in 1814 – the year of his daughter Jane's birth – but by the time of his departure Reid was again sufficiently well off to be conscious of the risk involved in going to Australia. Recalling later the events of that year 1821 when they sailed on the *Castle Forbes* from Leith on August 27, Jane Reid writes:

'It was not, as now, an event of everyday occurrence for a family to relinquish the attachments and comforts of their home in the old world to seek their fortunes in those far off islands of the South Sea, which were at the time when my recollections begin emphatically a terra incognita. It was consequently viewed as no small undertaking by all his friends. By some it was looked upon as a species of madness, by others as a rash and unwise act of which the cost had not been counted: all united in considering it a most dreadful description of banishment, and my mother a heroine to encounter the prospect of all things strange and horrible; for dim and misty were their conceptions of what was there to be endured.

'Without yielding either to the solicitations of relations, or to her own anxieties, but trusting that a merciful Providence would support her under all trials which were found in the path of her duty, my mother would not listen to the proposal that she should remain for two years in Scotland after my father's departure, to enable him to make things comfortable before she followed. Our family party consisted of my parents, myself (then a mere child), and my brother – an infant of a year old. A female was hired to attend on him, who having a knowledge of country matters was expected to be very useful on our arrival in the land of promise; she however deserted her post on the day of embarkation, and my mother was obliged to depend on the assistance of some female steerage passengers during the voyage, it being then too late to seek another girl to replace the truant. My father took with him a respectable person well acquainted with farming, who was to act in the capacity of overseer with a salary of £40[1]; and a *sheep dog* completed our number of live stock. The vessel was crowded with passengers. It was the commencement of that great tide of emigration which since has continued to flow towards these colonies.

'Six months! six long months passed away before we came in

[1] Twenty-four-year-old Philip Russell of Fife.

[76]

sight of Van Diemen's Land. . . . The time on board was chiefly occupied by the gentlemen in reading works on agriculture, drawing plans of mansions (never destined to appear in any other form), and talking over the readiest and shortest mode of making their fortunes – displaying their love of country by always taking it for granted that in a certain given number of years they would return to spend their wealth in their native land. Several architects who were among the passengers without doubt were the most busily engaged of any in the ship. One lady insisted that her house should be exactly on the plan of that she had left in the Canongate, with the simple addition of a *large ball room* – for she had several daughters! Another would content himself with a cottage ornée; but no mention was ever made of that description of architecture the only kind which all were destined to be acquainted with for many years – namely a mud or turf hut. I well remember the pleasure I had in walking along the streets of Cape Town with my father and mother. At Cape Town we took on board a Captain and Mrs. Sockett, who afterwards became our neighbours when we settled at the Clyde.

'We arrived in Hobart Town, then like a small fishing village, in March 1822. My father took such lodgings as he could obtain for his family in an abode called 'Vinegar Cottage', in Liverpool Street, while he busied himself in getting his baggage landed and stored, and about land to select as his grant. In those days 2000 acres was the maximum that was granted to settlers, and this my father obtained; but there was much difficulty in hearing of suitable land.'

Purchasing a horse for £70 ('a great sum in those days'), Alexander Reid surveyed ground offered to him to the north of Hobart on the river Clyde. This he took – 1400 acres on the west bank of the Clyde, which he named 'Ratho', and another 600 acres down stream on the east bank. A three day journey in a 'double gig', with one night sleeping beneath the stars *en route*, took the family to Dennistoun, on the opposite side of the river to Ratho, and here they stayed temporarily in a turf hut, with earthen floors and blankets for doors.

'My father's wagons had arrived, and the chests, boxes, and chests of drawers were piled up before the huts, there being no room for them within, and we being at Dennistoun only till my father had his turf cottage erected at Ratho. For this he had

[77]

brought doors and cottage windows. He soon found a final visit to town would be necessary before he could get all his remaining goods and furniture stored. The piano, for instance, plate chest and other luxuries were left with a Mr. M., and before things were so advanced as to bring such up the country, Mr. M. had died. His widow knew nothing of his affairs, and all was lost to my father.'

One unforeseen drawback to this district was that although a new penal station at Macquarie Harbour was some distance to the west, it was, in early years, to prove exposed to marauding convicts or bushrangers. This gave rise to one of Jane Reid's earliest memories of Ratho:

'In my father's absence the first event I distinctly remember took place. My dear mother was sitting one afternoon hearing me repeat the Shorter Catechism (Mr. Russell in the field holding the plough, while Captain Wood[1] was driving the bullocks) when an armed man looked into the hut, saying he was a constable looking for bushrangers. My mother told him he could see there was no one there, but he took up his station at the door, or where a door should have been, with his loaded gun ready to fire if any of us had attempted to escape. In the mean time others of the party went out and told the gentlemen that Mrs. Reid and the women were terrified by some bushrangers, whereupon Captain Wood came running to the hut, on which both he and Mr. Russell were seized and handcuffed, as were all the men, and brought into the kitchen hut and seated round the fire, while two of the men watched them. The others took axes and began to break open the chest of drawers, boxes, etc., when my mother with her usual admirable composure told them it was a pity to destroy the furniture, and if they were determined to help themselves she would open the drawers; and getting her bunch of keys threw everything open, while they turned out the stores of clothing and other comforts my father had provided, thinking to give us all the necessaries of life which could not then be obtained in the bush.

'They remained so employed during the night, drawing off also in buckets some wine my father had brought from the Cape, and giving the farm servants abundantly of it, but keeping themselves sober. My mother had just put my brother in bed in his little crib, while the men were ransacking all around him. Coming on a telescope, they said that would suit them well. Alick started up in

[1]Patrick Wood, a fellow emigrant on the *Castle Forbes* who, settling on the ground named Dennistoun, was a near neighbour.

his bed, crying 'No take Papa's mark!' – the name the child gave it
from hearing the captain call when taking the altitude of the sun,
'Mark!' My father used to tell this story in after days with much
enjoyment, and how the chief bushranger said, 'Give it to the little
boy', and so it was rescued from their grip. Captain Wood urged
my mother to put laudanum in their drink, or cut the cords that
tied his hands; but patient submission she thought better, and lest
there might be bloodshed would not agree. Eventually they went
away, in the morning, taking as much as fourteen men could carry
in sheets, and comforting us by saying they would soon come back
and take the rest.

'My father arrived from town that day, and vowed he would not
stay another day in such a place, but go and try Sydney. But my
mother said, "I've come so far with you, and I can go no further."
Some of the men were taken in the streets of Hobart Town,
wearing my father's shirts with his name in full on them. This
convicted them; but as there were no courts of law then in the
colony, Captain Wood had to go to Sydney to prosecute them.

'My mother always spoke of the great mercy it was that they
were quite civil to her and the women servants.'

Virtually nothing is known of Jane Reid's childhood, nor of how
she acquired the education and culture which she evidently
possessed in later years. Despite the lost piano, a love for music
was clearly instilled in her from an early age. Her Christian
instruction seems to have come chiefly from her mother, who did
not rest content with teaching her the Shorter Catechism, but
would say to her, 'O Jeanie, if you do not become a Christian you
will be the only one of our family who has not sought the Lord'.

MARRIAGE AND INDIA

We may assume that Jane's childhood experiences led to an early
maturity for she was only fourteen when her parents consented to
her marriage to Lieutenant William Williams of the 57th Regiment in April 1829. Williams was then serving as a police
magistrate in the Clyde district of Tasmania, but new orders were
soon to take the couple to India (January 1830). Letters back to
Ratho, via Bombay and Cape Town, were tantalizingly slow. Her
mother's correspondence shows how deeply she had entered into

the truth that 'man's chief end is to glorify God'. On hearing that Jane was ill and had lost a first-born, Mary Reid wrote in September 1831:

. . . To think I could be of so little service to you when you so much required a mother's care: but your heavenly Father is all sufficient, and will I trust be ever near you to supply all your wants . . . I trust you will both be enabled to maintain a spirit of gratitude to your heavenly Father for preserving you so well amidst so many dangers: our profit and not our pleasure ought to be what we should seek in this state of being, and then all would be well. I can say from experience, I have had more happiness in doing what I considered my duty than ever I had from self indulgence; and unless we seek a spirit of submission to the will of God, there will not, I fear, be much happiness for us in time or eternity.

In the social life and entertainments of the officers and their wives of the 40th Regiment with which her husband, now a Brevet Captain, served in India, Jane Williams encountered a world very different from the Australian bush and it did not appeal to her. When her husband had to be away, as became increasingly the case, she was consoled by his long letters and reading helped to fill her time. 'Do you not think a little absence now and then is very salutary to teach us the value of comforts?' William wrote from Bombay in September 1832. 'But upon my word, six weeks' absence is too long! I am very glad to hear you have been reading useful books. The others have a most prejudicial effect, except occasionally as a relaxation to the mind – and that very seldom, for they create a false view of life which never can be realized, and excite the mind in a manner that is dangerous to our very best principles, and occasion a craving for those comforts we there see displayed as the only means of happiness in this world, which we well know to be false, for there is no happiness equal to that which springs from peace of mind – that peace of mind which passeth the understanding of man.'

It needed peace beyond what the world could afford to sustain Jane Williams in what lay ahead. In November 1834 her husband died after an illness of ten weeks which had begun with fever. Sending this news to the Reids in Tasmania, Captain Williams' friend, the Rev. George Pigott, wrote from Bombay:

He died on the 23rd, and was buried at Colabah Burial Ground. The next morning your poor daughter, weak with unwearied attention and anxious watchings over him, has had in her affliction another loss which has at such moment come with a double weight of affliction and distress: her weak state induced a premature confinement and her poor little infant died almost immediately after its birth.

In January 1835 Jane Williams, bereft of husband and two children, commenced the long journey home by sailing for Cape Town. After various delays in her journey, she wrote a letter to her mother from the Cape on May 14, 1835 which included the following: 'There are two small vessels in the Bay bound for Van Diemen's Land and finding that the *Sir C Macarteny* is likely to sail first, I send you these few lines by her, 'tho it is probable I may be with you before this arrives . . . I am convinced that even those annoying delays, as well as the deep afflictions that I have been visited with, are all sent to answer some wise purpose, all intended to work together for our eternal welfare; and altho I cannot help praying that we may be allowed to meet again *here*, yet my dear Mamma, if this is not to *be*, you must not indulge one useless regret, for I trust we have the same *sure Hope* . . . I trust that He who has smoothed my path, and who, while He has afflicted has also given me a heart to bear those afflictions, will also support you. The greatest pleasure that remains to me in this world will be to find you *well*, strong and happy . . .

'Of my own feelings I might write to you for ever without being able to express the half of what I have felt . . . But my dear Mamma, He who has seen and knows them all, who having formed me, understands them all, is ever ready to listen to all which we find it impossible to express to any human being . . .

'I do not think you will have much difficulty in recognizing me again.'[1]

THE WIDOW AT HOME

For the rest of her long life, until her death in 1897, Jane Williams' home was in Tasmania. A page from her Journal, written at Ratho

[1]Mrs. Reid's letters to her daughter had often contained spiritual help. In one dated April 26, 1834, she wrote: 'I trust you have both belief in the wisdom of the Almighty that whatever *is is best*, and that nothing can be enjoyed without His blessing . . . May we daily seek grace to avoid all sin, in thought, word and deed.'

on January 1, 1837, reveals more to us of the inner life of this Christian woman:

'All are gone to Church, & I remained at home to commune with my own thoughts & to retrace the steps I have taken this last year; to look back & think of all that for ever is past to me in this life; to pray for grace to improve by my afflictions & losses – for support on my entrance on this new year; to thank thee, my righteous God & Saviour, for the blessings still spared me, & for the protection & *quiet* of the past year.

'I do thank thee for all the love still so undeservedly given me. Bless each member of my dear family this day;. . . bless my sisters – be their guide now in their youth: lead my dear Elizabeth to *thee* for the good gifts [*th*]ou only canst bestow & which she so much requires; make her to *love her Saviour* & to imitate his lovely character – to seek that best gift, a *meek* & quiet spirit; make her all that woman should be – gentle in her mind & manners, kind & affectionate to all, seeking to diffuse happiness around her by taking an interest in all that interests those with whom her lot is cast; *soften* her mind, make her humble & lowly in her own eyes. Hear my prayer for this poor dear child, oh Lord – for this creature whom I *might* have rased up an *idol* in my heart but for thy wisdom in shewing me that it was not thy will. I thank thee oh Lord for this as all other trials.

'Have mercy on me, oh God, thou God of my salvation! Keep me near thee, make me thine, increase my love to thee; & oh, when this heart feels that it has lost its greatest earthly blessing – a heart that felt *with it, that loved it, that was all its own* – oh when I feel how *very much* I have lost, in my sorrow be thou near me, my Saviour, my God, my only hope – have mercy on me! shall I meet the lost, the loved? oh it is a bitter thing to taste of the happiness that there is in having a *friend* to whom to go, & *trust* to, & depend on, & love with all one's heart; & then to be left alone! but Lord, forgive me; I thank thee for thy merciful support: the blessings I have, & the glorious hope before me, is surely enough . . .

'Lord, take my heart & keep it, for I cannot; it will go astray if thou hast it not – keep it this year: & oh, let my path be that of the just – as a shining light going on brigh[ten]ing till the perfect day!'

The memory of her husband, referred to in this prayer, was never far from her, waking and sleeping. In her journal for October 12, 1837, Jane Williams wrote:

'It is a subject of gratitude, among the numberless a gracious God

gives us, when He blesses us with happiness even in our dreams . . .
'I was walking with my beloved William in some beautiful bright
plains, & we were quite alone; & I was *so happy*, it seemed like
heaven. He looked as in his *best days*, & his arm was round my waist,
& looking at me so kindly, so fondly, as he used to do; & then, as I've
often seen him, his eyes turned from me to heaven, & his lips moved
in prayer, & the expression of warm affection became mingled with
solemn adoration as he implored a blessing on his Wife. I saw all this
in my dream, as I have often seen it in reality; & I thought we had
been separated a weary long time, & I was telling all that had
occurred in his absence & all that I had done. And then I awoke, to
find that it was all false; yet I was thankful to God for the happiness it
afforded me for the time the delusion lasted; & oh, surely I have
constant, never ceasing cause of gratitude to him for his mercies,
friends, & comforts, all which I so abundantly possess! . . . If,
through the mercy of our Saviour's death, *we* may hope to meet in
his happy mansions, how exactly did this dream shadow forth what
might most probably pass between my beloved husband & myself.'

The next year Jane's youngest sister, Elizabeth (the subject of
her recorded prayer of January 1, 1837), died. Jane's journal
entries, recording the event, were written shortly before the family
left on a visit to New South Wales and they provide a suitable
conclusion to these extracts:

'[Ratho,] *5th March, 1838*:
Since I last wrote in my journal, what a change has taken place in
our family! My dear, darling Lizzy is gone from us – the cold grave
is now the home of her whom we hoped long to behold growing a
comfort & ornament to her family. So sweet, so interesting, so
lovely & graceful, cut off in the bloom of her youth, when life was
just opening on her in all its brightest colors! . . . She went from
us in to (I trust) the arms of her much loved Saviour on the
morning of Sunday the 18th of February, about 1 or 2 o'clock.

'We leave dear Lizzy & Ratho on Friday morning for Town, as
we want to take the sacrament on Sunday,[1] & shall be in Town for

---

[1]St. Andrew's, Hobart, where John Lillie (1806–1866) had succeeded
Archibald Macarthur (resigned 1835) in September 1837. In October 1837
Lillie had visited and preached mid-week near Ratho, and Jane Williams says
his energetic sermon was 'much admired', though 'he began about half-past
seven, and we did not get home till *ten*'. Lillie became the Presbyterian leader
in Tasmania.

some time, as we do not sail till the 20th. My dear Mamma has been wonderfully supported during this trial – the loss of her *first* child – & such a child! Yet I have heard no murmur escape her lips; all has been thankfulness & submission. Dear Papa, too, has borne up far better than I expected. Lord, I bless thy name for ever & ever! Oh, be *our God!*

'*8th, Thursday afternoon*:

We have packed every thing, & sent it off today; the house looks desolate enough. We have taken our *last dinner* at dear Ratho, & are to sleep at Mrs. Russell's tonight, that we may be able to start early tomorrow morning. More than 16 years have we now sojourned here, & much mercy have we experienced: Lord, go with us & be our guide, wherever we go! . . .'

5

MEMORIES OF CHILDHOOD
IN PIONEER DAYS

'A Chain Gang, Convicts going to work near Sydney, N. S. Wales'.
From J. Backhouse, Narrative of a visit to the Australian Colonies, *1843.*
Despite the commonplace nature of such scenes, William Cowper (first
chaplain at St. Phillip's, Sydney) could write in February 1832: 'Real
religion has taken deep root here in the hearts of some. Can any good come out of
New South Wales or be found therein? Yes, I believe the eternal Trinity has
been pleased to visit souls, in these ends of the earth, and numbers have been
removed from New South Wales to Paradise!'

The first pages in this chapter are from *The Autobiography and Reminiscences of William MacQuarie Cowper* (Sydney, 1902). Cowper's father, William Cowper (1778–1858) was encouraged to come to Sydney by Marsden in 1809 and served St. Phillip's Church for nearly forty-nine years. In a notice of his death, *The Christian Advocate and Wesleyan Record* for July 21, 1858 reported: 'He possessed many excellencies, but his greatest praise is that he was a diligent, faithful Minister of the Gospel of Christ. Surrounded by temptations to the indulgence of a worldly spirit, he was true to his holy calling, seeking not the things of earth, but the spiritual and eternal happiness of men.'

Born in Sydney in 1810, William MacQuarie Cowper trained for the ministry in England (1827–1835), succeeding his father to St. Phillip's in 1858, when he was also appointed Dean and Archdeacon of Sydney. On his death in 1902, James Hassall could say that he was 'a man beloved and venerated above almost all others to this day'. Dean Cowper's ministry was, in part, an answer to his father's prayers for 'faithful, zealous, exemplary clergymen'.

The second selection of childhood memories comes from James Hassall's *In Old Australia*, Records and Reminiscences from 1794, 1902. The author, grandson of Rowland Hassall (died 1820), was one of the seven children of Thomas and Anne Hassall – his mother being the Marsden baby who Palmer carried ashore in 1794. Sent back to England to be educated for the ministry according to the guidance of Charles Simeon, his father, Thomas Hassall, 'the galloping parson', spent much time in itinerant ministry, with his base at Cobbity in the district then called the Cowpastures, NSW. James Hassall, after serving as prison chaplain at Berrima, spent the rest of his life in Queensland.

I

William MacQuarie Cowper
in Sydney

SYDNEY IN THE EARLY
NINETEENTH CENTURY

Before his departure [from England] my father was married to a
lady who proved herself a true mother to his children, and a
valuable helper to himself in his ministry. The voyage in those
days was long and tedious, although broken by touching at Rio
Janeiro or the Cape. The period from the time of their embarkation to their arrival in Port Jackson was nearly eight months. The
Indispensable dropped her anchor in the harbour on the 18th of
August, and Mr. Cowper at once reported himself to the Acting
Governor, and entered upon his ministry on the next day, Sunday,
the 19th of August, 1809.

In an interview with His Excellency, that officer gave him no
very encouraging view of the position he had come to occupy. One
piece of advice which he gave him was to 'regard every man as
rogue until he found him to be an honest man.' This, however, was
not the principle upon which he meant to act. His mission was a
mission of reconciliation between God and man. He came as a
messenger bringing glad tidings to the lost, preaching repentance
and the forgiveness of sins, if men would submit themselves to
God. He began his ministry in the old Church of St. Phillip's,
which had been completed in the previous year, preaching from
the words of St. Paul in his Epistle to the Galatian Church, Chapter
1, verse 10: 'Do I now persuade men or God? or do I seek to please
men? For if I yet pleased men, I should not be the servant of
Christ.' The note which he struck in that sermon characterized his
ministry throughout his whole career. It was responsibility and

devotion to *Christ* as the Saviour of mankind.

In the year 1810, there stood facing Bridge Street, on a portion of land which now forms the site of the new buildings of the Government Lands Office, a small verandah cottage, with a garden of fruit trees. In front of it, and on either side of the pathway leading from the gate to the house, stood two orange trees in full bearing. This was the residence of the chaplain, and these trees had probably been planted by the Rev. Mr. Johnson, who is known to have taken special interest in the cultivation of oranges with the seeds of which fruit he supplied himself at Rio Janeiro on the voyage to the Colony. In the cottage, my father resided with his family, and there I was born on July 3rd, 1810, and with it my earliest recollections are associated. In about three years however, we removed to a larger and more commodious dwelling in Macquarie Place, with a balcony and verandah in front and a considerable space behind.

Macquarie Place, although the high way to the Harbour, was very little frequented, for it will be remembered that the population of the town was only about 5000, and there was neither wharf nor quay on that side of the Harbour. All that shore which now provides accommodation for the magnificent steamships of the P and O, the Orient, and the French Companies, was fringed down to the water's edge with the natural bush. Such shipping business as there was, was transacted on the opposite side of the Cove, where the King's Wharf, and the Commissariat Stores were situated. There was also the Custom House, under the charge of the Naval Officer, Captain Piper. And further north, the residence and business premises of merchant Robert Campbell. Seldom were the placid waters disturbed by the splash of oars. So small was the amount of shipping at that early period, that sometimes a single vessel was anchored there. This happened in 1814, when a ship named the *Three Bees* was burnt to the water's edge, the fire being caused by a slight accident on board, and no appliances being available for extinguishing it. There was only a man and a boy on board at the time. I well remember the Governor's Orderly being sent to our house with a message directing us all to retire from the premises and take shelter at a distance, as it was believed that there was a loaded gun in the ship which might by explosion do some damage; we did not return until the evening.

The triangular piece of land which lies between Macquarie Place and Bridge Street, was then an open space, and was, occasionally, the resort of the aborigines from different tribes near Sydney for corroborees (dances), and other customary observances. On the eastern side were the residences of the Judges of the Supreme Court, and the Governor's Secretary, Mr. J. F. Campbell (from whom Campbelltown received its name), and further on a military guard house for the protection of the Governor's residence, which was about 40 or 50 yards within the Domain gate.

Two events connected with this locality are deeply impressed upon my memory, as having occurred early in my childhood; one was my own wonderful preservation from being drowned. There was then not far from Bridge Street, near the spot which is now adorned by the statue of Mr. T. S. Mort, an open well, which was used by the neighbours for household purposes. I had gone, accompanied by a man servant, across from our house to the garden in front of the cottage I have spoken of. He had forgotten something, and when he discovered the omission, boy like, I said I would run and fetch it. I did so, and on returning, going too near the well, my foot slipped and I fell into it. It was a lonely spot, and no passerby saw me. But at the instant that I slipped, a man was looking through a window in Mr. Uther's hat factory in that direction, and saw me disappear. Without a moment's delay he ran down and rushed across to my rescue. He found me in the water, which was several feet deep, clinging to the slab which was fixed across for the drawers of water to stand upon. Thus he saved me from a watery grave. This is what men commonly call a piece of good luck. But I have always looked upon it as the Providential act of God; it was He who directed that man's eyes towards me when I fell. And I can never pass that spot without calling to mind His mercy towards me and thanking Him for His interposition.

The other event to which I referred was my witnessing the barbarous method by which the Aborigines took to themselves their wives. There had been a gathering of two or three tribes for a day or two in the open ground, and I believe their corroborees were over. As I was walking down what is now known as Gresham Street to Macquarie Place, I saw a fine stalwart aboriginal, with a waddy (club) in his right hand, and with his left clutching the arm of a female whom he was dragging along the ground apparently senseless. He seemed to be carrying her off to some hiding place. This was an instance of what Collins describes in his history regarding their customs. He says:

These unfortunate women are selected by the men from tribes different from their own, and are stolen in the absence of their protectors. Secrecy is observed, and the woman, stupified with blows inflicted by a club upon the head and shoulders, is then dragged through the woods by one arm with a violence which might be supposed to displace it from the socket. This outrage is not resented by the female's relatives, who only retaliate by a similar opportunity.

THE CONVICT POPULATION

Many persons have exaggerated ideas about the convict population of that time. There were no doubt some of very bad character, and dangerous to society. But there were many who little deserved the degradation to which they were condemned by the terribly severe and cruel laws of that period. And the administration of those laws was marked more by the thought of vindictive punishment than by that of reformation. Offences which were really trivial were regarded as heinous, and sentences were often passed upon offenders out of all proportion to the offence committed. I have no hesitation in expressing my belief that as long as those draconic laws were in force in England, grievous injustice was often done to comparatively innocent persons. We live now in happier times, and thankful should we be to those Christian philanthropists through whose labours the old laws were abrogated and more humane ones substituted.

There were two different ways of dealing with the convicts practised by the Government. Some were employed upon Government works of various kinds as labourers, artisans, etc. Others were assigned under certain regulations to respectable persons as domestic servants, farm labourers, or mechanics, according to their different capabilities. The latter method was far preferable for the purpose of the reformation of individuals. Those who were thus assigned, in many instances became useful and respectable members of society. This, however, depended upon the circumstances in which they were placed, and the treatment they met with from their employers. Treated with justice, kindness, and consideration, they generally proved themselves grateful and trustworthy. But the results were very different if they were dealt with harshly and with any degree of injustice; such treatment produced insubordination, hostility, and dislike, which in various ways led to very disastrous consequences.

The system of working the convicts in gangs upon the public works always appeared to me to be very unfavourable to their moral improvement. It tended on the contrary to produce greater corruption and vice, to arouse the evil passions, and to provoke to deeds of criminality.

Men thus herded together were under less moral influence, were more exposed to temptation from those with whom they were surrounded, and were often stimulated to vicious indulgences by the tales of vice, often exaggerated, which the more corrupt delighted to tell for the amusement of their fellows. It was from such sources that the worst evils arose.

And here let me mention, though it is painful to call it to mind, an evil which existed for many years in the heart of the town in connection with the gang system. There was at the corner of George and Bridge Streets, a yard called the lumber yard, where the convicts in the Hyde Park Barracks were employed. It reached down to the Tank Stream. The men were employed in sawing timber, in carpentering, and making articles of furniture for the Government establishments. They were marched down to the yard in their clanging chains every morning, and back every evening. During the day, but more especially in the forenoon, one frequently heard the cries and moans of men suffering from the infliction of corporal punishment. It must have had a hardening and exasperating effect upon those who suffered it, and I fear that it was often very hastily administered without a trial.

It was a wise and humane policy which was adopted by Governor Macquarie some years after he took the reins of Government, when he held out hopes of reward to persistent good conduct through a certain fixed period. This was done by the issue of tickets of leave, and conditional pardons. The ticket of leave authorized the person who held it to employ himself on his own account within a limited area in any trade or calling of which he was capable. The conditional pardon set the holder free within the Colony, but forbade his leaving it. If this rule were infringed, the pardon was at once revoked. In order to obtain the first of these privileges, the applicant was required to obtain unequivocal testimonials founded upon personal knowledge, of well sustained good conduct, from the Chaplain and one or two Justices of the Peace in the district in which he lived for a specified period. The conditional pardon was only given after a much longer probation, and similar testimonials from a chaplain and a magistrate or magistrates.

As I write this, there rises up before me a scene which I often witnessed in front of the Parsonage in Gresham Street. I see before me a number of persons of both sexes standing before the gate, with their written applications in their hands, ready to be handed in to my father for his examination and testimonial. Their countenances so eager, their hopes so strong that they shall obtain the coveted certificate. And I see them one after another going away, with joyful faces if they had been successful, but deeply disappointed if they had failed.

ST. PHILLIP'S CHURCH

My earliest recollections are associated with the old St. Phillip's Church. There I was baptized, though, of course, I do not recollect it, being then only six weeks old; and there I was carried in my infancy in my nurse's arms, that she might not altogether lose the privilege of attending public worship. For my father made it a rule that all his household should, if possible, enjoy that privilege, both for their own benefit, and as an example to others. I was taught to take an interest in the service, and, more than that, to take a delight in it. He always expected his children to give some account of what they heard there.

The public duties which fell to my father's lot every Sunday were three services and sermons, one at the Gaol at 8.30 a.m. in the open yard, which was then situated in Lower George Street, the second in St. Phillip's Church at 11 a.m., the third at 3 p.m. That at 11 a.m. was usually attended by the Governor and Mrs. Macquarie with His Excellency's suite, the civil and military officers, a fair number of the commercial and trading community, while the soldiers also of the regiment stationed in Sydney who were members of the Church of England were regular attendants at that service. Conspicuous among the civilians were three leading merchants and their families, Messrs. Campbell, Jones, and Riley, the first of whom was a remarkable figure with his almost snow-white head of hair. He was scarcely ever absent from the morning service, bringing his whole family with him.[1] At a later period they were all, father and sons, distinguished by the great interest they took in the affairs of the Church in the Diocese, and by their large and spontaneous donations for extending its operations. In these respects, they have had few equals in the Colony.

In those days almost the whole of the service devolved upon the officiating minister, the parish clerk making the responses, accompanied by perhaps a few members of the congregation here and there. There was very little singing, only a few verses of Tate and Brady's metrical version of the Psalms at the end of the Morning Prayer, and again after the Ante-Communion. Chanting the Psalms was unknown (in Australia). The three services in which my father officiated thus involved four hours and a half of public reading and speaking on the Sunday, and they were frequently followed by churchings and baptismal services, adding another half hour. During the week he was constantly engaged in visitation of the sick and afflicted, in visiting the General and Military Hospitals, in watching over the Parochial, Military and Orphan Schools, and attending other duties attaching to his office as chaplain. Every Thursday evening he had a public service in the Church, with a sermon or exposition of Scripture.

He seemed to me to never lose five minutes in the day. And his work was so well distributed that one part did not conflict with another. He was always an early riser, and he did not retire to rest until eleven at night. The first hour of the day was always spent in his study, in private devotion, and study of the Word of God, as was also the last half hour before he retired. In the morning after family prayer and breakfast, all the day was planned out for particular purposes, and as far as possible the plan was adhered to, although interruptions would occasionally arise.

In the year 1817, he was largely instrumental, in conjunction with the Rev. Samuel Marsden, in the establishment of an Auxiliary to the British and Foreign Bible Society.

Although I was at that time but seven years of age, I have never forgotten the joyous spirit in which he came home from the public meeting at which it had been inaugurated. He seemed as glad as though he had found a great treasure. The meeting was of a most

[1]The reference is, of course, to Robert Campbell.

influential character. It was presided over by the Governor (Macquarie), and attended by the judges, and other civil, as well as military officers, magistrates, merchants, and other citizens, who thus manifested their interest in the object for which it was formed. A large committee was chosen from those who were present, which soon showed itself energetic and practical. Out of the large committee a sub-committee was formed to make a house to house visitation of the town for the purpose of ascertaining the extent to which the inhabitants were supplied with the Word of God, and what amount of copies of the whole Bible or of the New Testament would be probably required to supply the existing wants.

I have reason for thinking that from my earliest years my father entertained a hope that it might please God to incline my heart to the ministry of the Gospel, should I possess such qualities as would appear to fit me for it. At the same time his estimate of the sacred office was so high, that he would have shrunk from inducing me to seek it as a profession without such a distinct call from God as is required in the Ordination Services of our Church. I cannot remember that he at any time endeavoured directly to influence me in regard to it. What he did was to guide my education, so that, if it should please God to incline my heart to the work, I might be able to pursue the course of study which would be requisite to fit me for the proper discharge of my sacred duties.

When I had reached the age of 16 years, he began to make arrangements for sending me to England, there to take up such a course of preliminary reading with a clergyman as would fit me for entering one of the Universities – giving the preference to Cambridge. And, having, through a friend, completed those arrangements, he sought for a favourable opportunity for sending me thither. Such an opportunity occurred early in 1827, when a ship was to be despatched laden with cargo and passengers, some of whom were well known to our family. We sailed from Sydney in the good ship *Portland* of about 400 tons, on February 9th, 1827.

2

James S. Hassall in Parramatta

CHILDHOOD MEMORIES

One of my first recollections is driving from Parramatta to Sydney with my father, over seventy years ago, and I retain a clear remembrance of the latter town as it was at that time. We travelled the road from Parramatta without seeing a house except the half-way inn at Homebush and, nearer Sydney, the residences of Mr. Underwood of Ashfield, Dr. Ramsay of Dobroyd, Mr. Robert Johnson of Annandale, and a few slab huts on the roadside.

The old toll-bar stood in front of the Benevolent Asylum, built in 1819, and a low shanty public-house and blacksmith's shop on the rise of Brickfield Hill was all that was to be seen of Sydney before we came to the Cemetery, adjoining the site of what is now St. Andrew's Cathedral.

The foundations of St. Andrew's were first laid by Governor Macquarie, in 1819. The Sydney Town Hall was afterwards built in part of what had been the Cemetery.

About this time, I was staying at my grandmother Hassall's, at the old house in George-street, Parramatta, and I remember my uncles going off to look for pasturage, in what they called 'the new country'. They were then preparing for their start, taking pack-horses and a quantity of provisions, and armed to the teeth with fire-arms, for fear of wild blacks.

I learnt afterwards that they went to Burrowa, some hundred and fifty miles from Sydney. One of my uncles took up country there, and shortly after other members of the family selected the grants of land, to which the native-born were in those days entitled, of eight hundred acres apiece, in the same locality. People may be surprised, nowadays, to hear of such preparations being needed to go only fifty miles or so beyond Goulburn. Of the country on the other side of Burrowa, their destination, nothing was then known.

In the year 1826, my father purchased a property, Denbigh, in the neighbourhood of Camden, then called the Cowpastures. Upon it was a house, partly finished, built by a Mr. Hook, who had shortly before died there. The house was similar to an Indian bungalow, having two large rooms in front, with a spacious verandah. Immediately surrounding it was a paling fence, about seven or eight feet high, intended to keep out bushrangers or the assigned servants, who were not very trustworthy if their masters were harsh and tyrannical. After my father bought the place this fence was soon removed and the house completed. The man who did the work, a carpenter, formerly a convict, remained on the estate with his wife over fifty years.

At Denbigh, during this early period, the blacks were very numerous. One evening I witnessed a corroboree in which over four hundred of them took part. My father used to employ from a hundred to two hundred of them, occasionally, in burning off dead timber. They would begin work about nine o'clock a.m., and work till three p.m. When they left off in the afternoon, they had a good meal of hasty pudding, hominy, soup, and vegetables, finishing up with sugar-bag. This last, I must explain, consisted of empty sugar mats, soaked in a bucket of water. The sweetened liquid was sucked from a piece of bruised stringy-bark, dipped into the bucket.

I never knew any mischief to be perpetrated by the blacks in those days. An old fellow named Cogrewoy occasionally startled my mother by suddenly popping his head in at her bedroom window when he came begging for food.

It may be interesting to some to hear a little about the convict days, especially as so many horrible accounts of them have been written. All these may be true, but so far as my experience went, the days were not so dark as many chroniclers make out, nor the condition of many assigned servants so miserable.

For a number of years, my father had from a dozen to twenty convict servants, whom he had to clothe and ration. The rations consisted of tea and sugar, meat, and flour, or wheat which they used to grind for themselves in a small steel mill – windmills were few in those days. They worked from six in the morning in summer, and from eight in winter, until sundown. A large bullock's horn, blown by an expert on that particular wind instrument, used to arouse them – and the neighbourhood – in the early morning. The horn could be heard two miles off, and it used very much to astonish new arrivals in the colony.

The assigned servants at Denbigh were managed by a Scotch overseer, and a good deal of farming was carried on. The wheat crops then would average about thirty-five bushels per acre. Wheat sold at 8s. per bushel, and hay at £8 per ton. Horses realized a very high price. My father seldom sold any under from £60 to £70, and I remember his being offered a hundred guineas for one of his carriage horses, named Bombarcus.

The men assigned as servants to the settlers had great inducements to behave well, because by so doing, with the recommendation of their masters, they were enabled to obtain a reduction of their sentences, and to be granted a ticket-of-leave, sooner than they otherwise would have done, and most of our men were well-behaved.

There were some cases, however, which formed exceptions to this rule. I may mention, as one instance, that of a rogue who was our watchman. The watchman's duty was to cry the hours at night and look after the place, and he was answerable for the safe-keeping of the establishment. This fellow stole a gold watch from a table in the house, during one evening, and then in the night threw several large bricks at the window-shutters, and gave an alarm of bushrangers. His track was traced from a well, whence he had taken the bricks, but there was no direct proof against him. He was, however, returned to Government. We searched for days for the watch, in all directions, without avail. Years afterwards, when the man was about to be executed for some crime, he sent a message to my father, telling him that the watch was in a certain hollow tree about a mile from the house, where it was found. The case was in good condition but the works had to be renewed. It is still in the possession of a member of the family.

A man of ours, a bullock-driver, after regaining his liberty, went to Sydney and became a wealthy man. I met him many years afterwards in George Street, we recognized each other, he asked me to go home and dine with him, and I found that he had a very fine house and kept his carriage and pair. During dinner he talked with evident pleasure about the good old times, and recounted, almost with pride, the names of his favourite bullocks – 'Spot',

'Leopard', 'Monday', 'Boxer', and others. He had grown-up daughters, who plainly did not like his referring to his convict days, for I observed them kicking him on the shins, underneath the table, to make him hold his tongue. If he had been ill-treated and unhappy in his days of servitude he would not have felt so much pleasure in referring to his former life.

There was a negro who lived with us for fifty years. He was rescued by the Reverend Samuel Marsden from a ship at Tasmania (then Van Diemen's Land), where he was very cruelly treated, brought to Sydney, and placed with the Reverend Richard Hill, of St. James's Church. I remember him in the Sunday School there. He was very fond of the *Pilgrim's Progress*, and thought no-one so good as himself and old Bunyan. He was not sure where he was born, but sometimes claimed Jamaica as his birth-place, and at other times Maryland or the Brazils. He was a true Uncle Tom, and a very faithful servant.

We had an excellent garden at Denbigh, of about five acres, with an abundance of fruit trees. I have never seen fruit equal to what was grown there; the peaches and apples were of enormous size. I remember measuring one apple which was sixteen inches round. The melons were also large; one, a red-seed water-melon, measured twenty-two inches from end to end. The grapes, too, were very fine and of great variety. Three men were kept constantly at work in the garden, and sometimes half-a-dozen besides were sent in to help. Labour was very cheap in those days, because the men, who were convicts, had only to be kept in food and clothes, receiving no pay.

One of the farthest back recollections I have preserved of our life at Denbigh is of Christmas Day, 1827. We drove to service at Kirkham, the property of Surveyor-General Oxley, in the morning. The service was held in a large loft, over the stables. The convict servants all attended – perhaps fifty of them. In the afternoon we started for Parramatta, about twenty-five miles off, in a car which held the whole family. A big iron-grey horse named Blücher was in the shafts, and Peter, a bay, was driven outrigger. It was a dreadfully hot summer day, and we children soon began to cry out for water. I believe it was a season of drought. No water could be had at Nonorah when we passed through, nor at a hut ten miles farther on, where a basin of what looked like thick yellow mud was brought to us, which my mother would not let us drink.

One of my uncles, with his man, accompanied us on horseback. My uncle's horse got his foot in a rut and fell, injuring him so much that he had to be taken into the car for the rest of the way. We passed by the Orphan School, and reached Parramatta at dark, after a most miserable Christmas journey, which has remained impressed on my memory, by reason of the discomfort suffered, to this very day.

ACROSS THE BLUE MOUNTAINS

When I was eight years old, my father took me with him on a trip to Bathurst, on horseback. We first rode to Parramatta, and shortly after started over the Blue Mountains to Bathurst. The first day's stage was one of twenty-eight miles, to the Pilgrim Inn, on the top of Lapstone Hill. Next day we rode about fifty miles in a pouring rain.

The New Pass was in course of construction over Mount Victoria, and my father, having heard that it was passable for horses, decided to try it, instead of going the old road by Mount York. When we arrived at the pass, we found we had to ride on the top of a wall, recently erected, of large blocks of cut stone. This road was no more than four feet wide on one side, while the other side was not completed, nor was any earth filled in. It was a great risk to take horses along this place, as the declivity on both sides was perpendicular and of great depth. We did not, however, care for a day's journey back, in order to go by the other road, so my father led his horse over, as did the other members of the party, of whom Mrs. Samuel Hassall, my uncle's widow, was one.

For fear I might slip over, I was told to keep my seat on my pony. It was not pleasant, as I rode, to see the tree-tops immediately below me. Had the horse tried to turn back, he would certainly have gone over the precipice. Fortunately, we all got over safely.

At night we arrived at a station on Cox's River, a slab hut, where lived a little Irishman, known by the name of 'Terrible Billy', who gave us shelter for the night. I was soon in a tub of cold water, and then, as I had been wet all day, put on dry clothes, and after a good meal of beef and damper turned into a blanket and slept till morning, none the worse for as wet a day as I have ever travelled in.

Travellers cross the Blue Mountains in rather more luxurious fashion now.

Next day, we reached O'Connell Plains, our destination. A few days after, we rode over Bathurst Plains, and called at, or passed by, several stations – the Wests', the Lawsons', the Streets', the Mackenzies', and some others. There was a township called Kelso on the plains, but not a house where Bathurst now stands; only a few sheep-folds, and a flock or two of sheep.

In those days, there was usually a small hut for the hut-keeper and the shepherd, but the latter was obliged to sleep in his box by the sheep-fold. This box was raised from the ground, and was about seven feet by three, with a bunk in it, by way of bed. The dingoes were very troublesome, and great care had to be taken to guard the sheep from them.

★   ★   ★

PARRAMATTA

Parramatta, as I remember it in my earliest days, was a very small town, and was the head-quarters of the Governor, Sir Ralph Darling. Mr. Dunlop, the astronomer, who had been encouraged by Sir Thomas Brisbane, himself a scientific man, still lived there. A large brick parsonage stood on a hill overlooking the town, the residence of my maternal grandfather, the Reverend Samuel Marsden, and his family consisting of Mrs. Marsden and four unmarried daughters, with whom my sister and I often stayed.

The church, in which my grandfather officiated, old St. John's, was a large brick building, stuccoed, with two towers and spires. The church itself was removed afterwards, and was rebuilt of stone, all but the towers, which are still standing.

Within were high pews and galleries. The soldiers sat in one gallery, and, afterwards, the King's School boys in another. A high pulpit stood in the middle of the church. I remember my grandfather preaching from it about the patriarchs and saying that Abraham was a squatter on Government ground. The reading-desk was below the pulpit, and the clerk's desk somewhat lower still. The clerk's desk was occupied for many years by Mr. J. Staff, who repeated the responses and the amens in a loud voice and gave out the hymns. Most people attended the church in the morning, and many of the same congregation went in the evening to the Wesleyan services, conducted by the Reverend Mr. Leigh, who was a very worthy man and much respected.

There had been a church, built of timber, at the corner of George and Macquarie Streets, but it was gone in my time, and a Court-house built upon the site. Nash's and Mrs. Walker's hotels were not far distant and there were only small houses anywhere around, excepting a two-storey one belonging to Mr. Oakes. The bridge over the river was a low wooden one. On the bank near by stood an ugly stone gaol, with the stocks outside, in which drunkards and other offenders had their feet placed, and a low wooden seat on which they were obliged to sit all day, in the heat of the summer sun or the cold winds of winter. I suppose this was an old custom before my day, for we read in the Old Testament that Jeremiah was put in the stocks. Very few houses had been built on the north side of the river. The grounds of the present King's School formed a well-kept Government garden – I suppose for the use of the Governor. Beyond was the Female Factory, where were lodged a large number of convict women.

In those days, a man could apply for a wife from the factory. I remember a man applying for one to my grandfather Marsden, who was a magistrate. My grandfather told him to go to the factory and he would meet him there, and he drove me with him in his gig.

The women were all drawn up in a row, and the man passed along from one to another until he found one who was to his liking and was willing to marry him. As soon as her consent was given, the man took his bride to the church, where Mr. Marsden met them and married them, and then they set off for their farm or homestead. Such marriages were not unusual.

THE KING'S SCHOOL

In January, 1832, the King's School [Parramatta] was opened by the Reverend Robert Forrest, of St. Bee's College, Durham, England. It was founded, I believe, at the suggestion of Archdeacon Broughton (afterwards Bishop of Australia), King William IV., and the Duke of Wellington. The Duke was a great friend of the Archdeacon's, it was he who had him appointed the second Australian archdeacon and afterwards bishop. The Duke and the Archdeacon's other friends used their influence with the British Government to order its establishment, and as the King himself was among those who interested themselves in the matter it was called in honour of him 'The King's School'.

As only the Established Church was recognized at the time, it was made a Church of England school, as it has remained ever since, although boys of all classes and denominations were to be admitted.

The school began in a brick house in Lower George-street, Parramatta. I entered in April, 1832, three months later. Only a few boys were before me. The names of the first pupils will now be interesting to many, so I venture to mention them here:– Andrew McDougal, Edwin Suttor, George Rouse, Joseph Thompson, James Waller, Charles Lockyer, boarders; and six day boys: two Orrs, two Oakeses, George Macarthur, and John Watsford.

After the June holidays, I think we numbered over a hundred boys. Among them were: Arthur Blaxland, John Nicholson, William Cordeaux, John Oxley, two Bloomfields, John Antill, John Futter, and many others, some of whom I have not heard of since our school-days. A schoolroom had to be built and two adjoining houses rented for bedrooms. One of the houses was placed under the charge of 'Jerry' Hatch, a tutor, and the other under that of Mr. W. Woolls, afterwards the Reverend Dr. Woolls.

I wish I could present my readers with some portraits of the boys who came to the school. Knickerbockers were unknown. Short jackets were worn and often the little fellows had the jacket buttoned up and the trousers, or 'pantaloons', as Mrs. Forrest called them, buttoned over it; the suit generally made of blue cloth. One boy had jacket and trousers all in one, made of brown holland, with buttons only at the back of the neck and waist. This suit gave him a cool appearance on a hot summer's day, and Parramatta was as hot a place as I was ever in.

Some of the boys wore large pinafores. At nine years old, I used to wear, over my long-trousered cloth suit, a brown holland pinafore, down to my ankles nearly. All we pinafore-wearing boys had girls' names given us, by way of nickname.

The caps worn were of a peculiar style, having small leather peaks and large crowns with a cane round them, the pleats drawn into the centre to a button. After a time, these canes would be taken out, and then the caps used to hang loose at the side of the head. One boy, John Antill, who at once received the nickname of 'Magpie', came with a home-made cap, the upright made of square pieces of cloth – black, white, and red, with an immense cane top, no peak, and a ribbon at one side. Older lads wore what were called 'black billies' – the usual beaver or silk hats.

We walked to church two-and-two, in great order, while the soldiers marched there with a band playing and a crowd following, listening to the music. What would I not give to hear the old bugle-call again that used to summon us at nine o'clock at night to leave our lessons and go to bed.

School opened at seven a.m. and closed at nine p.m., but, morning, noon, and night, we had to learn the everlasting Eton Latin Grammar – parrot-like, as we learnt the Church Catechism. Of course there were some boys that read the Greek and Latin classics, but as I had not advanced so far I must confine my reminiscences to outside events.

We paid only £28 per annum, so we could not be expected to fare as well as schoolboys of the present day. For breakfast and tea we had merely dry bread, with tea in large basins containing about a quart apiece. Green tea alone was used then in the colony. The quantity allotted for our tea was very scant, but a liberal supply of brown sugar, about the colour of coffee, and a dash of milk, made it into a kind of syrup. Two or three basinfuls were considered necessary to wash down the dry bread, and the consequence was that the small boys became like podgy calves. For dinner we had roast beef one day and boiled the next, the boiled beef quite fresh, never corned or salted, sometimes mutton, and 'duff', that is suet puddings – with lumps of suet an inch in diameter, and not very nice, either. I have never liked duff since. We never tasted butter, unless by means of a shilling tip to the housekeeper, when one might find some buttered toast under his pillow at night.

On one occasion we had a great treat. A keg of butter – a hundredweight – was sent by a good mother directed to her son at the school, and with it a letter to say he was to see it delivered to a person in town. The letter did not arrive so soon as the butter, and the son thought the latter was a present for himself, and being a good-natured fellow he supplied the whole school, morning and night, till it was all gone. We went to him with a bit of paper in our hands and, with a large knife, he would place on it a good slice of butter, with which we marched into the dining room, using our pocket knives to spread it on our bread. The keg of butter lasted only three days.

No sooner was it finished than Mr. Forrest – 'Old Bob', as he was called – walked into the schoolroom one morning, and in his usual stentorian voice, called up Durham, the butter-giving boy, and said, 'Here is a letter from your mother to me, enquiring about some butter.' 'Yes, sir,' said Durham, 'I got it all right.' 'And did you see it delivered to Mrs. So-and-so?' 'No, sir. My mother did not tell me to send it anywhere.' 'Where is it, then?' 'We have eaten it all.' 'But it was a hundred-weight!' 'Yes, sir. It is all gone.' The master split his sides laughing, and told the boy that he must explain matters to his mother himself for he would have nothing to do with it.

The boys frequently received fruit and cakes from home, when it was the rule to share only with those in the same bedroom, after retiring to bed at night.

There was a playground of considerable size, which extended to the river. It was bounded by a fruit-garden on each side – unfortunately for the owners. In one of the gardens, a boy was once caught at the quinces, but as he had a £1 note in his pocket at the time he was able so to arrange matters that he was not only allowed to depart with his booty, but was favoured with an invitation to come again as often as he pleased.

The river afforded a good bathing-place. One of the boys, Alick Riley, was once nearly killed by plunging into the water from a high rock on the other side. He grazed his chest against a protruding rock under water, tearing his flesh several inches, and nearly fainted from loss of blood when he reached the landing.

It may not offend, in these distant years, if I mention a rather amusing mischance that befell one of my schoolfellows. The boy, one of the day-scholars, who had very red hair, was persuaded by a doctor named Stewart to have it dyed black. Unfortunately, the process turned it a puce colour – a sort of purple. He was so teased by the boys that he would not come to school again for about three months. When he came back again his hair had regained its natural colour with the exception of a fringe along the rim. This was worse still, and he had to stay away again until that also could be cut.

On one occasion, it being a holiday, the boys were allowed to pay a visit to the blacks' camp, some distance out of Parramatta, towards Prospect. The blacks had assembled from various parts of the colony, for the annual feast given them by the Governor, and to receive a blanket apiece. The latter gift is still customary wherever any blacks remain.

Before the feast came off, quarrels had sometimes to be adjusted, and on this occasion a fight took place, which we had the opportunity of witnessing.

There were probably six or seven hundred blacks assembled at their camps. The women of each party had first to be placed at a safe distance. The men painted themselves with white pipe-clay and red ochre and thus, without any clothing, the two parties advanced towards each other in a half circle, in ranks three and four deep, armed with spears, boomerangs, nullah-nullahs, waddies, and shields. When within a hundred yards or so of each other, the battle began. The spears flew across the half circle in great profusion, but were well parried by the shields. Then came the boomerangs, striking the ground first, and then rebounding in all directions among the enemy. These are dangerous weapons and cannot be warded off so well as the spears. After a little time, the contending parties closed in, and a hand-to-hand fight with their nullah-nullahs or waddies ended the affray. Three blacks were killed and a number wounded. Next day, notwithstanding, both parties assembled at the feast together and made friends.

Our usual recreation grounds were Harris's Fields, where cricket, rounders, steal-clothes, and leap-frog, were played. Once at leap-frog a boy broke first one arm and shortly afterwards the other. He was a bully, and used to 'punch', amidst other small boys, his three uncles, who were among his schoolfellows. The little boys were rather glad of this accident, and enjoyed teasing him whilst he had both arms in slings, and was no longer able to 'punch' them.

Outside the school-grounds, the younger boys often went picking ground-berries and 'five-corners'. Sometimes we walked to the North Rocks, Redbank, on the Parramatta River, or Newlands, on the opposite side of the river. Mr. and Mrs. Forrest frequently accompanied us on these occasions, or one of the ushers.

Crossing the dam to Newlands, we had to be on the watch for a savage dog that used to be chained up at Howell's mill. Only about two feet space was clear of his chain. Once I was going very cautiously by, when an old gander gave me a nip behind and made me jump almost into the dog's mouth.

I was born in a weather-board house near this spot, and opposite to the steamers' wharf. The soldiers' barracks were at the wharf, and long afterwards Byrnes's tweed factory was erected close by. Byrnes had also a brewery, adjoining the school, called by the boys 'big Bill Byrnes's Burton brewery.' My father had an old-fashioned brick house opposite the school, built by Government for his father – I think at the time when he had charge of the colonial cattle-stations, then all Government property. There was a great mulberry-tree in the garden and the largest English oaks in the colony were there. The property comprised about four acres of land. On a Guy Fawkes' Day, we used to make large bonfires from the dead lemon trees that had formed a hedge around it.

One St. Patrick's Day, the boys barred Mr. Forrest out of the schoolroom, because he had refused to give them a half-holiday. He was furious when he found the door closed against him. Shortly after, Mrs. Forrest came to a window and said that Mr. Forrest was dressing to go for Colonel Despard and the soldiers, so they quickly opened the door and took their seats.

He came into the school, I remember, in his Sunday-going clothes, which shewed that he really had intended to carry out his purpose.

My most frequent visits from the King's School were to the house of my grandfather, the Reverend Samuel Marsden. My grandmother and my aunts were very kind and used to supply me with the materials for a good feast as the holidays came round, for the breaking-up nights. The boys had to provide for these feasts themselves and held them in their several bedrooms. There would be from six to a dozen boys in each room.

I remember the Reverend Samuel Marsden very well at this time. He was about seventy years of age, short and stout, clean-shaved, and rather bald, with white hair. He wore a broad-brimmed beaver hat, and drove himself about Parramatta in one of the old-fashioned gigs, with a splendid horse. He had two rings placed in the splashboard, to pass the reins through, for he would sometimes drive home without them in his hands, in the forgetfulness of old age. His horse, however, would always stop safely at the front door of the parsonage, quite the same as if driven there.

Mr. Marsden imported a close carriage for Mrs. Marsden, as she was an invalid, but it was seldom used. It cost £200. Whenever he went far from home, he took with him a very faithful old servant, Paddy McCabe.

I remained at the King's School about three years, and left before the new building was occupied. I must not, therefore, refer to boys or matters connected with it.

I have never forgotten the names of the boys who were at the old school in my time. I know that two of them afterwards entered the army and were for a long while in India. Two others were doctors there. Two became clergymen and remained in livings in England. One was for a time Premier of New South Wales – William Foster. As a body, I believe, most of the boys turned out well, and to the end of their lives preserved a great respect for their old master, Mr. Forrest, and were proud to call themselves 'King's School boys'.

6

THE NEW AND CHANGING POPULATION OF NEW SOUTH WALES

John Dunmore Lang

1. Port Jackson (Sydney Cove) in the 1790's, Thomas Watling

2. Parramatta in 1793, Fernando Brambilla

4. *Robert Campbell,*
   Australia's first merchant

5. *Sophia Campbell*

◀ 3. *A Prison Hulk at Portsmouth*
   From the early 1770's, in an attempt to relieve pressure on prisons, old ships
   were turned into floating prisons. The end of the transportation of convicts to
   America upon the outbreak of the War of Independence increased the pressure
   in England. There were four such 'hulks' – dark, smelly and unhealthy – in
   Portsmouth in 1783.

6. *View of Sydney, 1802, Charles Alexandre Lesueur*

7. 'English officer and lady in New Holland'
From Malaspina, Expedition Drawings, 1793 (Courtesy of the Library of
New South Wales).

8. Silver-Stem Eucalyptus

9. Part of a View of Port Jackson, Richard Read, 1820
*The building in the foreground (right) is the home of Robert and Sophia
Campbell and (left) the Campbell warehouse. The two towers on the left across
the harbour were the entrance to Fort Macquarie on which site the Opera
House now stands.*

10. Emu Plains

*11. The Valley of the Grose,
Blue Mountains*

12. *Clyde Street, Miller's Point, Sydney, Samuel Elyard*
Built by some of Lang's 'virtuous Protestant artisans' the street resembled a
Scottish village.

13. *Melbourne, 1840*

14. *A Squatter's Station*

I

John Dunmore Lang and Immigration

Born in 1799, John Dunmore Lang arrived in New South Wales as a minister of the Church of Scotland in 1823 and he soon became one of the most influential, determined and colourful figures in the life of the colony. In Sydney he founded the Scots Church (opened 1826) and until 1878, that is, for the remainder of his life, he was its minister, even though nine voyages to Britain meant that he spent a third of that time overseas. It was not any mere love of travel which prompted these long sea voyages for both his father and grandfather had gone down with ships. Lang returned repeatedly to Britain chiefly to crusade for able Christian immigrants and for evangelical ministers, and with these endeavours he coupled a resolute opposition to the British policy of the continued transportation of convicts. While aware of the spiritual change in some convicts and emancipists, he early came to share the view that without the arrival of a large number of free settlers it would be the outlook and standards of the convict class which would mark the nation of the future. The overwhelming preponderance of convicts in the population was a dead weight upon all attempts to raise the moral tone of society. In Australia's first eighty years, some 100,000 men and women (men in proportion of ten to one) were transported as criminals. With a few exceptions, it is said, 'most were a disreputable lot, poorly educated, young, urban ne'er-do-wells, with a virtually non-existent family life'.[1] By comparison, in the first twenty years, there were fewer than a

---

[1]*A New History of Australia*, F. K. Crowley, 1974, p. 22. Yet, so common was a profession of religion of some kind that the 'religious affiliation' of convicts in NSW in 1827 is recorded as Episcopal, 2,199; Presbyterian, 172; Roman Catholic, 1,746; Jews, 46; Pagan, 1!

hundred free settlers who came to stay. After that time the immigration of free settlers rose steadily, yet in 1830, when there were under 40,000 people on the mainland and nearly half that number in Van Diemen's Land, at least 90 percent in both places were convict connected and 40 percent were of direct convict origin.

It was thus clear to all who were concerned for the Christian future of Australia that more than the conversion of a few individual convicts was needed if the prevailing moral climate of the country was to be changed. As free settlers were the backbone of the first churches in Sydney and Parramatta, so it would be upon larger numbers of such people that the future chiefly depended. Scotland had already started to send her sons to Australia in the 1820's, predominantly men of middle class background, but the next decade, in part as a result of Lang's energetic appeals for free, Protestant settlers, saw a vast increase in numbers.

Some of the newcomers, 'fifty-four adults, with their wives and families, being stonemasons and bricklayers, carpenters and joiners, blacksmiths, plasterers, etc.', travelled with Lang when he returned to Sydney in 1831 after a second visit to Britain. They were, as he later reported, 'all members of Christian churches and congregations'.[1]

John Dunmore Lang was a prolific writer and he early saw the necessity of combining the influence of the press with that of the pulpit. It was on his third voyage to Britain in 1833 that he wrote his major work, *An Historical and Statistical Account of New South Wales*. Seven chapters were complete before his ship, the *Alice*, rounded Cape Horn and by the time they reached England a large two-volume work of over eight hundred pages was complete. When published in London in 1834, its title page carried the biblical text, 'We have seen the land, and, behold, it is very good'. The History drew the attention of many to the young colony and immigration increased. There were 8140 migrants from Britain to New South Wales between 1831–35; the numbers rose to 29,663 between 1836–40 and the rise was to continue.[2] By 1847, when

[1] For the fullest detail on Lang see *Days of Wrath*, A Life of John Dunmore Lang, D. W. A. Baker, 1985, but Lang still awaits a spiritually sympathetic biographer.

[2] Other regions of Australia were also expanding, thus total immigrant figures to Australia as a whole in 1831–35 were 14,047 and in 1836–40, 53,835.

New South Wales had a population of 153,894, free settlers accounted for 51.6 percent of the increase in population over the previous sixteen years. In Australia as a whole, although the convict population was at a peak about 1840, the percentage of convicts in the total population had fallen by ten percent and this fall in percentage continued until transportation finally ended in 1853.

Lang's pleas for migrants were not motivated solely by the needs of the colony. He was shocked by the poverty and destitution in parts of Scotland and convinced that many of his upright and hard-working fellow-countrymen would fare better in the southern hemisphere. Aided by a bounty system, no less than 20 ship loads, some 5263 people, sailed from Scotland between March 1837 and January 1840. Some were Lowlanders, skilled in trades or crafts, and frequently belonging to the Secession Churches. Others were Gaelic-speakers from the Highlands and Islands, including areas recently touched by revival. In many instances the promise of better temporal interests in Australia appears to have been fulfilled. In 1851 the Rev. George Mackie sent a report to the Rev. John Bonar in Scotland concerning the Illawara and Shoalhaven areas of New South Wales where he was then serving. He reported 'large numbers' of Scots 'scattered all through the district and all doing well'. 'Many of them (if not the whole), who came penniless to the country, are now living far more comfortably than many first-class farmers in Scotland. The Gael is the most industrious, most comfortable man in this colony, and also the most willing to contribute of his substance for supporting the cause of Christ.'[1]

As the last sentence above indicates, many of these new settlers were not primarily concerned with their material interests. They were God-fearing people, ready to 'subordinate worldly comforts for spiritual advancement'. Mackie speaks of prayer meetings and sabbath schools springing up along the Shoalhaven river and not depending upon any ministerial oversight. Wherever such settlers were concentrated a new community outlook replaced the previous

[1]MS letter, dated January 8, 1851 (University of Edinburgh). Mackie finished his letter to Bonar (secretary of a Free Church committee) appealing for 'a few of the best works of divinity', and adding, 'Could I at present possess myself of *Owen*, I should deem myself happier and wealthier than Croseus'.

'indifferentism and latitudinarianism'.

One conspicuous example of such a Christian community occurred on the Limestone Plains which were to be the site of the future federal capital of Canberra. Here Robert Campbell, the Sydney merchant, acquired the choicest part of the land and built a country house which he called Duntroon in the years 1830–33. By 1839 he employed about seventy Scottish families of 'the finest pioneering stock', people whose days began with prayer, who kept the Lord's Day and whose graves bore such texts as, 'For here have we no continuing city, but seek one to come'. It was the Campbells who introduced half-day work for their employees on Saturdays so that their household duties could be complete before Sunday, and who made possible the building of Canberra's first church, St. John's. Robert Campbell died at Duntroon in 1846 and chose to be buried beside his wife and many old friends in the graveyard of St. John's, Parramatta.[1] The wording of a tablet to his daughter-in-law, Catherine Campbell, who came to fulfil the duties of the first lady of the Duntroon district, begins

> Making religion the governing principle of her life,
> She was a humble Christian . . .

The same characteristics of esteem for the Bible and for the Lord's Day developed in many other places. A writer, recalling the first settlers at Scot's Corner, a district in the New England area of New South Wales, says:

Our pioneering forefathers reverenced the Fourth Command very deeply. . . . All manual labour, unless in dire emergencies as a bush fire or a flood, was suspended on Sundays and even domestic tasks were cut down to a minimum. The housewives would have been horrified of having any washing seen out on the line on the Sabbath, while Sunday sport was then a thing unheard of.[2]

*   *   *

Sydney was undoubtedly slowest in responding to the new influx

[1] The grave is beside that of his brother-in-law, John Palmer, and close to those of Francis Oakes and Rowland Hassall. In 1912 the Campbell estate was compulsorily purchased for the establishment of Canberra as the Federal Capital. Duntroon House became part of the Royal Military College.

[2] *Scot's Corner*, A Local History, B. L. Cameron and J. L. McLennan, 1971, p. 80.

of men and women and many of the newcomers had no higher convictions than their predecessors. But here also a change for the better had begun. Moral and Christian standards openly scorned at an earlier date were gradually coming to be respected. One of the newcomers who contributed to this change was the Rev. John Saunders, an English Baptist, who arrived in December 1834, and became the first pastor of the town's first permanent Baptist congregation. Born in London in 1806, and well educated, it appears that Saunders had been considering missionary work in India before circumstances – including a reading of Lang's *Historical Account of New South Wales* – turned his attention to the Antipodes. In an issue of *The Baptist Magazine* for 1834 he wrote:

Australia affords a fine field for Christian exertion; the messenger of truth enters into a sphere where in many respects Satan's seat is; he stands in the gap to prevent his fellow countrymen from falling back into barbarism, or from descending to the level of degraded and forced labour population. Moreover, in so doing he forms the society of a State rising in extent, in commercial prosperity, and destined to bless or be the bane of many generations.[1]

Saunders' first sight of Sydney confirmed his sense of its need:

Sydney appears, at the first sight, like some oriental city rising from the wilderness at the command of a despotic power. On landing its streets appear wretched, sandy and loose, and a hovel next to a respectable shop; a hut next to a mansion a Prince might be proud of. It appears at present as unlike an English town as it could possibly be made. And then to look at the people; so thin, so sunburnt, and many of them so drunk – not a lady to be seen, hardly a woman.

Two years later in 1836, when Saunders – with inter-denominational aid – opened a Baptist Chapel in Bathurst Street, Lang was engaged in sensational conflict with one of Sydney's leading citizens, John Wilson, whose sexual promiscuity Lang exposed in the columns of the *Colonist* – a weekly which the Presbyterian leader had founded in 1835. What was involved, in Lang's words, was 'a struggle for moral ascendancy, in which the powers of evil,

---

[1]*Some Fell On Good Ground*, A history of the beginnings and development of the Baptist Church in New South Wales, 1831–1965, A. C. Prior, p. 29. See also *The First Australian Baptists*, K. R. Manley and M. Petras, Baptist Historical Soc. of NSW, 1981.

numerous and influential in the colony at the time, were arrayed in mortal hate on the one hand against the interests of public and private virtue on the other'.[1] The outcome was Wilson's departure from the colony in a hurry, with thousands of pounds of debts left behind him.

Saunders' work in Sydney only lasted till 1848, when, in poor health, he returned to England, but these were the years when the new 'moral ascendancy' was occurring.[2] Not only did Saunders' preaching, 'characterized by great power and impressiveness', build a strong congregation in Bathurst Street, but he gave energetic support to the numerous Christian agencies which were now operating. Saunders was active in the Bible and Tract Societies, in the Auxiliary of the London Missionary Society, in the Benevolent Society and the NSW Temperance Society. His many friendships indicate how evangelical Christians were united in spiritual and moral endeavour. The circle included John Lang, John Fairfax (owner of *The Sydney Morning Herald*) and the Methodist, the Rev. Ralph Mansfield who had made a life work of journalism.[3] *The Sydney Morning Herald*, the *Colonist* and other papers were significant factors in the moral change. James Swan, another settler who arrived in Sydney in 1837, became the publisher of the *Moreton Bay Courier* and a foundation member of the first Baptist Church formed in Brisbane.

Lang's hope that he might 'leave footprints on the sands of time in Australia' was certainly fulfilled. The extent of his labours was phenomenal. For fifty years he was committed to every movement, religious, educational and political, which he conceived to be for the advancement of the country. Along with others, it was

---

[1] *An Historical Account...*, vol 1, 1875, p. 447.

[2] Michael Roe, in his work, *Quest for Authority in Eastern Australia 1835–1851*, argues that this was the period when the nature of the colony changed dramatically. Three weeks before Saunders' death in 1858 he asked his physician if it might be possible for him to return to Australia. 'He would have liked to have his dust laid to rest in that bright land.' When it was known that his wife was left destitute, his friend, John Fairfax opened a subscription list in the *Sydney Morning Herald* and £650 was sent to her. In the words of the *Baptist Magazine*, Saunders was 'a Christian gentleman who sacrificed possible worldly greatness for the service of Jesus Christ'.

[3] Mansfield, mentioned earlier as the second Methodist preacher in Tasmania, had settled in NSW and, although leaving the regular Methodist ministry, remained active as both a preacher and writer.

Lang who did much to secure the change in the Colony's constitution which gave it a representative Parliament in 1850. For that achievement he was, says the Methodist leader, J. E. Carruthers, one of the four men 'to whom Australia will be indebted for all time to come'. Speaking of the many-sidedness of Lang's life and work, Frank Halan has written: 'As preacher, politician, journalist, organizer, immigration agent, anthropologist, geographer and historian, he indeed played many parts. For half a century he had a finger in every political pie. His domineering, self-righteous pugnacity kept him continually in trouble; his outstanding ability and sacrificial patriotism enabled him to render very real and lasting services to his adopted country.'[11]

Lang's *Historical and Statistical Account of New South Wales*, 1834, was revised and reprinted in 1837, 1852 and, finally, in 1875. It is from the final edition that the following pages are taken.

For the last time Lang was in the Scots Church, Sydney, on August 4, 1878, although not well enough to preach. He died on the following Thursday. For his funeral all shops and businesses closed in respect, the city churches tolled their muffled bells, the flags of ships in the harbour flew at half mast and several thousand people walked in the funeral procession.

The plinth beneath his statue, erected in Wynyard Square, Sydney, in 1891, bears the simple words:

JOHN DUNMORE LANG, 1799–1878,
PATRIOT AND STATESMAN

[11]'Sidelights on Dr. John Dunmore Lang' in *Royal Australian Historical Society Journal and Proceedings*, vol xxx, 1944, p. 221.

2

The New Settlers

John Dunmore Lang

It was during the administration of Governor King,[1] that about a dozen families of free emigrant settlers, chiefly from the Scottish border, arrived in the colony; having been induced to emigrate to New South Wales, on receiving a free passage from Government, with the promise of a grant of one hundred acres of land each on their arrival in the colony, and rations for a certain period afterwards from the King's stores. They arrived in the year 1802. Governor King mustered them on the quarter-deck of their vessel, shortly after their arrival, to ascertain their respective views, resources, and abilities. Observing an old grey-haired man in their number, who acknowledged he had been thirty years in business in London, the Governor exclaimed in astonishment, 'One foot in the grave, and the other out of it, what brought you here, old man?' It is somewhat remarkable that Captain King himself should have been the first of the two to have both feet in the grave. For many years after the death of the moralizing Governor, the old grey-haired man was still alive in the colony, and able to perform frequent journeys on horseback from his farm to Sydney, a distance of forty miles.

The free emigrants I have just mentioned were Presbyterians, and settled on farms of a hundred acres each of alluvial land near Portland Head, on the banks of the Hawkesbury. Their settlement was, in these early times, the most exemplary and successful in the colony; and some of them, or rather their sons, were afterwards among the wealthiest proprietors in the country. The reader may form some idea of the fertility of the district, from the fact that, from its first settlement in the year 1802, much of the land in cultivation had borne a crop of wheat every year for twenty-five or

[1] 1800–1806.

thirty years in succession, and in many years even a second crop of maize, or Indian corn.

The settlement of Portland Head also deserves peculiar credit, for having been the first in the colony to make a voluntary and self-originated effort to provide for itself the regular dispensation of the ordinances of religion. So early as the year 1809, the settlers in that district had erected a church, a stone-built edifice – the first that was ever erected in Australia by voluntary subscription – at a cost of upwards of 400*l.*, in the hope of obtaining a minister of their own communion from the mother country[1]; and from the very commencement of their settlement they assembled regularly every Sabbath for the public worship of God; one of their number, Mr. James Mein, a venerable old man when I first knew him in 1823, reading a sermon and presiding in the exercises of praise and extempore prayer, agreeably to the practice of the Church of Scotland. In a report of a Committee of the House of Commons on the state of the colony, which was printed by order of the House in the year 1812, the circumstance is mentioned to the honour of that individual and of the settlement to which he belonged; Governor Bligh having stated in his evidence before the Committee, that 'it was the only case of the kind he had heard of during his government of the colony'. I had the singular gratification of dispensing the sacrament of the Holy Communion to this little community in the year 1824, according to the hallowed customs of the Presbyterian Church. There were twenty communicants; and the very peculiar circumstances in which the ordinance was solemnized in the little church – situated on a rising ground on the edge of the forest, and overlooking a beautiful and romantic reach of the noble river – rendered the whole scene the most interesting and affecting I had ever witnessed.

From the progressive settlement of families and individuals of this industrious class in various parts of the colony, the agricultural resources of the country began to be developed, and additional

[1]This church, given the name 'Ebenezer' ('Hitherto hath the Lord helped us', 1 Sam. 7:12) by its builders, still stands on a bend in the Hawkesbury River, 40 miles from Sydney. George R. S. Reid describes these early settlers as, 'God-fearing folk . . . They were frugal, hard-working, intelligent and serious-minded. It would have been well for Australia had their robust faith and religious convictions been more generally maintained' (*The History of Ebenezer*, booklet, seventh edition 1977, pp. 3–4).

quantities of land were progressively brought into cultivation. Large importations of stock of all kinds had been made from time to time at the public expense, both from India and from the Cape of Good Hope. . . .
The state of morals in New South Wales was sufficiently low, previous to the era of free emigration in the year 1821. It is almost unnecessary to speak of the state of religion in such a condition of society as was then prevalent in the colony. There were 'a few names', however, 'even in Sardis', who had uniformly maintained a higher character.

From the era of free emigration, however, in the year 1821, the colony began to assume a more favourable aspect than it had ever presented previous to that period. Concubinage was gradually discountenanced in the higher circles of the colony – in so far at least as regarded the open and shameless avowal of it, which had previously been comparatively frequent – and of course gradually disappeared from the face of society; for, although still practised by a few *old offenders*, the daily increasing array of well-ordered families, both among the free emigrant and the more reputable portion of the emancipist population, at length forced that particular form of colonial immorality into the shade.

It was scarcely, however, from the higher classes of colonial society – whether Government officers, lawyers, landholders of the higher class, or merchants – that a healing influence could be expected to emanate in that comparatively early period of the history of the colony, to cleanse and to purify the land. The men who are *'clothed in purple and fine linen, and who fare sumptuously every day'*, may be powerful to do good from their wealth and their station in society; but that good is but rarely done, and the influence they exert on society is of consequence far more frequently evil. Even their profession of Christianity – a sort of fashionable accompaniment of gentility in the present age – is perhaps more hurtful than beneficial to the cause of pure and undefiled religion; for the vessels of the House of God are for the most part polluted by their desecrating touch, and the day of God profaned by their unholy example.

The moralist will ask, therefore, how it fared in such circumstances with the humbler classes of the colonial community; and, in reply to such a question, it must be acknowledged that, in directing the eye to those who occupied the lower steps of the colonial ladder, during the first ten years from the period of my first arrival in the colony, in the month of May, 1823, the prospect was sufficiently discouraging. Most of the free emigrants who arrived in New South Wales during the administrations of Sir Thomas Brisbane and Sir Ralph Darling settled in the interior as proprietors of land and stock, and diffused, in many instances at least, a salutary influence over the country; but the towns, and especially Sydney, continued much the same, both in population and morals, as before. The first object of the ambition of a newly-emancipated convict, at that period, was to be employed as a constable – a situation which insured him sufficient pay for his maintenance, and enabled him to lead a life of comparative inaction. The next object of his ambition was to obtain a licence to keep a public-house, which was easily obtainable for 25*l.* per annum, provided his house and character were sufficient to satisfy the visiting magistrates – and they were generally very easily satisfied, especially as they were not unfrequently wholesale importers of wines and spirits. The number of these nuisances consequently increased prodigiously in the colony, and the consumption of ardent spirits increased proportionably; insomuch that in the year 1836, when the population of Sydney amounted to 20,000 souls, the number of public-houses in the city was upwards of two hundred; the licences alone producing an annual revenue to the Government of more than 5000*l.*, exclusive of the direct duties on spirits, which then amounted, for the whole colony, to 117,000*l.* per annum.

Whether the number of public-houses ought to be limited by authority is a question which has often been asked in New South Wales, but which I confess it is somewhat difficult to answer. I am inclined to believe, however, that the influence, to be employed successfully, in counteracting so enormous an evil, must be of a totally different kind, and that the cruse of purifying salt, which alone can be expected to heal the bitter waters, must be cast in at the fountain-head, or at least much higher up the stream. It was on this principle, at least, that I endeavoured to act in the matter myself.

I had ascertained very early in my colonial life, that a large proportion of the money expended in the numerous public-houses of Sydney was expended by mechanics – chiefly of the class of emancipated convicts – whose wages were then sufficiently high to enable them to spend several days every week in low dissipation, to the great annoyance and the serious loss of their employers. It appeared to me, therefore, that the only effectual remedy for so great an evil would be to introduce into the colony a number of reputable and industrious free emigrant mechanics from the mother country, who, by working at their several handicrafts six days every week, and expending their earnings in a proper manner, would in due time render the means of dissipation less easily attainable by the emancipated convict-mechanics, and withdraw the means of support, to a certain degree at least, from the colonial publicans. Attempts had doubtless been repeatedly made by individual colonists to carry out mechanics to New South Wales, under engagements to serve for a sufficient length of time in the colony to repay the expense of their passage out; but these attempts had always been unsuccessful, the mechanics uniformly breaking through their engagements as soon as possible. It appeared to me, however, that if mechanics only of proper character were selected, they would faithfully fulfil their engagement, provided that engagement were an equitable one; for it often happened, in the instances I refer to, that a breach of engagement on the part of the servant or mechanic had been occasioned by a previous attempt to over-reach him on the part of the master or employer – the mechanic being generally hired in the mother country to labour for a term of years in the colony at English instead of colonial wages.

It was in these circumstances that I was induced to propose the arrangement which I succeeded in making with Lord Goderich, in the year 1831, and to which I have already referred in the first volume of this work, for carrying out a number of reputable mechanics, with their wives and children, for the erection of the requisite buildings for an academical institution, or college, for the education of youth in the town of Sydney.

I accompanied these mechanics myself, in a vessel chartered for the purpose, which arrived in the colony in October, 1831; and in seven days thereafter the buildings in question were commenced, the average rate of wages for good mechanics being then 2l. sterling a week. In six or eight months, all the unmarried men had paid the whole of their passage-money by weekly instalments from their wages; and when the buildings were at length necessarily discontinued for a time, the greater number of the married mechanics had paid about two-thirds of theirs. In short, the experiment proved completely successful.

The Scotch mechanics, as they were called in the colony, were men of superior ability in their respective handicrafts; for I had required them, previous to their being engaged, to produce certificates of their mechanical skill, as well as of their moral character, and their connexion with some Christian congregation. In addition, therefore, to the other consequences of their importation, they greatly improved the style of architecture throughout the colony; and, by becoming contractors for public buildings, they enabled the Government to erect superior buildings at a much cheaper rate than had previously been current in the colony.

But it was the moral influence of their example, as sober and industrious men, that was of greatest importance to the community. A few months after their arrival, no fewer than sixteen of them joined together in the purchase of an allotment of ground in the town of Sydney, which was afterwards surrendered to eight of the number. Seven of them subsequently entered into partnership, as contractors for the erection of the stonework of various public and private buildings both in Sydney and in the interior. Several others had purchased allotments on their own private account, after paying for their passage out, and erected good houses of stone for their own residence; and individuals of their number had sent home money to their poorer relatives in Scotland. Nay, before fifteen months had elapsed from the period of their arrival, several other families and individuals of a similar class in society had arrived in the colony from various parts of Scotland; having emigrated to New South Wales solely in consequence of the favourable intelligence they had received from their relatives there of the state of the country, and of the prospect which it held forth to persons of a similar station in life.

The emigration of reputable and industrious persons of various other classes of society, from the United Kingdom to New South Wales, kept pace with that of mechanics, during the whole period of the administration of Sir Richard Bourke; and their influence on the colony was salutary in the highest degree. In short, from the period of the arrival of the Scotch mechanics in the year 1831, a visible and striking change for the better was gradually effected; not only in that important and influential portion of the population of the colonial capital to which they belonged, but throughout the colony generally. For example, the entire population of New South Wales amounted in the year 1833 to 60,861. It amounted on the 1st of March, 1851, to 189,951, having more than tripled itself, from immigration chiefly, during the intervening period of eighteen years; but the duties on spirits for 1851 amounted only to 107,013*l*. 10*s*. 1*d*., that is, less by 10,000*l*. than the amount collected for a third of the population eighteen years before.

In forming an estimate of the state of morals in the Australian colonies, it must not be forgotten that, although very many of the free emigrants who have hitherto settled in these colonies have been men of reputable character and respectable standing in the world, others have been driven to emigrate, as a sort of *dernière ressource*, after every expedient for gaining a livelihood in the mother country had completely failed; and it sometimes unfortunately happens that such persons are just as bankrupt in character as in purse.

The general prevalence of a spirit of grasping avarice among the buying and selling portion of the community had also a most unfavourable influence on the morals of the colony for a series of years after my own arrival in the country. The idea of asking a fair price for an article was then seldom thought of: the grand question was, how much could be got for it by any means; and, I am sorry to add, it was not always considered, even in quarters where one should have expected better things, whether the means were fair or otherwise. As immigration from the mother country increased, however, the mercantile transactions of the colony, both in the wholesale and retail departments, came to be conducted, with not a few exceptions, of course, on a much better system. The profits on particular speculations gradually became more and more reasonable, in proportion as the field of mercantile enterprise widened, and competition increased; while the numerous reputable free emigrants, who from time to time arrived in the colony, and established themselves as dealers in general, or as manufacturers of articles for sale in various branches of business, made sad inroads on the province of the old colonial extortioner, by asking only a reasonable profit on their articles of merchandise, or a reasonable price for their labour. In short, the mercantile pulse of the colony did not then beat quite so high as it had done at the period referred to, but it indicated a much higher state of moral health in the body politic of the country.

In regard to the gold-mining community of New South Wales, and its bearing and influence on the moral and religious welfare of the colony, of which there were at one time the most dismal apprehensions entertained, I made it my business, before undertaking my present visit to England and the publication of this work, to visit a whole series of the gold-fields, both active and extinct, of the colony; and in all of these, without exception, I found an orderly, reputable, and church-going people, with their places of worship and their Sunday-schools for the children.[1] I have already stated what I found at the extinct gold-fields, but now promising towns of Young and Forbes. There was precisely the same at the still active mines of Grenfell, Gulgong, Hill End, and Tambaroora. At Hill End in particular, I found a Presbyterian church, in which I officiated twice to numerous congregations during my stay. It was built of brick, remarkably appropriate in every respect, and had cost 1300*l.*, to which a successful gold-miner, and a Christian man, had contributed very liberally, while the other denominations of the place had their places of worship, also of a creditable appearance. In short, gold and tin mining having now become regular colonial industries, many of the miners have their wives and children with them at the gold-fields, living in cottages of their own on allotments they have purchased at the Government land sales.

In one word, the colony has undergone a wonderful change for the better during the last thirty or forty years. All traces of its origin as a penal settlement have long since disappeared; and I have no hesitation in stating my belief and conviction that, not only in externals, but in reality, it would stand a comparison with most parts of the United Kingdom. . . .

The following is a list of the different religious denominations of the colony for the year 1872, showing the number of ministers of these denominations respectively, as also the number of places of worship, of individual sittings, and of the number of attendants at the principal service on Sundays:

[1]Gold was first discovered near Bathurst in NSW in February 1851. Lang made his first visit to the gold mines that year when, he says, 'the mania for the diggings was at its height'. The visit referred to above was made in the 1870's.

Denomination.	Number of Ministers.	Number of Churches or Chapels.	Total Number of individual Sittings.	Number of attendants at the Principal Service on Sundays.
Church of England –				
Five Bishops.				
Diocese of Sydney				
Diocese of Newcastle				
Diocese of Goulburn	164	295	52,320	37,019
Diocese of Grafton and Armidale				
Roman Catholic Church –				
Five Bishops.				
Diocese of Sydney				
Diocese of Maitland				
Diocese of Goulburn	115	207	28,090	35,514
Diocese of Bathurst				
Diocese of Armidale				
Presbyterian Church	72	120	21,818	10,733
Wesleyan Methodist Church – Ministers & Local Preachers	82	241	33,337	19,256
Congregational Church – (Independents)	24	25	10,143	5,985
Baptist Church	14	24	3,480	1,912
Primitive Methodist Church	15	42	6,200	5,300
Particular Baptist Church	2	3	930	525
Unitarian Church	2	1	250	110
United Methodist Free Church	3	5	630	184
United Free Gospel Church – Country	1	1	70	25
German Lutheran Church – Country	1	2	150	80
Independent (Unconnected) Country	1	1	200	75
Evangelical Lutheran – Country	1	4	219	94
Jew's Synagogue – City of Sydney	5	2	510	330
Christian Israelites – Country	1	3	210	70
General Total	503	976	158,557	117,212[1]

[1] The total population of NSW in 1871 was 503,981.

7

DEVELOPMENTS IN TASMANIA AND VICTORIA

Corra Lynn, Tasmania

I

Tasmania

Despite initial success in the 1820's through the work of Methodists (who Lt. Governor George Arthur believed could do more good than Anglican chaplains), the spiritual scene was far from promising in the early 1830's. The Launceston chapel had closed and Carvosso had returned to England from Hobart, leaving a divided and troubled church. In the words of one contemporary: 'The duty of a clergyman in Hobart Town is indeed most arduous. He is placed as it were in the very gorge of sin, in the midst of the general receptacle for the worst characters in the world. . . . He has here to struggle with the enemy at close combat, face to face, foot to foot, and to brace himself up to the utmost point of exertion.'

During the 1830's, largely under the leadership of three men, Nathaniel Turner, John Manton and Joseph Orton, there was a major advance. It took place through ordinary preaching services[1] attended by the power of the Holy Spirit in answer to earnest prayer. As Turner worked in the south of the island, and Manton in the north, there were many conversions.

Speaking of the exercise of the church in prayer, Turner's biography records:

At the six o'clock prayer-meeting on the quarterly fast day, the vestry was more than crowded, and the people had to go into the chapel. So at the noon-day service, several who had lately been brought from the

---

[1] But these Methodists, it should be said, also preached in many situations other than their few chapels. Turner was often in the convict barracks, and Sir George Arthur gave him permission to stop the work of road-gangs in order to address them. 'In exhibiting the hope set before them in the Gospel,' says Turner's biographer, 'he would mingle his tears and prayers with theirs. This kind of service occupied a short half hour, and he not unfrequently held several such during the same day.'

very gate of destruction into Gospel liberty, gave up their employment for the day, and spent the whole of the forenoon in the schoolroom, in prayer and praise. On the Monday morning following, at six o'clock, a special prayer-meeting for the outpouring of the Spirit was held, and a blessed influence prevailed.

Our June quarterly visitation was, I believe, the best our society ever knew in this part of the world. Glory be to God! At our quarterly fast the power of the Spirit came down so that many were led to cry aloud for mercy. Several souls found peace with God. The spirit of prayer was given in an extraordinary degree. Such wrestling and pleading with God I never beheld in these regions. Our people seem all on fire. At most of our prayer-meetings, which are numerously attended, souls are crying out for mercy. At one meeting a man and his wife were kneeling side by side. The man was made happy, and immediately prayed aloud for his wife. She too found the Saviour.

The same source summarizes the situation in 1834 as follows:

The Melville Street chapel [Hobart] was ordinarily crowded on Sabbath evenings, and special efforts were put forth to secure a more copious outpouring of the Holy Spirit. Under the preaching on the first Sabbath evening in September many were awakened; and at the prayer-meeting eight or ten found peace with God. Throughout Van Diemen's Land there was a good work at that time. At Glenorchy, the darkness of many was turned to day. At New Norfolk, where for six months public worship had been held in the Court House, steps were taken to build a chapel. Mr. Butters wrote from Port Arthur that more than twenty had begun to seek salvation. At Launceston, Mr. Manton was meeting with encouraging success.

Two years later the Methodist records for 1836 say:

The Lord has poured out His Spirit in a more glorious manner, and many have been turned from darkness to light and from the power of Satan unto God. We live in peace, we dwell together in unity.

From 1835 to 1839 Turner was in New Zealand and New South Wales. On his return to Tasmania he was again to see crowded prayer-meetings and unusual blessing.

On Monday, June 20th, after a series of blessed services on the Sabbath, a gracious revival broke out in Launceston. 'At the prayer-meeting several were in deep distress, and three or four found peace with God. Many of the old members appeared on full stretch for holiness. May the sacred fire continue to burn, and set us all on a flame!'

The record of one of his country Sabbaths is as follows:

Sunday, 25th, Longford. – Here morning and evening. In afternoon at Mr. Ball's prayer-meeting at Mountford, where we had a most lively season. Thank God, here are souls of the right sort; men of strong faith, and mighty in prayer, whom God is using for His own glory. Colonel Hazelwood, father of Mrs. Ball, a man of nearly eighty years of age, has become the subject of saving grace.

It is clear that neither Turner nor his colleagues believed that such days of revival could be organized or 'worked up'. Twenty years later in Queensland, on hearing news of an awakening from his daughter in Melbourne, he replied to her: 'Your last did me good, raising my drooping spirits. It led me back to days gone by, when my soul lived in revival scenes like these, though on a smaller scale. In Hobart Town, Launceston, and Sydney, we were privileged to see the Lord's hand made bare in the conversion of many souls, for which I still bless His name.'

A widespread spiritual change evidently took place in Tasmania between 1820 and 1850. Speaking of the situation around 1820, John West says, 'The return of the Sabbath was unattended in the country with a religious welcome'. In contrast with this condition he tells us that thirty years later the immigrant population was 'usually in attendance' upon one hundred Christian clergy. This means that a large part of the island was in the habit of church attendance by the 1850's. The convicts mostly by compulsion, but West looked forward to the time when 'moral power' would take the place of 'prescriptive authority' and when 'a vast apparatus, already supplied by the state and private zeal, will bring within reach of every colonial family some form of Christian doctrine'.[1]

[1] *The History of Tasmania*, John West, 1852 (ed. A. G. L. Shaw, 1971, p. 72, p. 164).

2

Port Phillip (Melbourne and Victoria)

For the first half of the last century the whole south-eastern corner of Australia was known as New South Wales, with the large area south of the Murray river called the Port Phillip District. It was this district which, in 1851, became the separate colony of Victoria.

An initial attempt to form a settlement in the Port Phillip District in 1803 was given up in preference for Van Diemen's Land. In 1835 a very small settlement was commenced by John Batman on the river Yarra (to be named Melbourne in 1837). One of those who had crossed from Van Diemen's Land at this time was an evangelical Christian by the name of Henry Reed, who went over, he says, 'to devise some means for preserving the natives from destruction'. With some five men, possessed of three huts, Reed 'had prayers every day, read the Scriptures and preached Christ to them'. The following year the Rev. Joseph Orton (the Methodist preacher) accompanied Batman, who crossed with his family from Van Diemen's Land to become a permanent settler. While those who participated in the beginnings of the new settlement were of different Protestant denominations, their over-all unity in Christian commitment was expressed together in public worship. Among those present at the first organized services held on April 24, 1836, was John Pascoe Fawkner, a Congregationalist (Independent), who became the father of the Victorian press; James Simpson, the colony's first magistrate, who helped Orton by repeating the responses to the Anglican liturgy; and Presbyterian Dr. Alexander Thompson, future mayor of Geelong, who 'raised the tunes and led the singing'. These historic services were held on the eastern slope of ground belonging to Batman and are described by Joseph Orton who was the preacher:

Sunday, April 24th. – At eleven o'clock the people of the settlement were assembled for public worship on the premises of Mr. John Batman. The service was commenced by reading the Liturgy of the Church of England, after which I addressed the audience from the young ruler's question, 'What shall I do to inherit eternal life?' At the conclusion of my discourse I took occasion to dwell on the propriety of a consistent deportment on the part of the settlers in this new settlement, particularly enjoining them to acknowledge God in all their ways, that they might insure the Divine blessing with their undertaking; otherwise they might expect His curse in all they undertook.

In the afternoon, the people again assembled, to whom I preached from John 1:12. The number of Europeans present was greater than in the morning, but the largest portion of my congregation consisted of natives, about fifty in number, who sat very quietly during the time of service, and seemed particularly interested by the singing. I took the opportunity to make an appeal to the intelligent part of my audience in behalf of these poor depraved creatures, among whom they had come to reside, and whose land they had come to occupy; endeavouring to show their incumbent duty to use all possible means to promote their temporal and spiritual welfare. I have not been more interested by any sight than the one presented this afternoon. My soul truly went out after their best interests. I felt as though I could sacrifice every personal comfort for their welfare. I longed to be able to communicate my views and feelings to them. I could but pray and anticipate the happy day when these poor creatures, or at least their rising progeny, will come to a knowledge of the truth and participate in the blessings of the light of the glorious gospel.

Orton was not able to stay in Melbourne, and the first minister to settle was the Rev. James Clow (1790–1861) who arrived in 1837 with his wife and family of six daughters and two sons. It was the same year that the Government authorized the first sale of land lots and J. P. Fawkner became the first purchaser. Clow, from the Church of Scotland, had been a chaplain of the Bombay Establishment of the East India Company from 1815 to 1833, when he appears to have retired on a pension. He had not long begun preaching at Melbourne (in a structure shared by other denominations) when he was followed from Scotland by the young Rev. James Forbes who was to become his son-in-law. A meeting of Presbyterians presided over by Clow called Forbes to be their minister in June 1838. About the same time Congregationalists gathered under the Rev. William Waterfield (meeting in the home of John Pascoe Fawkner), while Baptist services were taken by Peter Virtue and James Wilson.[1] James Forbes built a strong evangelical and Presbyterian congregation which by 1841 had outgrown two buildings. J. Campbell Robinson has written of Forbes: 'In prayer he was a great man. . . . Apart from the usual week-night prayer meeting he often called his elders together for what he termed "Concerts for prayer". These usually lasted several days, when the needs of the congregation and of the young country were specially pleaded at the throne of grace.'[2]

A good illustration of Forbes' thought and spirit can be seen in the following extract from a letter of September 10, 1839, addressed to a young 'squatter' who had moved inland:

I rejoice to hear that you are so comfortably situated. Earnestly do I hope you will realize abundantly the comforts of the Spirit. You want the outward and ordinary means, it is true – such as the ordinance of the sanctuary and the preaching of the Word. You have access, however, to the two most efficacious sources of divine influence – private prayer and *study* of the Scriptures. If these two means are neglected, the use of the others will be productive of little benefit; if these are attended to the want of the others will be but little felt. The Hearer of Prayer is ever present. The all-prevailing Mediator is ever nigh. The Holy Spirit is always at hand. This, I doubt not, you have abundantly experienced in the bush, and the more you are thrown on the secret means – the more you are driven to fall on your knees amid the solitudes of the forest and on the wide expanse of the wilderness – the more richly you will feel that the Lord will ever remember His own, and that you can never be alone, seeing your best and kindest Friend is ever nigh.

I am sure I need not remind you of Him who said, 'Ye are the light of the world', and dark as is the place where you are, I fondly trust you will be enabled to shed a little brightness amidst the gloom. Private Christians can do a great deal for the Lord's cause, perhaps in some respects they can do more than ministers. The ungodly and profane regard religion as 'the parson's *trade*', and treat his admonitions as

[1]The first Baptist preacher to come to Melbourne (in 1840) was John J. Mouritz who helped to form the original congregation which met in a tent, in a furniture shop, and then in a weatherboard schoolroom loaned by the Presbyterians. Dying at the age of 71 in 1868, his gravestone bears the text, 'By the grace of God I am what I am'. *Baptists in Victoria, Our First Century*, F. J. Wilkin, 1939.

[2]*Melbourne's First Settled Minister*, Paper read at the Victorian Historical Society, 1928, pp. 16–17.

very much in the way of business. They cannot regard the kind advice and the reproving *example* of laymen in the same light. I hope I shall not be forgotten in your prayers. There are too few praying Presbyterians, I fear, but I fondly believe that better days are before us all.[1]

When Orton returned to Melbourne on a visit in 1839 he was astonished at the change. Instead of the wilderness encountered on his previous visit there was already an extensive town, with four or five hundred houses, and a Methodist Church (without minister) existing alongside the others. Already new settlers were pouring in from New South Wales and more from Britain. In the year 1841 alone, 8000 passengers landed from 44 ships in Melbourne. By 1850 the city's population of 23,000 matched that of Hobart which it was quickly to overtake. Sydney at the same date had some 54,000 residents, but such was Melbourne's continued growth that it was soon to be the serious rival of Australia's first settlement. In a journal entry of March 13, 1856, Jane Barker in Sydney complained that mail to and from Britain lost 'much time by visiting Melbourne both coming and going . . . and I hope some better plan may be devised, but Melbourne is destined to cut out Sydney, and I think deserves to do so from its larger amount of energy and public spirit . . .'

Certainly Melbourne lacked the dead weight of a large convict population and in the person of Charles Joseph Latrobe, from 1839 Superintendent of the Port Phillip District and from 1851 Victoria's first Governor, it benefited from a leader who believed that true religion and biblical morality are the foundations for any happy society.

By 1886, when the population of Victoria was over one million, there was church accommodation for almost half that figure and a weekly attendance of around 315,000 people. Ministers included 185 Anglican, 177 Presbyterian, 161 Methodist, 54 Independent and 38 Baptist. The Methodists appear to have been the most exact in recording the growth of their membership. The figure stood at 3937 in 1858, 8088 in 1865 (1750 having been added the previous year, of which 'two-thirds had been converted to God from out of the world') and 16,095 in 1886. In 1886 the members were still a comparatively small proportion to those in regular attendance at

[1]*Colonization and Church Work in Victoria*, C. Stuart Ross, 1891, pp. 78–79.

Methodist churches (97,115). It is a striking fact that the churches made a deeper impression upon society when people were *not* hurried into membership. The fact that 'ten per cent of the population were Wesleyan' in their church adherence was less important to the spiritual leaders than the lower number of communicant members who, by life and word, could bear personal testimony to their salvation in Christ.

During these years there were many local revivals recorded in Victoria, but, as the century advanced and more of the influence of Charles G. Finney was felt in the churches, revivals tended to become confused with organized evangelistic campaigns, and, for the first time, records of the number of 'converts' began to be announced. The enquirer's public acknowledgement of his need, as known to Methodism, was changed into a 'decision for Christ' and, instead of such a person being told that he must receive assurance through a 'witness' which only the Holy Spirit can give, the public act itself slowly became regarded as sufficient evidence of a changed relationship to God. John Watsford spoke of the danger towards the end of the last century, 'lest the pledge of consecration be taken for conversion'. This tendency had already begun in the 1860's and it would seem to have been present in the 'revival work' associated with the coming of the Californian, the Rev. W. Taylor, to Melbourne in 1863. The Methodist leader D. J. Draper welcomed Taylor to his pulpit – 'a *real live Yankee*' – and wrote of his ministry to a friend: '*many hundreds* have been awakened and led to seek the Lord'. But Draper had reservations, saying in the same letter, 'I hope we shall not go too fast in spiritual things'. The justification for his reservation was subsequently confirmed. 'As time wore on,' says Draper's biographer and fellow-Methodist minister, 'he became convinced of what previously he had only feared, that the amount of real and permanent good effected by Mr. Taylor's labours was in no proportion to the apparent results which followed them'.[1]

Notwithstanding this necessary qualification, it is clear there were large and permanent additions to the churches of Victoria during this period. We close this chapter with one illustration:

[1]*Life of Daniel J. Draper*, John C. Symons, 1870, p. 267. On the subject of 'Calling for Decisions' see the valuable chapter in D. M. Lloyd-Jones' *Preaching and Preachers*, 1971. A wrong kind of pressure exerted on people during evangelistic campaigns unquestionably led to discrediting the whole idea of revival in the present century.

Notable and large additions came through God's blessing upon ordinary services, and the Revival movements which now took place. That at Brighton may be placed in the front of our notice, as it was one of the earliest in order of time. The rising cloud of blessing appeared at a lovefeast held at Great Brighton, on May 22nd, 1859. The sorrow for sin shown by numbers expressed itself in tears and prayers for mercy. The Sanctuary became a Bochim, a place of weeping. Nine persons professed that night to have their mourning turned into joy, by the sweet assurance of God's reconciling love, and others went to their homes 'sorrowing after a godly sort', and seeking the conscious salvation of Christ. Then special services were held daily, and private devotions increased in intensity and spiritual power, so that soon there was 'a sound of abundance of rain'. The work went on amazingly, affecting all classes, the tender child and the aged sire, the educated man and the unlettered peasant. Answers to prayer were swift or immediate in a wife's conversion, a husband's decision and prayerfulness, and in whole families brought to love and serve God. 'Showers of blessing' came on devout worshippers, and on most of the congregations in this Circuit. The Rev. E. King, the Minister, who had the lead of this movement, is in temperament calm, placid, even; in manner and spirit, courteous and kindly; not given to rant, nor favouring unseemly extravagancies in public worship; but he is a devout man, a faithful preacher, a diligent student of the Greek Testament, of sterling piety, a witness and embodiment of Christian holiness, and has been favoured, not so much with the smiles of the populace, but by the praises of good men, and with the benediction of several notable revivals under his ministry. The President of the Conference and other Ministers, came to the help of the Circuit Preachers, so that the good work spread to Little Brighton, Moorabbin, and the other places adjacent. The results of this religious revival were peace and goodwill where brethren had been at strife; the greatly quickened piety of professed disciples of Christ; the spirit of praise, prayer, love, self-denial, benevolence, triumphant in them; scores of careless, hardened sinners brought to seek the everlasting welfare of their own souls and those of their families and acquaintances; many trained in godly families taking the important steps of religious decision and surrender to Christ; between one and two hundred new members added to the Churches; and the fruits of good living thereafter manifesting the genuineness and power of the work.[1]

[1]*The Early Story of the Wesleyan Methodist Church in Victoria*, W. L. Blamires and John B. Smith, 1886, pp. 90–92. Other illustrations of revival in Victoria will be given below.

8

PARRAMATTA AND NEW TESTAMENT CHURCH GROWTH

A Sharp Corner
James Watsford (who arrived in New South Wales, January 18, 1812)
established the first transport running from Parramatta to Sydney in the 1820's
and then the first across the Blue Mountains to Bathurst in 1832. His pair-horse
light coaches were certainly more primitive than the above.

I

John Watsford

John Watsford, the third in James and Jane Watsford's family of twelve, was the first outstanding preacher to be born in Australia. He served in Fiji, Queensland (Brisbane), New South Wales, South Australia and Victoria and saw genuine revivals at several periods during his ministry. On retiring from active circuit work in 1891 he continued preaching, and his autobiography, *Glorious Gospel Triumphs, As Seen In My Life and Work*, was published in 1900. In an Introductory Sketch to that book the Rev. W. H. Fitchett wrote:

As a preacher and theologian, John Watsford does not, perhaps, belong to the 'modern' school; and, though well read in general literature, and singularly versed in Scripture and in Methodist theology, he has no claims to be, in any wide sense, a scholar. But he represents and embodies all the best and most characteristic qualities of Methodism: its pity for men; its passion for conversions; its faith in Divine Saviour and a personal redemption; its proclamation of the sanctifying offices of the Holy Ghost; its conception of religion as a present spiritual victory over sin, a creation of saintly character, here and now; its faith in the swift coming and assured triumph of the kingdom of God. And John Watsford has done, and still does, more perhaps than any other single figure to maintain these great and kindling conceptions in the Methodist Churches of Australasia.

These spiritual elements, which became so marked in Watsford's character, he first saw as a youth in the lives of the Methodist preachers he mentions in this chapter and, most notably, in Daniel J. Draper and Nathaniel Turner. Parramatta, 'to many the dearest spot on earth', writes Turner's son, J. G. Turner, was not without its serious problems in the early 1830's. Marsden was an old man and the Methodist work had come to a virtual standstill. Speaking of the year 1831, J. G. Turner writes: 'Mr Leigh, who was stationed at Parramatta, had lately followed the remains of his dear wife to the tomb, was reduced to great weakness both of body and mind, and was utterly unfit for any ministerial duty'.[1] When Draper was settled in the circuit in 1836 he found affairs 'in a very disorganized state' and an apathy in the congregation, yet he wrote in his diary, 'I cannot but think that this colony will yet be favoured with an outpouring of the Holy Spirit'. By 1838 there was some change. In the words of Draper's biographer, 'Earnest effort, fervent prayer and strong faith were not in vain'. In 1839 Draper could say, 'congregations are overflowing' and later that year there was a congregation of 450 at the opening of a new church, while elsewhere in the town, on the same day, the foundation stone of a second chapel was laid. Events were to prove that this was an over-optimistic estimate of future growth.[2] Draper's biography does not speak of 'revival' during his period in the Parramatta circuit which he left early in 1842. It is clear that church growth at this time was, however, considerable. Methodist membership in New South Wales rose from 121 in 1834 to 707 in 1841 and, as a writer pointed out in the 1850's, the standards required for members were such that they constituted only 'a very small part of those attending services'. Turner returned to the Parramatta circuit in 1849 and his biography confirms Watsford's testimony:

In Parramatta were a few devoted men who felt for God's cause. Their Minister's stirring pulpit appeals, and earnest labours for souls, awoke and stimulated their reserve force of spiritual life, and they worked hard. Frequently the Sabbath evening prayer-meetings became services of revival power. Several wanderers were restored, and some few penitents found the Saviour. At these times Mr. Turner had not always the self-restraint called for. His strength for the day having been pretty nearly exhausted by fifteen or twenty miles' travelling and three services, he would just open the prayer-meeting

[1]*The Pioneer Missionary: Life of the Rev. Nathaniel Turner*, J. G. Turner, 1872, p. 130.

[2]The biographers of both Draper and Turner speak of work on a second Methodist chapel being commenced simultaneously with the opening of the new one as 'a mistake'. The High Church Bishop Broughton, alarmed at such signs of growth, told Hannibal Macarthur who laid the foundation stone of the second chapel that he would repent of his action on his death-bed. Hannibal Macarthur, friend of Marsden, was obviously maintaining the earlier policy of co-operation between evangelicals.

he had called after the sermon, leave the Hymn-Book with some Local Preacher or Leader, run into his house next door, exchange his flannel vest, wringing wet with perspiration, for a dry one, and then return to do battle with the devil and unbelief. He often earnestly engaged in prayer several times in the same meeting.[1]

When allowance has been made for Watsford as an old man looking back to the romance of his spiritual youth, the following pages from his autobiography remain valuable as an indication of the type of Christianity which was then a force in the land.

[1]*The Pioneer Missionary*, p. 276.

After Stray Cattle

2

Prayer and the Outpouring of the Holy Spirit

John Watsford

SCHOOL-DAYS

To be used by God in saving others we must ourselves be saved. To Abraham the Lord said, 'I will bless thee, and thou shalt be a blessing.' David prayed, 'Create in me a clean heart, O God; and renew a right spirit within me . . . then will I teach transgressors Thy ways, and sinners shall be converted unto Thee.' Let me then first and briefly tell of my early days, and how the Lord Jesus sought and saved me.

I was born at Parramatta, New South Wales, Australia, on December 5, 1820. Parramatta is small and insignificant compared with other towns even in Australia, but as the place of my birth it is to me

A dearer, sweeter spot than all the rest.

It is about thirteen miles from Sydney, the capital of New South Wales. Its beautiful river, with villas and orange groves on the banks, has been much admired. In the days of my youth the Governor's country residence was there. The barracks were generally occupied by a large company of soldiers, who, while they did not improve the morality of the place, gave to it an air of life and activity. By the people of Sydney, however, it was regarded as dull and slow-going.

Methodism was no sooner introduced into Australia than it found its way to Parramatta, and the labours of God's servants were there crowned with success. The town has given to the

[144]

Methodist Church some earnest workers, among whom I may mention Mrs. Draper, the excellent wife of the Rev. D. J. Draper; Mrs. Cross, the wife of the devoted missionary to Tonga and Fiji; and the Rev. W. J. and Mrs. Webb, who long laboured in our Mission in Fiji. The Rev. J. G. Millard came from England when a lad, but he was converted in Parramatta, and was there received into the Christian ministry.

I was the third child in a family of twelve, – a large number for our very kind and, I fear, sometimes over-indulgent parents to care for. We were all sent early to the Wesleyan Sabbath School, and were never allowed to be absent from church, morning or evening, on the Sabbath day. My mother's father lived with us for many years. He had been a soldier, and was a stern old man. We children, however, could always reckon on his being on our side, and I think that he often encouraged us to rebel against our parents. Some grandfathers and grandmothers are very foolish, and, however wisely and well they may have brought up their own children, they are not to be trusted in the training of their grandchildren.

As a boy I had my share of troubles, accidents, and hairbreadth escapes.

One day I was standing in a narrow lane near a coach and four horses. The coachman, leaving the box, carelessly threw the reins on the backs of the horses, which in a moment were off. I ran for a wide gate near at hand. The horses running for the same, I was caught by one of the wheels of the coach and jammed against the gate-post. When the coach passed in I was thrown insensible on the ground. All thought that every bone in my body was broken, and that I was dead. Soon, however, I regained consciousness, and was lifted tenderly and carried into the nearest house. I was in an agony of pain, and yet I remember laughing at an accident that occurred. At the side of the house was a low fence that anyone could easily step over, and inside of it, at one end, was a large tub let into the ground and filled with water for the ducks. One of the neighbours, a funny old lady, came rushing in, and, forgetting all about the fence, fell over it into the duck tub. I heard the splash, followed by the cry, 'Old Biddy's in the duck tub', and even in my intense suffering I could not help laughing at poor Biddy's misfortune, although at the same time I felt sorry for the old woman, whom we all liked. When the doctor examined me he found that no bone was broken, but that I was sadly bruised. It was feared that I should feel the effects all my life, but in six or seven months, through the goodness of God, I was all well as ever. My Sabbath School days were days to be remembered. I am afraid that I gave my teachers much trouble, and I am sure that many of them never understood me. As a boy I was full of life and fun and mischief, though my heart was always easily touched. When cuffed and scolded, my proud spirit rebelled; but gentleness and love soon melted me. I remember that I once tore up a feather pillow that an old man used as a cushion in church. When the stewards found the feathers flying in all directions they vowed that they would punish the offender, intimating that they knew pretty well who he was. All their threats had no power to move me, but when I heard the old man say, 'I would not have cared, only it was the pillow on which my dear old wife laid her head when she died', it almost broke my heart, and I was willing to suffer anything for the bad deed I had done.

When a boy, I heard and knew most of the pioneer ministers of the Wesleyan Church in Australia, and my love and respect for them was very great. They were indeed earnest, hard-working, noble men. It was a great joy to me in early life to see and hear them, and now, in my old age, I delight to think of them still. The Rev. S. Leigh, the first Wesleyan minister in Australia, did a great work, and did it well. He left for England when I was eleven years old. The Rev. G. Erskine was one of Dr. Coke's missionaries to India. He was the first Chairman of the Australian District. We boys used to think him a stern old man. He would have order in church, and has startled us many a time by calling from the pulpit in his loud, gruff voice, 'Drive that dog out of the chapel!' 'Take that hat off the window-sill!'

The Rev. Walter Lawry, Mr. Leigh's first colleague, I knew better in after-years, when he was the General Superintendent of Missions. He was a popular preacher, full of wit and humour, and often said queer things in the pulpit. It is reported of him that once, when preaching, a child cried loud and long. Mr. Lawry bore it patiently for a while, and then, kindly addressing the mother, said, in a way with which no one could be offended, 'My dear sister, it's like the toothache, there is only one cure for it, you must have it out.' I heard him preach at the opening of York Street Church, Sydney. His text was Ezekiel 34:26. Speaking of 'the holy hill', the stability and permanency of the Church, he referred to Popery and its sad work. 'But,' said he, 'at the glorious Reformation, Protestantism arose in all its strength and smote the whore of Babylon in the mouth, and, I was going to say, knocked the teeth down her throat.' The well-known Dr. Lang sat near me that morning, and he shook his sides more than once during the service. When I was in Surrey Hills Circuit, Sydney, Mr. Lawry was living near me, and I often saw him. When he had the first attack of paralysis, the effects of which clung to him to the end, I called at once to see him. I said to him, 'Mr. Lawry, is it all right with your soul now?' Looking at me in his peculiar way, he replied, 'Would you not think me a fool if I had not made that right?' Some six weeks after, when much better, though still very feeble, he insisted on going to church. When I had preached on the Conversion of Saul of Tarsus, he came from his pew near the door. Staggering up the aisle of the church, and standing inside the communion rail, he said, 'God has raised me up from the gates of death to warn you once more.' Then, while a wonderful influence rested on the people, he prayed them to be reconciled to God.

The Rev. W. Horton, another of the pioneers, left for England when I was about eight years old. I remember well the night when he preached his farewell sermon, and how I longed to hear it; but I had not that privilege, for a neighbour of ours wished also to hear it, and as his wife was too nervous to be left alone, I, an eight-year-old guard, was sent in to take care of her. Another of these first ministers was the Rev. Joseph Orton. He had been a missionary in the West Indies, and had suffered for Christ's sake. He was the first Wesleyan minister who preached in Victoria. I remember how he used to preach at people in the congregation. I have heard him say, 'I want ten of you, twenty of you, to come to Christ to-night. You men and women sitting on the last form there, and that soldier in the corner.'

Another of the first ministers was the Rev. N. Turner, at one time a missionary in Tonga, then in New Zealand, and afterwards stationed in Australia. He was an eminent Christian, and a thoroughly devoted minister of Christ. He had a powerful voice. It was said that when he preached in the open air he could be heard a mile away, but I think that was an exaggeration. Mr. Turner was always seeking to save souls, and in most of his services sinners were converted. I have known him compelled to stop in his sermon and come down from the pulpit to comfort penitents in great distress. Oh that we had more of that in our day! Mrs. Turner, who came with her husband from England in 1827, and who saw the wonderful changes that took place in this southern wild, lived for some years with her son-in-law, the Rev. John Harcourt, in Kew. She died at Kew, on October 10, 1893, in her ninety-fifth year.

I cannot speak very highly of most of the week-day schools I attended in my early life. There was generally plenty of cane, and little else. The teachers thought they could drive knowledge into children; in these days they have learned the better plan of drawing it out of them. Of one of the masters I have a very vivid recollection. He was a brutal tyrant, who delighted in severely flogging the boys for every trifling offence. When I was between ten and eleven years old, the King's School was established at Parramatta. Its first master was the Rev. R. Forrest, MA, a clergyman of the Church of England, a gentleman of noble bearing, a thorough scholar, and a most successful teacher. This school at once took its place as one of the first Grammar Schools in Australia, and I am pleased to say that it has never lost its proud position. Gentlemen of the highest attainments have been at its head, and it has always had a large staff of thoroughly efficient teachers. The most popular and generally beloved of the staff in my day, and one to whom I delight to refer, was the Rev. W. Woolls, DD, who died in Sydney, New South Wales.

To this school I was sent, my father saying to a friend, when he sent me, 'That boy will one day be a missionary'; a prophecy which was certainly fulfilled. I remember my first examination in history at the King's School, and how lamentably I failed; but a kind word of encouragement from the Head Master stimulated me to plod on with the determination to succeed. I remained at the school as a pupil for six years, and was afterwards employed as one of the teachers under Mr. Forrest for two years.

While at 'King's' I attended the Episcopalian church every Sunday afternoon. The well-known Rev. Samuel Marsden, then very old, was officiating. We boys got to know some of his sermons almost by heart, for he often repeated them, and there were two that we specially looked out for: 'David and the ewe lamb' and 'Onesimus'. A grand old man was the first Colonial chaplain. He excited a great influence for good in those early days of our history, and was much respected by everybody. When his funeral sermon was preached the Methodist church was closed, and all went to the service at St. John's.

All the time I was at 'King's' the Head Master was exceedingly kind to me, lending me books and helping me in my studies. I thank God that I was ever placed under his care.

CONVERSION

In 1838 occurred the event of my life, for which I shall have to praise God 'long as eternal ages roll'. One evening, with one or two other young fellows, I went to the Methodist Church, Macquarie Street, Parramatta. The Rev. D. J. Draper was conducting a prayer-meeting. I had no serious thoughts; I went to mock rather than to pray. What was said or sung I do not know; all I know is that after a while a mighty power came upon me. The sins of my whole life pressed heavily on my soul. I trembled before God, and thought I should sink through the floor into hell. I tried to leave the church, but could not. No one came near me. After the service I left my companions at once and hurried away to my home. Someone followed me. I quickened my pace, but the faster I walked the faster he pursued, until, just as I was about to pass through my father's gate, a strong hand was laid upon me, and one who was a leader in the Church said to me, 'My young friend, I've been thinking about you and praying for you. I am going to commence a young men's class, and I thought I would invite you to join it. Others have tried to persuade me not to invite you, but I have been moved to follow you to-night and press you to come.'

I could not speak a word, my heart was too full, for I felt that God had sent him. I tore myself away, and running into the house went at once to my room, and there poured out my heart to God and cried to Him for mercy. For hours I continued pleading, but no answer came. I was afraid to go to sleep lest I should wake up in hell before the morning. That night, and many a night after, I drew my little bed near the fireplace, and, setting the candlestick on the mantelpiece, read and read my precious Bible until I fell asleep.

It was our long vacation at 'King's', and day after day I spent alone in my room reading the Bible, and praying to God to save me. I was the first to join the young men's class. There they showed me the way of salvation, and prayed for me; but no rest came to my troubled, burdened heart. For six long weeks I was in this distress and bondage, and my poor mother thought I was going out of my mind. One day – how well I remember it! – I went into an upper room, and falling on my knees cried, 'O God, I cannot live another day like this. The load of sin is crushing me down into hell. Have mercy upon me, and pardon all my sin, for Jesus Christ's sake, who shed His blood for me.' In a moment I saw all my sins laid on Jesus, and I laid hold of Him as my present Saviour. My chains fell off, and my burden rolled away. Glory be to God! The witness of the Holy Spirit was so clear and distinct, that I thought at the time God really spoke to me from heaven: 'Thy sins, which are many, are all forgiven thee.' My joy was very great; it was 'joy unspeakable and full of glory'.

Baptized with the Holy Ghost, I had a great longing to bring others to Jesus. I began by distributing tracts. Procuring a large bundle, I set out on my mission, with the determination not to pass by one person, and with the thought that almost everyone would be converted to God. I had given away many tracts without any rebuff, when I came to an unfinished house, on the roof of which a man was shingling. Ascending the ladder I presented a tract, and asked the shingler to read it. Turning on me with fury he said, 'Look you, young fellow, if you are not soon off I'll send you down quicker than you came up.' I had to beat a hasty retreat, and a feeling of great discouragement came over me. But it did not last long. I was soon at work again, with an earnest desire to save souls from death.

I became a teacher in the Sabbath School, where I sought to win the young for Jesus.

In July 1839 I was received as a local preacher on trial. At that time we had a band of earnest local preachers in Parramatta. Labouring with these, I was much strengthened and blessed in my work.

CALL TO THE MINISTRY

In 1841 I was recommended to the British Conference as a candidate for the Wesleyan ministry, and was very soon afterwards sent out to supply for a minister who had to leave for South Australia.

The ministers of that day were the Rev. John McKenny, Chairman of the District, one of Dr. Coke's missionaries to India, a fine old gentleman, but almost worn out by his labours in India; the Rev. D. J. Draper, who did a great work in New South Wales, South Australia, and Victoria, and who died preaching Christ to his perishing fellow-voyagers on board the ill-fated *London*, which foundered in the Bay of Biscay; the Rev. F. Lewis, a Welshman, full of fire and love, who knew how to bring sinners to Christ, and to whom I owe a great deal; the Rev. G. Sweetman, a sweet man indeed, and one of the best preachers of the time; and the Rev. W. Schofield. The Rev. James Watkin, who wrote the appeal, *Pity Poor Fiji*, that thrilled thousands of hearts, and mine, was another. He was a missionary in the Friendly Islands, and afterward in New Zealand, but was then in Sydney. He was one of the first preachers, and far away the best platform speaker of the day. I was strongly drawn to Mr. Watkin, and used to consider it one of my greatest privileges to be allowed to walk with him on a Sunday night to his home in Surrey Hills, though it gave me a long walk afterward to my lodgings at the other end of the city. The Rev. Samuel Wilkinson is the only one left of the ministers forming the District Meeting at which I was received. Though now getting very feeble, he is doing a good work among the soldiers and sailors of Sydney.

At that time there came among us the Rev. John Waterhouse, the General Superintendent of our Polynesian Missions. Mr. Waterhouse had the soul of a true missionary. He had just come from Tonga and Fiji, and preached to us on the Sunday from 'They that sow in tears shall reap in joy'. I never saw a congregation melted as that was. Old and young, ministers and laymen, wept like children. The sobbing of the people sometimes almost stopped the preacher in his sermon. The next day I was introduced to Mr. Waterhouse by Mr. McKenny, who asked, 'Do you want a man for Fiji?' Laying hold of me, Mr. Waterhouse said, 'I'm afraid he won't do; he's short of a rib, I think. Never mind, be ready when I come again.' He died praying, 'More missionaries, more missionaries!' and that prayer was answered.

I might tell of many of the laymen of that day who were earnest workers in our Church, and to whom Methodism is largely indebted. Brother Pidgeon, who laboured as a city missionary in

Sydney, was the instrument of great good. He was always at work, and many from among the lowest and worst were brought to Christ through his efforts. Some of the local preachers and leaders in Sydney and Parramatta were men of great spiritual power, men who believed in prayer and fasting, and who did not depend upon a stranger coming now and then to hold special services and bring sinners to Christ. They believed in the Holy Ghost, and pleaded for His coming in connection with the ordinary services. As a result, there were 'showers of blessing', glorious revivals, wonderful displays of the Holy Spirit's power in convincing and saving men. We used often to see a whole congregation broken down and unable to leave the church; and numbers, night after night, coming to the house of God and finding salvation, and this no matter who was conducting the service. A more particular account of some of the revivals with which I was at this time connected will not be uninteresting to the reader.

REVIVAL

The first revival in Parramatta that I know of was in 1840. Religion had been in a low state. The minister of the Circuit was a good man, but old and nearly worn out. He was greatly opposed to noise, and marked the men who were very much in earnest. It was the custom then to call by name a few persons to pray in the prayer-meetings, and any who were at all noisy were never asked. Two of our most excellent and devoted local preachers, who were always seeking to save souls, were placed on the list of persons not allowed to take part in the prayer-meetings. Very soon I was added to the number. One day the two brethren to whom I have referred said to me, 'We are going specially to pray for the outpouring of the Holy Spirit and the revival of God's work, and we want you to join us. This is our plan: Every morning and evening and at midday to spend some time in pleading with God to pour out His Spirit; to observe every Friday as a day of fasting and prayer; to sit together in the meetings, and, though not permitted to pray aloud, silently to plead for the coming of the Holy Ghost.' I think they were a little afraid of me, as they gave me this caution: 'Now mind, you must not say a word against our minister, or have any unkind feeling toward him, because he does not allow us to take part in the

[152]

meetings. He knows what he is doing, and has his own reasons for it. If we complain, or speak against him, the Lord will not hear our prayer.' We carried out our plan for one, two, three weeks, no one but God and ourselves knowing what we were doing. At the end of the fourth week, on Sunday evening, the Rev. William Walker preached a powerful sermon. After the service the people flocked to the prayer-meeting, till the schoolroom was filled. My two friends were there, one on each side of me, and I knew they had hold of God. We could hear sighs and suppressed sobs all around us. The old minister of the Circuit, who had conducted the meeting, was concluding with the benediction, 'The grace of our Lord Jesus Christ, and the love of God' – here he stopped, and sobbed aloud. When he could speak he called out, 'Brother Watsford, pray'. I prayed, and then my two friends prayed, and oh! the power of God that came upon the people, who were overwhelmed by it in every part of the room! And what a cry for mercy! It was heard by the passers-by in the street, some of whom came running in to see what was the matter, and were smitten down at the door in great distress. The clock of a neighbouring church struck twelve before we could leave the meeting. How many were saved I cannot tell. Day after day and week after week the work went on, and many were converted. Among them many young persons. Thank God when the children are saved. Some persons think and speak lightly of the conversion of the young, and, instead of doing all they can to help and guard them, are always expecting them to fall away. Many of the boys and girls converted in that revival at Parramatta are still members of the Methodist Church, and others are 'around the throne of God in heaven'. I had a little trouble with the boys one Sunday. A friend had taken me in his buggy to Liverpool, where I preached in the open air. Just as we finished the service about sixteen of our boys ran on to the green. They had followed me all the way from Parramatta to be at the service. I had some difficulty in getting them home again, for most of them were wearied with the long journey of nine miles. I took a number of them into the buggy, and drove a mile or so, then put them down and bade them walk on as fast as they could while I went back for others; thus driving backward and forward I got them all home at last. One of these boys was the President of the Victoria and Tasmania Conference some years ago.

In 1841 I went to assist the Rev. F. Lewis at Windsor, and we had a blessed revival there. In those days we did not so much arrange for special services or missions; we looked for God's blessing in connection with the ordinary services. At one of the meetings the Holy Spirit came mightily upon us. We were compelled to continue the meetings night after night. Numbers flocked to them, and we had some remarkable cases of conversion. Among these were some of the best customers of the publicans, and no wonder that they cried out against us.

In the Sabbath School at Windsor we had a most blessed work. I was giving an address in the school one Sunday afternoon, when the children were greatly impressed. I closed the school, and asked those who wished to decide for Jesus to remain. Very few left. About seventy young persons, from eight to sixteen years old, gathered in great distress around the Superintendent of the school and myself, while we prayed for them. Many of them were soon rejoicing in Jesus. Two cases were particularly interesting. A little girl, seven or eight years of age, was weeping bitterly and praying to God to save her. Her mother, who was a teacher, was kneeling by her side and praying for her. Presently the dear child cried out, 'O mother, I do believe; Jesus does save me.' The mother, doubting that her child understood what believing was, asked, 'But what is believing, dear?' 'O mother,' replied the little one, 'believing is just seeing Jesus with your eyes shut.' Had not the Good Spirit opened the eyes of her heart so that by faith she saw Jesus and trusted Him? That child is now growing old, but she is still a member of the Church, and has been ever since that memorable hour when Jesus saved her.

Castlereagh was a part of the Windsor Circuit, and there we had a good work. The whole neighbourhood at one time seemed moved by Divine power. A good brother lived there named John Lees, a grand man, 'full of faith and of the Holy Ghost'. To his house penitents in distress came from far and near, and many were born for glory there. Among others converted at that time was one who had been a great sinner. He was gloriously saved. Strange to say, his wife, who had suffered much from his sins, now became his persecutor. She would snatch the Bible from his hand and throw it out of the window, and do all she could to annoy him. One day he was reading the Bible, when his wife laid hold of it and threw it on the floor. He immediately rose and went into his garden. He had not been there long when one of his children came running to him and said, 'Mother's crying so; come, father, and see her.' He went into the house, and found his wife with the Bible in her hand, weeping bitterly. She had taken up the book to throw it out of the window, when a sentence caught her eye and pierced her heart like a sharp sword. The hand of God was on her. 'Come away to John Lees,' said her husband, and, taking a child under each arm, he led his wife without shawl or bonnet, crying as she went, to John Lees, and there, very soon, while prayer was being offered, the peace and blessing of God came into her soul.

The Lower Hawkesbury was another part of the Windsor Circuit where we had a good work. At one place, then called 'Green's', when we went to prayer at the opening of the service, the power of God so came upon us that the people could not rise again from their knees for two or three hours. What a time it was! All seemed broken down; many were saved. One peculiarity about the place was that many who came to service there had to stay all night, for they came from far. The people of the place gladly provided for all who came, and provisions had often to be made on a large scale.

These were true revivals. The fruit soon appeared in changed lives, in earnest work for Jesus, and in cheerful giving to His cause. What collections we used to have! At one of our missionary meetings at Castlereagh, Mrs. G—— brought in her missionary box. She had collected all the year, and had the silver changed for gold. When the box was at last opened, sovereign after sovereign rolled out, until we counted forty. At one of our meetings Mr. Lewis and I had to stop the people in their giving. We positively refused to take any more.

9

THE ABORIGINES, OUR BRETHREN

A Waddy Fight

I

Evangelistic Outreach and William Hamilton

The history of the Aboriginal people of Australia, following the establishment of the colony, is, for the most part, a sad record. The First Fleet arrived with virtually no accurate knowledge of the people who were to be so suddenly placed under British rule. Captain Cook's impression that they were comparatively few in number and naturally timid was wrong. Their numbers were perhaps around 300,000, and, instead of being mere disorganized, wandering and lawless nomads, we now know that they had clan structures within the larger groupings of some 600 tribes. Their supposed timidity consisted of an understandable reluctance to mix with newcomers whose way of life was so incomprehensible.

From the time that Richard Johnson first took Aboriginal children into his home, and called his own daughter by an Aboriginal name, Christians were foremost in attempting to befriend and help the country's native population. In the first three decades of the nineteenth century many individuals and agencies were working to bring both material and spiritual help to Aborigines. The number included: the 'Native Institution' at Parramatta; Robert Cartwright, first Anglican minister resident at Windsor; Lancelot Threlkeld among the Awabagal tribe at Lake Macquarie from 1825 to 1841 (one of the first missionaries to learn a tribal language); John Handt with the Church Missionary Society mission at Wellington Valley and later (1837–40) in the Aboriginal mission near Brisbane; and the Buntingdale Aboriginal Mission commenced by the Methodists in Victoria.

Despite the commitment of these, and other workers, the surprising fact is that scarcely any of the early nineteenth century work among Aborigines appears to have had success. Most of these

[159]

missions ended in failure in the 1840's.[1] There is the mystery of divine sovereignty in this fact, for, at the same period, several parts of the Pacific were witnessing many conversions to evangelical Christianity. But it is notable that in the Pacific islands it was white traders who were a main obstacle to missionary endeavour as they spread alcohol and exemplified standards of behaviour which frequently incurred justifiable hostility in the local population. In Australia the concentration of a much larger, godless, white community undoubtedly provoked a deep resentment among the Aborigines. Land was taken from them with little consciousness of what it meant in terms of their culture or their traditional means of support. Further, despite the efforts of successive Governors, justice was unequally administered between black and white. Lang, Threlkeld and other Christians were foremost in insisting that the murder of Aborigines receive the same penalty as it would if the victim had been white, yet there was a large public outcry when seven whites were hanged for the murder of Aborigines in 1838. Unknown numbers of Aborigines did meet violent deaths – especially in Van Diemen's Land – and this has to be considered as one of the factors in the fall of the Aboriginal population from some 300,000 to about 60,000 in 1921.[2] Disease and malnutrition were prominent among the other contributing causes of the decline.

The early Christians were not themselves innocent with respect to the removal of Aborigines' traditional means of support and livelihood. Their approval for a policy of gathering Aborigines into

[1] An early exception was the Moravian mission established in 1851 at the junction of the Loddon and Murray rivers of which C. Stuart Ross says, 'beyond all others, it prospered and was attended by encouraging results' (*Colonization and Church Work in Victoria*, 1891, p. 318).

[2] A balanced view of the history of the Aborigines is hard to obtain. In their criticism of whites and in their sympathy for the Aboriginal cause, many modern writers say little or nothing of the Aborigines' degradation in heathenism. The existence of cannibalism among them, for example, is denied, although attested by a number of early sources. The daughter of Andrew Love, one of the first ministers in Geelong, says that a man was once killed and eaten in their manse garden (*One Hundred Years of Presbyterianism in Victoria*, Aeneas MacDonald, 1937, p. 171). For an accurate comment on Aborigine life by one sympathetic to them, and who lived with them for many years, see William Thomas (1791–1867), 'Brief Account of the Aborigines of Australia Felix', in *Letters from Victorian Pioneers*, T. F. Bride, 1898, reprinted 1969.

settlements might have been well-intentioned, but it was probably misguided. By the 1850's Marsden's biographer, among others, could see the mistake, but it was too late.

*   *   *

The following sermon by William Hamilton was first published as one of twelve sermons by the same preacher in a volume entitled, *Practical Discourses, Intended for Circulation in the Interior of New South Wales*, 1843. He not only acknowledged wrongs done to 'our heathen brethren', who suffered 'temporal disadvantages through our colonization', but in speaking of the wrong racial attitude manifested by too many whites he points to a deeper problem.

Part of Hamilton's purpose in publishing his volume of sermons was his hope that it might encourage donations to the Church-extension and Aboriginal-mission Committees of the Presbyterian Synod of Australia. Over sixty years were to pass before another Presbyterian, Dr. John Flynn, with his motto, 'For Christ and the Continent', was to found 'The Australian Inland Mission' in 1912 – an organization which was to bring such large help to the scattered descendants of Australia's first people.

*   *   ·   *

The life of William Hamilton (1807–1879) is one of the many largely untold stories of Australian church history. His manuscript journals and letters preserved in the National Library at Canberra still await and justify an evangelical editor. Hamilton was an assistant minister in Greenock, Scotland, when he heard the call of Australia. He sailed in 1837 with 'the prospect', in his own words, 'of being engaged in laying the foundation of the Church of Christ in what is destined to be one of the greatest countries of the earth'. In his journal of the voyage there is a note on a sermon preached by an older minister (James Clow, his future father-in-law) which reveals his own view of good preaching: '. . . a truly excellent sermon . . . the discourse was elegantly composed, powerfully argued, and skilfully and faithfully applied. It only wanted liveliness and ardour of style to render it suitable to the generality of audiences.'

Reaching Sydney, at length, via Van Diemen's Land, Hamilton was sent by the Presbytery of New South Wales to Goulburn

(October 1838). Here he found a large population of whom he wrote, 'They border on heathenism, and have hitherto been without a minister.' For the next eight years, his evangelical preaching appears to have been accompanied with considerable success. At Goulburn he could speak of his congregation as in a 'thriving state' and by energetic itineraries other churches were established sixty miles and more distant.

The Disruption of 1843 in Scotland brought a controversy among the New South Wales Presbyterians which could not be concluded without a parting of the ways. Hamilton took a middle position, not wishing any overseas controversy to divide their slender numbers. When this policy failed, rather than accept a division in his congregation, he generously gave up the house and garden which was his own and, without support for the future, began a nine-week over-land trek of more than 500 miles to Melbourne. Accompanied by his wife, their four children, and another family, they reached Melbourne on January 1, 1847.

Hamilton had married the sixteen-year-old daughter of the Rev. James Clow in 1840. At Melbourne she was re-united with her family, for the Clows had made their home at the foot of the Dandenongs after their arrival in 1837. In 1836 the future capital of Victoria had consisted of thirteen buildings and 177 people (only 35 being female). By the time of Hamilton's arrival the scene had entirely changed as already described. Despite work enough to engage him in the town's immediate vicinity, Hamilton deliberately moved to the out-back region of western Victoria where he could evangelize among the unchurched settlers in a district extending over a thousand square miles. With Kilnoorat (a few miles from Mount Noorat) as his base, he laboured so extensively that it could later be said 'that, with two or three exceptions, he formed all the congregations in the very large Presbytery of Mortlake'. When, at the age of fifty, Hamilton had to give up his days of hard-riding in the bush, he 'retired' to a property of his own near Mortlake, where he commenced services in his open woolshed. A church was soon built where he was to continue to serve although the original building was outgrown within two or three years.

Such, in outline, was William Hamilton's fruitful life. Of his spirit, this early sermon will tell us more.

2

On the Obligation of the Scottish Presbyterian Church of New South Wales, to Use Means for the Salvation of the Aborigines of the Territory.[1]

William Hamilton

Acts 13:1–3; 14:21–27; 26:15–18

From these passages of Scripture, more especially the last, it appears that it is the will of God the Gospel should be preached to all the nations of the earth, that, by faith in Christ, men of all nations may receive the forgiveness of their sins and an inheritance among them which are sanctified. Paul and Barnabas were specially called and sent forth to preach the Gospel to the Gentiles, and they fulfilled this good work in their time with exemplary zeal and great success. Having made known Christ to many, and led many to believe in Him in the numerous towns they visited, they associated the converts in Churches, and ordained over each Church elders or overseers to teach and rule in the name of the Lord, for the common edification of all the members.

Since the age of Paul and the other Apostles, we may infer from these passages, it is the will of God, that the work of instructing and converting heathen nations, and organizing Churches in them, should be prosecuted by those teachers, whom God calls to it by the imparting of suitable qualifications and dispositions, and whom a Church of Christ, like the Church of Antioch, can afford to send forth, and sees it to be its duty to designate and send forth to such nations. When God gives gifts of any kind to men, he intends

---

[1]This sermon has been slightly abridged from its original form.

[163]

they should be employed for his glory, and the common benefit of the human race. And accordingly, having formed a Gentile Church at Antioch, and raised up in it, or drawn together to it, a considerable number of teachers, eminently qualified to declare his will to the Gentiles, and these teachers earnestly waiting on their ministry, and engaging in fasting and prayer, with a view to its success, and the direction of their services in future, He commanded them to separate Barnabas and Paul for the work whereunto He had called them. Are there, then, now many ministers and candidates for the ministry in the Church of Scotland, highly qualified to preach the Gospel, and richly furnished, through the mercy of God, with the graces that are needful for that service; and has our Church been blessed with times of spiritual revival; and in seeking God by prayer and supplication, has it been led, among other missionary projects, to propose, both in the mother country and in this colony, to separate one or two of its ministers to the work of teaching the aborigines of New Holland the way of salvation, and seeking otherwise to promote their transformation into a Christian and civilized people? – undoubtedly it is our duty, as a small branch of the Church of Scotland, to rejoice in this proposal, and to contribute all that God enables us to carry it into effect.

In order to satisfy your minds the more fully respecting this duty, and show you that it is indeed the will of God that we, and every Church of Christ, should do all that we have opportunity and means of doing for the conversion, and of consequence that salvation of heathen nations, and in particular of heathens who stand in the relation to us that the aborigines of this country do, I propose:

I

To advert to the facts that all mankind, not excepting the aborigines of New Holland, are descended from common parents, and that all are sinners, who stand alike in need of salvation.

These facts are not doubted by any who reverence the sacred Scriptures as the word of God. They believe, according to the Scriptures, that 'God hath made of one blood all nations of men, for to dwell on all the face of the earth'; and that 'by one man sin entered into the world, and death by sin; and so death passed upon all men, for that all have sinned'. The sacred history fully satisfies their minds that Adam and Eve were the first parents from whom all the nations and tribes of the earth have sprung, and that, as they transgressed the covenant of life into which God entered with them, and by their transgression fell into a state of sin and misery, so they involved in sin and misery, all their posterity descending from them by ordinary generation; that is, all mankind, excepting only the man Christ Jesus.

With the testimony of Scripture respecting the common origin and universal sinfulness of the human race, nothing that we observe in the world disagrees. The dispersion of mankind over all the earth can be accounted for, consistently with their common origin; and so can the different complexions, and languages, and other differences, as of stature, hair, and figure, by which men of different countries and climates are distinguished. Nay, the observable progression of population, and the migrations, and transformations of individuals and tribes of the human species, which are known to have taken place in modern times, as well as the notices of changes in the position and condition of men in ancient times, which have come down to us through profane history, corroborate the Mosaic record, and lead us, independently of it, to the conclusion, that all men, however now diversified, are of one family, and the offspring of the same original pair. . . .

To those who are unacquainted with the prejudices and the sophistry of infidels, I fear these remarks must appear very idle. Yet, if you bear in mind, in what terms our fellow-men, the first inhabitants of these lands have frequently been spoken of – what absurdities you have heard or read respecting the native blacks around us, as if they were not of the same species as ourselves, but only a kind of ourang-outang, or creature possessing a constitution somewhere about midway between man and monkey – you will not wonder that, in a discourse advocating missionary exertion for the salvation of the New Hollanders, I should have thus adverted to the relation in which they stand to us. They are our brethren, of the same flesh and blood as ourselves, descended from the same parents, and inheriting from them, in common with us, every property which distinguishes us as human beings. Have they not the same perception of external objects? do they not receive like impressions from external things in like circumstances? are they not affected with joy and sorrow, with love and hatred like ourselves? Do they not give utterance to their thoughts and feelings by articulate words, by laughter, and by tears, like ourselves? Are they not all possessed of human intelligence as well as the human face, and distinguished, one from another, as we ourselves are, by different degrees of intellectual acuteness and vigour? and are they not more or less characterized by knowledge, skill, and address, according as they have more or less cultivated their understanding and other powers? Do we not also find that they are attentive to what they witness, recollect what they have seen and heard, and pursue what interests them with steady purpose, accommodating themselves to changing circumstances, and rendering all their resources, internal and external, subservient to their purpose? In a word, is it not obvious beyond all doubt to those who have had intercourse with them, that they have souls as well as we? and are we not bound to believe that these souls are immortal? Shall it be supposed for a moment, that, while Hindoos and Negroes, and multitudes of white men of greatly inferior mental endowments to a large proportion of New Hollanders, are immortal beings, they, (the aborigines of this country), have no more existence beyond the grave than the beasts that perish? No, my brethren, we are neither so prejudiced nor so irrational as to entertain this supposition.

If we believe that the native blacks are our fellow-men in other respects, we will not doubt that they are characterized, in common with ourselves, by the sin and misery of man's estate. If it is human to err – human to transgress the law of God, written on the heart, and revealed in the Scriptures, – they may be known to be men by their thus acting. In opposition to the light of nature they are often cruel husbands and parents, false friends and implacable enemies. They desire not to know God, and are averse to hear of his law and recognize his authority. Sound in their reasonings about other matters, and capable of bestowing anxious attention on them, they will not reason soundly respecting the existence of God, or listen patiently to instruction respecting their obligation to Him. In short, they manifest all the alienation from God, and insubordination to his law – all the carnal-mindedness and rebelliousness against restraint from their own pleasures and the evil ways of their own hearts, which characterize unregenerated men of the more civilized and better instructed nations of the earth. It is obvious, therefore, that they stand in need of the same salvation with ourselves, – salvation from the merited curse of God, salvation from sin in heart, habit, and practice, and salvation from a future state of endless misery. They need, like us, to be brought nigh to God, to be ennobled with his image, blessed with grace to do his will, prepared for fellowship with God, angels, and saints, in heaven, and invested with a title to admission into heaven, and to a place in its lovely and loving society through eternal ages.

2

I proceed now to show, in the second place, that the salvation which is through Christ Jesus is adapted and intended for men of all nations and that God has required his ministers and people to communicate the glad tidings of it to all.

The Mosaic dispensation being temporary, and designed to prepare for that grand revelation of divine grace which is through Christ, was confined to one particular nation. But not so the Christian dispensation. 'God sent his Son into the world, that whosoever (in it, whether Jew or Gentile, bond or free, rich or poor, learned or unlearned,) believeth in Him should not perish, but have everlasting life.' Accordingly, the angel who appeared to the shepherds to announce his advent, declared, 'Behold I bring you good tidings of great joy, *which shall be to all people*; for unto you is born this day, in the city of David, a Saviour, who is Christ the Lord.'

Christ came into the world to save *sinners*, and by his obedience and death he provided for their salvation, in consistency with the holiness, justice, and truth of God, and the honour of the divine law, without respect to their country, clime, or outward condition. The salvation, which we have just seen men of all nations, and the aborigines of this country no less than others, need, is exactly the kind of salvation which He procured power by his work on earth to effect, and for the effecting of which He has been exalted to the exercise of mediatorial authority at the right hand of the Majesty on High. It is salvation from all the sin and misery consequent on the fall of the first parents of men, and which is more peculiarly adapted to any particular branch of the human family, according as it has become from any circumstances more deeply degraded and burdened with sin and sorrow. Hence the declaration, 'I came not to call the righteous but sinners to repentance.'

Christ having come with the intention of saving the lost sheep of the house of Israel, and those of every other fold or nation whom the Father had given to Him and would draw to Him, and having provided for the salvation of all such from all the evils in which they are in common involved, – having provided for their restoration to the favour of God, their renovation in knowledge, righteousness, and holiness, after the divine image, and their advancement to heaven, howsoever sinful and wretched, and though to human apprehension hopelessly degraded, – an offer of his salvation is made to all men without exception. He made offer of it Himself, 'I am the bread of life,' said He, 'he that cometh to me shall never hunger, and he that believeth on me shall never thirst. All that the Father giveth to me shall come to me, and him that cometh to me I will in no wise cast out.' 'If any man thirst let him come to me and drink.' And he commanded the Gospel, or glad-tidings of his salvation, to be published by his apostles to all men, and in its publication required encouragement to be given to all to look to Him for salvation, and to expect, that trusting in Him for it, they should experience it.

'All power is given to me in heaven and in earth; go ye therefore and teach all nations, baptizing them in the name of the Father, and of the Son, and of the Holy Ghost; teaching them to observe all things whatsoever I have commanded you, and lo! I am with you always, even to the end of the world.' 'Go ye into all the world and preach the gospel to every creature. He that believeth and is baptized shall be saved, but he that believeth not shall be damned.' (Luke 24:46, 47. Matthew 28:18–20. Mark 16:15, 16.)

Slow to understand the extent of this their commission as the apostles undoubtedly were, it was at length fully discovered to them. One important means employed to show them its extent, was the gift of tongues, by which they were qualified to preach the gospel to men of many different and remote nations, another means was the vision vouchsafed to Peter at Joppa, teaching him to call no man common or unclean, another was the descent of the Holy Ghost on Cornelius and the other Gentiles assembled with him to hear Peter declare the way of salvation, another was the calling of Paul to be an apostle to the Gentiles, the appointment of Barnabas with him to this office, and the success of their efforts to form churches in the cities of the Gentiles, and consisting chiefly of Gentile converts. The effect of these occurrences was completely to liberate the apostles and other believers of the Jewish nation from the narrow prejudices under which they for a time laboured, to silence all objection to the baptism of Gentiles, and to constrain those most opposed to their admission into the Church by baptism, to glorify God, saying, 'Then hath God also granted to the Gentiles repentance unto life.' When some bigotted Jews still proposed to impose circumcision on the Gentile Christians, and thus deprive them in some measure of that liberty wherewith Christ makes free all who believe in Him, the effect further was to induce the Church at Jerusalem to recognize them as brethren in Christ, and declare them free from circumcision and the whole law of Moses, as a condition of salvation, and only require of them, as things particularly necessary to prevent scandal, that they should abstain from meats offered to idols, and from blood, and from things strangled, and from fornication. From the time that this deliverance was given in answer to a reference from the Church at Antioch, no obstruction has been offered to the conversion of Gentiles; but it has been the clearly understood duty, and the practice of the ministers and people of Christ, to teach the doctrine of Christ to all men, and invite all to turn from sin unto God, and believe in Christ that they may be saved: and in every age God has given efficacy to his word, and by it enlightened and converted some even of the least hopeful of mankind, and taken them out from the ranks of the Gentiles to be a people for his name.

Every obstruction to the free promulgation of the gospel of salvation by Christ having been removed, the Apostle Paul, as the apostle more especially called to lay the foundation of the Gentile Churches, entered with his whole soul on his lofty career, and set an example of missionary zeal which it is the duty of every minister of Christ and of all Christian people, according to the grace and opportunity given them, to imitate; but to which they can never come up.

Since Paul finished his course, it is our duty to follow him in the prosecution of the work to which he was devoted, and to exert ourselves, with the help of his writings, and those of the other Apostles, to turn from darkness to light, and from the power of Satan to God, the multitudes of Gentiles, to whom neither he nor any of the Apostles could reach, and who through many ages have been kept from the knowledge of Christ, by means of the corruptions and schisms, by which the Devil contrives to exhaust the energies of Christians, and divert them from his work.

That many promises given by God in the Scriptures warrant the expectation, that a time will come, when men of all nations will gladly hear the Gospel, and receiving Christ as offered, will experience the salvation which is through Him.

Considering the obstinate impenitence and unbelief of many highly intelligent, cultivated, and honourable men of our own nation by whom we would expect the force of truth to be felt and acknowledged, and considering the ungodly and superstitious customs, the restless and lawless habits, the darkness of understanding, and the torpidity of moral feeling – all the circumstances which degrade heathen nations, such as the aborigines of this country and stand in the way of their religious improvement – considering these things, we are very apt to despair of success in any attempts we may make to instruct and convert men of such nations. They are often pronounced incapable of improvement, and we may be much disposed to think there is no hope of making them Christians, intelligent, gentle, and rightly affected in every good thing. It is therefore desirable to know what the word of God warrants us to expect respecting such men.

We find Christ encouraging his Apostles, to go into all the world and preach the Gospel to every creature, by telling them that, according to the Scriptures, it behoved Him to suffer and rise again, and that repentance and remission of sins should be preached to all nations. And when the Gentiles began to be visited with the gracious influences of the Holy Spirit, and were thus sealed as genuine believers in Christ, and acceptable worshippers of God, the Apostles, we find, recognized in the occurrence the fulfilment of promises given by God in the Old Testament scriptures. Thus James, on occasion of Barnabas' and Paul's relating the miracles and wonders God had wrought among the Gentiles by them, acknowledged the grace of God in the matter, and said, 'to this agree the words of the prophets, as it is written, after this I will return and build again the tabernacle of David which is fallen down, and I will build again the ruins thereof, and I will set it up, that the residue of men might seek after the Lord, and all the Gentiles upon whom my name is called, saith the Lord, who doeth all these things.' (Acts 15:15–17. Amos 9:11, 12.) I might refer to many other like prophecies of the Old Testament.

One in Isaiah, in the second chapter, at the beginning, is as follows: 'It shall come to pass in the last days that the mountain of the Lord's house shall be established in the top of the mountains, and shall be exalted above the hills, and all nations shall flow unto it, and many people shall go and say, come ye and let us go up to the mountain of the Lord, to the house of the God of Jacob, and he will teach us of his ways, and we will walk in his paths; for out of Zion shall go forth the law and the word of the Lord from Jerusalem, and He shall judge among the nations and shall rebuke many people, and they shall beat their swords into ploughshares, and their spears into pruning hooks, nation shall not lift up sword against nation, neither shall they learn war any more.' To show how promise of the universal diffusion of Christianity has been given in the New Testament, I may quote the words of Christ, 'Other sheep I have which are not of this fold; them also I must bring, and they shall hear my voice, and there shall be one fold and one shepherd,' (John 10:16.) 'I, if I be lifted up from the earth will draw all men unto me.' (John 12:32.) I may further remind you that it was decided by the Apostles that the dispensation of divine grace in Christ extends to the Gentiles no less than the Jews; that the doctrine they preached to all men was, that the righteousness of God, without the law – the righteousness which is by faith of Jesus – is unto all and upon all them that believe, there being no difference between one class of men and another, forasmuch as all have sinned; and that, preaching this doctrine, and believing that 'one God justifies the circumcision by faith, and uncircumcision through faith', they predicted and looked forward with lively hope to a time when 'the fulness of the Gentiles should be come in, and so all Israel should be saved'. Paul tells us that 'the Gentiles are made partakers of the promise in Christ by the Gospel', and that 'the Scripture foreseeing God would justify the heathen through faith, preached before the gospel unto Abraham, saying, "in thee shall all nations be blessed",' by these statements showing, that the very term Gospel implies that the dispensation to which it relates, extends to all nations, and that we ought to consider the admission of one class of heathens to the privileges of God's people an earnest of the admission of all, and should anticipate the conversion and salvation of all.

I come now, my brethren, to ground on the foregoing premises, the conclusion:

4

That we should suffer nothing to deter us from doing whatever we have opportunity and ability to do for the propagation of our holy religion among heathens, especially such as are nearest to us, and possess from their nearness and other circumstances, a primary claim on our Christian charity.

I trust the obligation the churches of Christ are now under to promote, by the labours of their teachers, and the prayers and pecuniary contributions of all their members, the salvation of men of every heathen nation, has been made abundantly obvious. I trust you see that all men, however they may differ in colour, and other circumstances, are your brethren and fellow-sinners, who stand in the same need of salvation as yourselves, and that it is the will of God they should be saved, and should come to the knowledge of the truth in order to their being saved. And I trust you perceive, that as there is one God, and one Mediator between God and man, the Man Christ Jesus who gave Himself a ransom for all, to be testified in due season, so it is the duty of you, who now worship God in the hope of salvation by faith, to instruct all men in the character of God, and make known Christ the Saviour to all, and warn, invite, and encourage, all to believe in Him, and seek God by Him. I trust, moreover, you feel warranted to expect that the God of all grace, who is not willing that any should perish, but that all should turn to Him and live, and who has promised to bless all nations in Christ, will be with you in every effort you may make to diffuse the knowledge of his word, and will make his word, faithfully preached, effectual for the pulling down of the strong holds of Satan in every people, and for the salvation from sin and misery, of the most degraded of all the sons of Adam. If so, what withholdeth that you should not give your zealous support to some missionary enterprise?

Much has been done in modern times, by our fellow-Christians, and much success has attended their exertions. Not fewer than a thousand missionaries have been sent out to heathen nations in different parts of the world, and are now maintained labouring for their salvation; and it has been calculated from authentic data, that the living converts of these missionaries, from among the South Sea Islanders, the Hindoos, the Hottentots, Caffers, and Negroes, and from the Greenlanders, and Esquimaux of Labrador (a no less degraded people than the aborigines of New Holland) amount to a hundred thousand. Referring to these converts, whose hearts have been purified by faith, we may say as the Apostle Peter did, with reference to Cornelius and his company when they received the seal of the Holy Ghost, 'Forasmuch as God gave them the like gift as He did unto us who believed on the Lord Jesus Christ, who was I that I could withstand God.' We are encouraged and required by the fact that heathens have been converted, not only to admit the possibility of their conversion, but to labour with animating hope for its accomplishment. When we see realized to some extent the results which faith led us to anticipate, we are without excuse if we do not prosecute with fresh alacrity the work of Christianizing the world.

Shall *we* do nothing for the spiritual welfare of our heathen brethren? Shall we not consider the condition of *the aborigines of this territory*, who being near to us, and having suffered some temporal disadvantages through our colonization, possess the first claim to our charitable exertions, if we feel it our duty to make any exertion of this kind at all? To bring them to the knowledge, love, and service, of God, and the hope of righteousness and everlasting life through Christ Jesus, shall we not pray for them and use other means, such as we have reason to believe God will own and bless?

There are two reasons for which we should not be satisfied to leave the aborigines dependent on the instructions which the ministers now in the colony, and private Christians, can give them: the *first*, that these ministers have enough to do if they wait on their ministering to the colonists, widely dispersed as they are, and that due attention can only be given to the aborigines by missionaries who shall give themselves wholly to the work of promoting their spiritual interests; and the *second* reason, that much less hope of success can be entertained from efforts directed to the aborigines who now remain, even more vitiated in some respects than they originally were, in those parts of the colony which have been some time settled, and in which ministers already are, than from efforts directed towards those aborigines, who, in the remote parts of the country, have scarcely come in contact with white men at all. These reasons I hope will satisfy you of the propriety of the course proposed.

Once more, I call on you to do your duty in this case. Here is a section of the human family living in sin, and exposed to the wrath of God. You are beside them, possessed of knowledge by which they may be saved, not only saved from eternal destruction, but very probably saved as a people inhabiting the earth (for experience has gone far to prove that continuing without Christianity they will be extirpated, whereas, receiving it, they will be preserved); – will you then do nothing to impart to them knowledge so invaluable? Rejoicing in Christ Jesus, will you not take proper steps to make them also glad in Him? Redeemed from the power of sin and Satan, or at least waiting for the hope of redemption through Christ, will you not seek to bring them to Him that they too may be set free from these enemies, reclaimed from iniquity, and led to follow after all things excellent? Blessed with the hope of immortality, will you not do what in you lies to open up a future world to their view, and beget them to the hope of its glory, – a hope which would cheer them in affliction, moderate them in prosperity, encourage them to do the will of God through life, and render them peaceful and happy at death? By such exercises of charity as the work now recommended, and that of using means for the extension of our Church among fellow-colonists, I am persuaded you contribute in the most effectual manner to your own salvation, – you are not impoverished, but greatly enriched through the spiritual advantages which accrue to yourselves; – by the perishing riches of time you thus purchase riches which are imperishable.

3

'A Remarkable Awakening'

Aboriginal Mission Station, Ramahyuck, Gippsland,
January 30, 1886.

DEAR SIR, – I gladly comply with your desire, to furnish you with some reliable information as to my views and experiences among the aborigines in reference to their capability of understanding and receiving Christianity as a power to change the hearts and lives of these people.

The beneficial influence of true Christianity, through the progress of education and civilization, has worked a wonderful change in the lives, manners and customs of the blacks. Any one not acquainted with their former cruel and most abominable habits, but knowing them only as now settled in peaceable communities, would scarcely believe that the description of heathen life which the apostle Paul gives in the Epistle to the Romans was a correct picture of their mode of life. Given to the continual licentiousness of their carnal minds, they were slaves to their lusts and passions, which, working with their superstitious and cruel nature, made them ever ready, and their feet swift, to shed blood. Without a settled home, they wandered about from place to place in a most miserable and depraved condition, adding to their native vices drunkenness and other evils, which they had learned from white people. The different tribes, either from superstitions or family quarrels, or from violation of tribal territory and the sacred surroundings of their dead, were at continual warfare; and their fear of revenge by secret enemies was sometimes terrible to behold. Their howling noises for many days and weeks before and after the deaths of their friends and relatives, which told but too plainly that they were without hope in this world, were most pitiful to hear, and the disgusting scenes in connection with their nocturnal corroborees cannot be fully

[175]

described. Added to this came the tormenting custom to which some of them were subjected at their peculiar native festivities, and especially the barbarous treatment of females by their tribal lords. It is not necessary to refer to the many atrocities and crimes committed by them in days gone by, for it is well known that they gave trouble to the earlier settlers, and were a terror to lonely women and children in the bush; nor need I say anything about their loathsome diseases, which were prevalent among them in consequence of their immoral lives and habits. Having lived for so many years among them as a close observer, I can testify that the above statements give only a faint picture of what actually took place, for there is not one hour of the night or day in which I did not witness one or other of their cruel customs.

In the midst of their quarrels and bloody fights, at their ghastly corroborees, and during the time of their most pitiful cries around their sick and dead ones, we have been able to bring to them the Gospel of life and peace, and many times did they throw down their weapons and stop their nocturnal dances in order to listen to the Word of God and the joyful news of salvation through our Lord Jesus Christ. In the beginning of 1860 a remarkable awakening amongst the blacks began with earnest cries to God for mercy, and sincere tears of repentance, which was followed by a striking change in their lives, manners and habits. The wonderful regenerating power of the Gospel among the lowest of mankind worked like leaven in their hearts, and, through patient labour and the constraining love of Jesus, we were soon privileged to see a small Christian church arise and a civilized community settled around us. To the glory of God it can be said that a comparatively large number of the remnant of this rapidly decreasing race has been brought to the knowledge of the truth, and a good many honoured the Lord by their humble Christian life for many years, and a still greater number died in full assurance of eternal happiness through faith in Jesus Christ.

The old manners and customs of the blacks have changed even among the remaining heathen under the influence of the Word of God. The war-paints and weapons for fights are seen no more, the awful heathen corroborees have ceased, the females are treated with kindness, and the lamentable cries, accompanied with bodily injuries, when death occurred, have given place to Christian sorrow and quiet tears for their departed friends. With very few exceptions, all the wanderers have settled down as Christian communities on the various stations, and, where they are kept under careful guidance and religious instruction, the change from former days is really a most remarkable one.

Whilst, on the one hand, we have reason to rejoice that God has blessed His work to such an extent, we feel sorrow at stating that our joy is often mingled with disappointment, in so far that so very many of these people pass away either through the consequences of their former diseases, or for some unknown reason. The Lord does what seemeth good in His sight; and we have reason to thank Him for so many tokens of His grace, and for the triumphs of the Gospel in the redemption of those members who passed away in peace to their eternal home, to be for ever with the Lord.

The carrying out of the Saviour's commandment to His Church, to preach the Gospel to every creature, has accomplished that which was considered by many an impossibility; for the influence of the Word of God proved its Divine power, and many of these poor depraved blacks soon began to sit at the feet of Jesus, 'clothed, and in their right mind'. General civilization and education, in and out of school, for young and old, followed step by step as a fruit of true Christianity, and showed in reality a greater progress than we ourselves could have expected in accordance with the generally adopted opinion in reference to the capability of the aborigines.

I may state here that in every case of conversion we have been most careful and cautious not to administer the ordinance of baptism too soon, but only after long trials and careful instruction in the Word of God. Some of the converts have honoured their confession of faith by most honest, faithful, and consistent lives from beginning to end; some have been, and still are, weak in their Christian discipline, in consequence of backslidings and sins; but even of those it can be stated truthfully that, though weak, they did cling to Jesus for salvation, and cried for mercy to Him who alone can forgive sins.

To enter into particulars of individual conversions and triumphs of faith would be out of place in such a short statement as this; but there are very many instances, both of young people and of the very oldest aborigines, who lived and died as faithful humble Christians. On the whole I believe that there is not any great difference between these blacks and any new converts from the heathen in other lands, or even among some classes of white people. It may also be stated that many people here and elsewhere at once expect the converted aborigines to be model Christians, whilst they forget that Christianity truly teaches all to grow in grace and in truth, and with patience and perseverance to press forward to the great aim; and this certainly is carried out by the converted aborigines in this colony.

I remain, dear sir, yours very truly,

F. A. HAGENAUER.

4

An Appeal from the Northern Territory[1]

West Arm, Port Darwin
June 3rd, 1909

Dear Mrs. Kelly,

I expect you will be surprised at this letter from a total stranger, but I was, before my marriage, a member of the Richmond Presbyterian Church. I received some copies of its monthly paper, and am writing now some news of this lonely land.

I am eighty miles from a town by land, twenty by sea, three miles from the nearest white woman, two miles from the nearest white man. Chinese and blacks are my nearest neighbours. There are three churches in Darwin, C of E, RC, and Methodist. There is also a convent, conducted by RC sisters. There is a Catholic priest, a Church of England clergyman, and lay preachers at the Methodist Church.

The Methodist preacher paid four visits to West Arm last year, this year no one will come. The trip by boat costs 7/– return. There are no other ministers in the NT – 500,000 square miles of country with 1500 whites, 2000 Chinese and 5000 blacks living here. Of the whites, fully 500 of the men keep lubras or use them as they want them, and nearly all have half-caste illegitimate children, whose only future in life is prostitution. There are not 50 Chinese without lubras. There is no law against this evil, and there are no missionaries to teach the people right from wrong. There is said to

---

[1]Mrs. Kelly, the recipient of this letter, was the wife of the Rev. Hugh Kelly, editor of the Victorian Church Paper, *The Messenger*, who, in turn, gave the letter to John Flynn. W. Scott McPheat says that it sounded a challenge which was 'to haunt Flynn for years' and thus it contributed, significantly, to the formation of the Australian Inland Mission (*John Flynn, Apostle to the Inland*, 1963, pp. 40–42).

be a black mission station on the Roper River, but what is needed is a mission station close to each of the principal towns, Borroloola, Pine Creek and Palmerston . . . I know that drink, drugs and lubras are responsible for nine out of ten hospital cases, and responsible for seven deaths out of ten.

Why cannot the Presbyterian Church send up a missionary to the NT, an earnest, enthusiastic married man (he is better married than single), give him £100 for living expenses, a certain sum for travelling expenses, and let him make his headquarters in Darwin, and have regular periods for visiting the outer places of the NT? He would do good, if he were a man who put Christ first, and who worked for the good of others, and spared neither time nor money nor labour in the cause of Christ.

You may be shocked by this letter, but I have under- rather than overstated the facts.

Yours faithfully,
JESSIE LITCHFIELD

10

THE NEED OF NEW ENGLAND, NEW SOUTH WALES

A New Clearing

'Colonial ministers require to be men of great zeal; there are no large congregations in the bush to awaken the enthusiasm of the preacher – it must be awakened at a holier shrine. The love of Christ, the love of His Word, the love to win souls to Him – these must be fed in private by "*praying down*", as Dr. Chalmers used to say to us, "the Holy Spirit".'

THE REV. GEORGE MACKIE (Kiama, NSW)
to the Rev. John Bonar, January 8, 1851.

I

Robert Blain

The following letter gives an account of a missionary tour of 1500 miles made by Robert Blain on horse-back in 1846. It describes one of the early journeys of any minister of religion through New England. The area, covering some 200 miles north from the Barnard River and varying in width from 40 to 80 miles, owes its name to its weather which, on tablelands above 2000 feet in New South Wales, was reminiscent of Britain.

Blain, born in Northern Ireland in 1797, had completed his studies for the ministry, and was already doing effective work in forming a new congregation in a needy locality, when he was arrested by an article written by John Dunmore Lang. Printed in *The Orthodox Presbyterian* for January, 1837, it gave an account of the state and prospects of the Presbyterian Church in Australia and pleaded for ministers. Speaking of the Episcopalians and the Presbyterians in New South Wales, Lang wrote: 'The zealous and unremitted exertions of the members of both communions will be indispensably necessary, for the future, to maintain the ascendancy, and to secure the general reception of the great doctrines of the Protestant Reformation, which are alike held by them both, in those vast territories of which Great Britain has been enabled by Divine Providence to obtain possession in the Southern Hemisphere.'

With the approval of the General Synod of Ulster, Blain determined to respond to this Macedonian call. A testimonial from Dr. Samuel Hana, his former professor of theology in Belfast, commended him, particularly, for his learning, piety and zeal, and affirmed that his 'unceasing diligence in the prosecution of his ministerial labours qualify him for planting and watering and establishing new churches'. Blain sailed with Lang (returning from a fourth visit to Britain) and eight other ministers in 1837.

One of these men, George MacFie, was to become minister of Ebenezer on the Hawkesbury River and Blain's life-long friend. Blain's sphere of service was to be further north, in the Hunter River district, where from Hinton, near Maitland, he was to pioneer among the widely scattered people who had begun the long task of turning the Hunter valley into prosperous farming and dairy country. It is recorded: 'At every little centre of population Blain established a preaching station at which, sometimes by day, and sometimes by night, almost throughout the whole week he conducted divine service; travelling on horseback, and contending with difficulties from bad roads, or lack of roads, with dangers from suddenly swollen creeks.'

In the early 1840's Blain's aged mother (born 1769) joined him from Ireland, dying in 1844. In 1845 he married Miss Sarah Keys, whose brother was married to a sister of the Rev. Irving Hetherington.[1] Thereafter there was to be a close tie between these two early ministers. Sarah Keys' family were known for their concern for the needy, her sister (Mrs. Keys) being 'the loved benefactress of the aborigines. Often, with her bag of necessaries, Mrs. Keys would go off in the middle of the night to the Black's camp with an anxious blackfellow to nurse and care for his *lubra* (wife) in illness or in child-birth.'

A letter to Blain from J. Radcliffe, a close friend in Ulster, is a reminder that it was not only those who had emigrated who felt the loneliness of separation. Writing on February 10, 1843, Radcliffe asks:

And *how* is your mother. Often and often did I think of them when out on the waters. Do you know, though I am seldom now up in the neighbourhood – yet I cannot bear to go along that road hard by Guiness. I spent many a happy hour there: and utterly devoid would I be of the commonest principles of affection were I not often very often to think of its former inhabitants, and to pray most devoutly that the God of Friendship and glory would conduct them at last to that land, where 'we shall know even as we are known' and spend an eternity in the presence of the Father and Son and Holy Ghost – – – – – Believe me I am somehow sad when I took back to those old – – – – – times, now sleeping away chastened in a sort of subdued memory. Somehow the fields were greener then than now – and the sun far clearer – and faces far blither – and the streams more silvery. I do not know how it is

[1]See p. 253.

– but I hail any scene or thought which sends me away back to old sweet times! and right glad am I, yea delighted exceedingly, to get some starting point from amid the thronging bustle of anxieties and cares, to embrace the Ela, and wander through the *Land of the Past.*

Blain's work in NSW certainly justified the testimonial from his professor of theology. An ailment which he brought with him from Belfast seems to have done nothing to limit his labours, although it was to cause him to lay down his pastoral charge in 1861. 'You have borne it thro' much hard work,' Hetherington wrote to him in 1859, 'and it is little to be wondered, though much to be regretted, that it has at length reached a stage which compels you to desist from your labour.'

Blain died at Sydney on April 25, 1871, aged 74, and was buried beside his friend, George MacFie in the Balmain Cemetery.[1]

It is impossible to say how far Blain's account of his journey through New England contributed to subsequent Christian work and witness in that area. 15.6 percent of the New England population was said to be Presbyterian in 1841, yet no Presbyterian minister was settled there until 1850, four years after Blain's visit. The Rev. A. Cameron was to be at Wellingrove from 1854 to 1905 and the Rev. Thomas Johnstone was to serve Armidale and other districts for 46 years from 1857. An admiring Methodist minister (J. E. Carruthers) speaks of 'Good old Dr. Johnstone' as 'the pioneer of his order . . . he retained the greater part of his vast geographical charge until he could travel it no longer. His story ought to be written.' As with much else in Australian Christian history, it would appear that this was never done. Our own source of information on Robert Blain is an unpublished MS. Memoir, written by his grand-daughter, Muriel F. Power in 1941.

[1] An obituary to him appeared in *The Presbyterian*, May 1871. Today there is no Presbyterian work at Hinton and no trace of the large church and manse remains. The headstone of Blain's grave was removed to the graveyard of Ebenezer Church on the Hawkesbury when the Balmain cemetery was subsequently cleared.

2

A Missionary Journey and Appeal

Hinton, February 20th, 1846.

My Dear People and Friends.

Some of you are aware that our Presbytery had been long and earnestly entreated to send someone of its members to visit those extensive districts beyond the boundaries of the colony, commonly heard of by the names – Liverpool Plains, Namoi, Big River, New England, Beardy and Byron Plains. For about ten years past, these extensive regions have been gradually increasing in population – men with families and others forming stations, and settling down upon numerous establishments – men and families carrying more or less of the knowledge of Christian doctrines, and the principles and practices of Christian precepts with them: and also more or less fixedness of resolution to keep true to the principles which they acknowledged, and to make the most of the privileges that still remained to them; such as family and private prayer and reading the Scriptures.

Many engaged in Sydney and went off not knowing whither they went – the bush was all before them to choose their place of rest, and Providence their guide. They never dreamed of the utter destitution of the ordinances of religion and other means so necessary in the training and education of those dearest to them, to which they and theirs would be subjected; and only discovered how difficult it was to sing the Lord's song in a strange land, when they found themselves beset with surrounding wickedness, and pointed at by direct ridicule whenever they engaged in the exercise of religion. Long and sorrowful have been the lingering looks cast behind upon the place hallowed by the dispensations of the ordinances of religion, and longer and heavier would their sighs have been, had they but known the dark and howling wilderness which lay before them. In many, it is hoped, the resolution was fixed to maintain their integrity at all hazards, with the mental and spiritual being of whom Christian precepts and Christian doctrines had been so long interwoven that they could not be torn from them; to separate such from Zion would be to destroy their existence; while they live, or wherever they live, they will praise the Lord: – whether they live they live unto the Lord, and whether they die they die unto the Lord, so that whether living or dying they are the Lord's. They know that their true happiness and prosperity is bound up with and measured by the prosperity of Zion. They know that the decree has gone forth from the Supreme Ruler that 'they shall prosper that love thee, O Jerusalem'. Such live and move and have their being in the courts of God's house, to them every wilderness blossoms, every dwelling place, even a camp in the bush for a night, is a church; they will dwell in the house of their God *for ever*.

Was the mixed multitude to perish in the wilderness, to which, for years, with painful anxiety I have seen them borne away on the returning wool drays of the upland settler; and shed there in silence the unavailing tear of regret over their remembered, their beloved Zion, as they sit down by the rivers and creeks of this Southern Babylon, and the harps that were wont to be tuned to Zion's sweetest songs to hang in dull forgetfulness upon the pensive willows, afraid to let their sound be heard, because that the white man's wickedness and the black man's ignorance abounded in the land? If we have hitherto allowed these sheep of *our* pasture, which are men, to wander in the cloudy and the dark day, shall none seek them, and find them out and bring them back? We are most pointedly and expressly taught in Scripture to leave those for a season that are safely folded, and seek even the one lost sheep in the wilderness; and shall we leave the *multitude* to be scattered and become a prey to the active agency of Satan, which we know is at work in every corner of this godless land? As shepherds we are not only to minister to those around us in strengthening the diseased, healing the sick and binding up the broken; but we are also to seek out that which was lost, and bring back again that which was driven away (Ezek. 34.4.). Read the whole chapter.

Having thus long seen a visit to those destitute places of the land to lie most clearly in my path of duty, the necessary arrangements were at length made, and on Thursday, November 27th, I left Hinton, and the Sabbath following preached at Muswellbrook, for the Reverend I. Hetherington, where by a most laudable effort of the people, a church has three years since been erected; but for which a minister has not yet been found, which is much to be regretted, as there is reason to fear that the Puseyite heresy will gain a footing in the place. . . . May God in His mercy, and by His grace save the people from it.

December 3rd. Visiting Blairmore and Dartbrook, I lodged for the night at the village of Scone, where I was hospitably entertained and much edified by the Christian conversation of one who had for years enjoyed the ministry of the late Robert Hall. It is most refreshing and encouraging thus to find the seed sown at such a distance rooting itself in the desert, and how these eminent servants of God, being dead, yet speak.

Next day, I came late at night to the Page, but not too late to be immediately surrounded by a very interesting congregation, many of whom expressed much anxiety for the regular dispensation of Gospel ordinances and the means of education for their children. May God in mercy strengthen the things that remain amongst them, and soon grant them their desires. The Government has here granted ground for a Presbyterian School, and Mr. Heden, a neighbouring proprietor, has also liberally given for Church purposes.

On the Saturday following I reached Tamworth (Peel River) in time to advertize for preaching the next day, December 7th, when I met as many as could reasonably be expected on so short a notice in the place. The day was excessively hot, the thermometer standing at 107 deg., but the fatigue of my journey, and the labours of the day were lightened by the kindness of the people and the attention of the resident physician.

Leaving the Peel on Monday morning, where every green thing was withered and burned up, at midday I encountered a thunderstorm and a deluge of rain on the Moonboy Mountains; on reaching the top of which, I found myself in quite a different element. The sterility and drought which for months had been sorely felt over the 200 miles I had travelled, was changed to abundance of grass and water, and the hottest Australian sun to the mildest European summer.

Passing the night at the Macdonalds, I next day reached Kentucky, where I preached at night, and received all the refreshing hospitalities of a comfortable home.

Next evening I arrived at Saumerly and found myself surrounded by known faces; the superintendent and family having
been my fellow passengers. Here I preached twice, in consequence
of being detained three days by the rains, once on a week day, and
again on Sunday, December 14th. During the next week I visited
many stations and more huts, preaching, baptizing, and marrying.
For one shepherd on Swan Brook, Byron Plains, I baptized *three*
children, and married one. Next Sabbath, December 21st, I
preached twice, and solemnized some baptisms between, at
Newstead, the well ordered and happy home of W. M. Sinclair,
Esquire. This is one of the Sabbaths of my life never to be
forgotten. May God grant many such refreshing and encouraging
sabbaths to faithful ministers in those districts. In the discharge of
similar duties, I travelled northward as far as Mr. Bloxsome's
station, and then returning by Benlomond Road, reached
Armidale on Saturday evening late; preached next day, December
28th in the Court House to a considerable number, and lodged
with Mr. Ross from Inverness, to whom I had been directed by the
good report of all. May he see the desire of his soul in the
conversion to God of many around him, and be instrumental in
planting true religion with the foundation of this mighty city of
coming ages! During the next week I went in an Eastern direction
to within 90 miles of Port Macquarie, finding by the way a most
interesting group of stations, sufficiently near each other for
church attendance, in a central position, and all anxious for the
dispensation of the ordinances of the Gospel among them. The
stations alluded to are those of Scott and Fletcher, Nevison, and
Jamieson and McKenzie; at the latter of which I preached to a
most respectable audience on January 4th, 1846, and after the
performance of some local duties in this pleasant neighbourhood I
bent my course again for the Macdonald, seven miles from the
usual crossing place, on which I found a whole family connexion
sat down on one station, consisting of an aged female, a son-in-law
with wife and family, one married son and family, and one son not
married. They assist each other in labour, unite in worship and
dwell in perfect safety, and though they vie not with the wealthy
squatters around, yet they are really living in luxury and laying the
foundation of an honourable independence. They all appear to
have enjoyed the important advantage of a sound religious
education; such as is found in the parochial schools of Scotland;

and afford the only specimen of the simple pastoral life I have found in my journey. Taking leave of those deeply interesting families, I crossed over the dividing range between the Macdonald River and the head of the Namoi, and descending the dry bed of the latter until its junction with the former, I arrived late at a cattle station of Mr. T. Hall, where at night I addressed some eight or ten individuals.

With a blackfellow as guide I next day set out for Mr. Kidd's, on the Manilla River, where, on Sabbath, January 11th, I preached, and baptized several children, hoping on the morrow to turn my steps homeward; but so pressing was the cry from the Big River district, that I could not resist going about fifty miles further in the direction of the far west. Having spent a few days in this quarter, and met with several anxious persons, I retracted my way to the Peel, and Saturday night found me at the station of Alexander Pringle Esq. where, next day, Sabbath, January 18th, I addressed the few that could be collected, and at night preached at Tamworth.

During the three succeeding days, I passed through the Australian Company's stations, and others, in the direction of Murrurundi (Page) and found many parents lamenting over the ignorance of their children, and some much desiring the enjoyment again of the means of grace.

At this time I suffered very much pain from sandy blight, which I bore the worse of never having experienced anything of the sort before; but as I had now been more than eight weeks away from my accustomed sphere of duty, there was no alternative but burn in the hottest sun, day after day, and try to shade my eyes as I could.

On the evening of Wednesday I arrived at the Page, rejoicing in the prospect of a few days easy labour, and determined to save my eyes, for one day at least, from the penetrating light and burning heat. As I had promised, if possible, to spend a Sabbath here on my return, I awaited the coming day, when finding myself, from the care and kindness of my friends, much recruited, I preached twice in the Court House to respectable and attentive congregations and leaving early next morning, rested for a little at the Burning Mountain Inn and also at Scone, and came to Saint Helier's that evening, where nine weeks before I had parted from my friends.

During this missionary tour of between twelve and thirteen hundred miles I experienced the greatest hospitality everywhere and from all classes, white and black, Roman Catholic and Protestant. Was their reception of Christ and the saving power of his grace upon their souls, to be tested by this reception of his poor unworthy minister, it would be truly gratifying. In return for this uniform kindness, of which I shall cherish through life the dearest remembrance, I can only record my sincere thanks, and pray that they may receive Christ Jesus, and walk in his commandments, and that they may through life enjoy such a *wholesome* prosperity as shall not one day leave them 'wretched, miserable and poor'. Some I found maintaining their integrity and walking in the good old ways of their pious fathers, gathering their families and dependents together for devotional exercises as frequently as possible, and training their children in the knowledge and fear of God: whilst, alas! the heart-rending fact cannot be denied, that many are fast descending and dragging their families with them into the godless wicked community around them. The want of the weekly returning Sabbath, with its hallowing influence of sweet counsel, thoughtfulness and rest, is always telling fearfully upon our emigrant population; dress, idleness, and other self-indulgences constitute too frequently the observance of the day commanded to be kept HOLY, and to be devoted to religious reading, meditation and prayer.

My dear people and friends, in the official visit thus paid to those destitute regions, I have endeavoured to discharge a duty which long pressed heavily upon me. If I had accepted fees for baptizing, I would have been pretty well remunerated for my toil, but as I did not in any instance, sell the sacred ordinance, I returned in this respect nearly as I went; five pounds for marriages being the sum total of my receipts. Whether or not some poor shepherd may have been led to seek and obtain the peace promised to the shepherds in the plains of Bethlehem, or one head of a family encouraged to preserve in the good old way of solid Scripture instruction, and praise, and prayer; or one proprietor induced to bring the hallowed and sanctifying power of religion to influence the regulation of his establishment, is only known to Him, who seeth the end from the beginning; who can acknowledge and bless the most humble efforts for the establishment of his Kingdom, and the advancement of his glory; and to whose purchased and promised blessings in Christ Jesus we must leave the issues of our humble endeavours.

I remain, dear people, and friends,
Affectionately and sincerely yours,
Robert Blain.

II

AUSTRALIA IN 1853–54

Queen's Wharf, Melbourne, 1856

From the appointment of Samuel Leigh, Methodist work in Australia, New Zealand and the South Pacific was controlled by the Church's missionary committee in London. This arrangement was not without early difficulties, but by 1850 – with 80 ministers and 10,000 members in Australia and New Zealand, and similar numbers in Fiji and Tonga – it was becoming impossible. Accordingly the British Conference sent out Dr. Robert Young in 1853 to see the situation and advise on a constitutional change. A separate Methodist Conference for Australasia was in view, and following Young's visit the 'distinct but affiliated' Australasian Wesleyan Methodist Connexion was set up in 1854. Its first Conference was held in Sydney in 1855, with the Churches organized in nine districts.

The following material is taken from Young's book, *The Southern World, Journal of a Deputation to Australia and Polynesia*, 1855.

A Visitor's Impressions

Robert Young

FROM WESTERN AUSTRALIA TO MELBOURNE

Australia contains four British colonies – New South Wales, Victoria, South Australia, and Western Australia. King George's Sound is in the latter colony, which, according to Martin, contains an area of 1,000,000 square miles, or more than eight times the size of the United Kingdom of England, Wales, Scotland, and Ireland. Perth, its capital, situated near Swan River, is 300 miles distant from King George's Sound. This colony was begun in 1829, and the first settlers were subjected to many hardships. They were landed on the beach, in mid-winter, in the neighbourhood of a bare limestone rock; and the country around was devoid of agricultural or pastoral capabilities, but filled with hostile savages. 'Several ships were dashed to pieces on the beach, which was crowded with masses of human beings, – families with infant children, ladies, civil officers, sailors, soldiers, and farmers; while blood and cart horses, milch-cows, prize bulls, sheep, goats, poultry, pigs, pianofortes, ploughs, mills, barouches, casks, furniture, bedding, tools, and seed-corn lay heaped together, drenched with torrents of rain. The confusion was complete: the leaders of the enterprise were equally at a loss with settlers to know what to do or advize. Some demanded to be led to their lands for which they had agreed; others gave way to despair: servants attacked the spirit-casks, and masters followed their example.' Such was the unpropitious commencement of the colony of Western Australia, or, as it is sometimes called, Swan-River; and although it has not made the same rapid progress as the other Australian colonies, having only 5000 white population, it nevertheless contains the elements of great wealth, and is no doubt destined to become a prosperous and mighty country. Its climate is of acknowledged salubrity, and is not subject to the droughts which prevail on the eastern coast.

April 26th [1853]

Went on shore . . . Albany, the name of the town, consists of straggling houses, built without order, very near the beach; and it is said to contain about 300 inhabitants. Finding that the people were without a Minister of any kind, the Archdeacon, who is the Incumbent, having been from home three months, I preached to them in the evening, and hope that my labour was not in vain in the Lord. During the day I walked some miles into the country. The land is not rich, nor suitable for grazing; but much of it might nevertheless be rendered productive, if properly tilled. I found an extraordinary variety of beautiful heaths and ferns; numberless wild-flowers of exquisite loveliness; and the gum and grass trees scattered through the wilderness in great profusion.

April 30th

In passing to-day through the great Australian bight, I was forcibly reminded of the Bay of Biscay, and thought it likely to be as greatly dreaded in turbulent weather as that boisterous sea undoubtedly is. The rolling of the vessel was terrific.

May 4th

We passed Althorp Island on the left, and Kangaroo Island on the right, as we entered the Gulf St. Vincent. The latter island received its name from the number of kangaroos found upon it at the time of its discovery by Flinders. At noon we came to anchor off Port Adelaide, and had some difficulty in getting on shore. Only two boats came to the ship, and each passenger had to pay ten shillings for the privilege of being landed. Nor did the boatmen appear to care whether or not we availed ourselves of their services.

May 5th

This morning, with the exception of four men, all our sailors refused to work, and wished to leave the ship; their alleged cause being the leaky state of the vessel, – but their real cause, doubtless, the attractions of the gold-fields. The Captain reasoned with them, and offered to double their wages, – but in vain. He then had the ringleaders taken before the Magistrate, who sent them to prison, to be kept at hard-labour thirty days. The others, being assured that they should receive their discharge at Sydney, with but one exception returned to their duty.

I went on shore, and was met by the Rev. Messrs. Draper and Hull, who gave me a most hearty welcome. We immediately started for Adelaide, seven miles distant, and I was much pleased with my ride on the top of an omnibus. The road from Port Adelaide to the city is macadamized, and quite level, but is soon to be superseded by a railway: the land on either side is generally rich, and, when properly cultivated must yield an abundant increase.

In the evening I preached in Pirie-street Wesleyan Chapel; and, although it was not the regular evening for service, yet, after about two hours' notice, we had a both large and respectable congregation. After service I was accosted by several persons who had previously been under my pastoral care in England; and deep emotion was excited, and many tears shed, as they detailed scenes of joy or sorrow through which they had passed since their departure from their native land.

May 6th

I walked through the city, and examined its various streets, which are wide, and cross each other at right angles. The plan, including both South and North Adelaide, is well arranged; and, when filled up, will form a most beautiful city, with the river Torrens flowing through it, and surrounded by a magnificent park. At present, however, it is but a skeleton, containing not more than 14,000 inhabitants.

It is not yet seventeen years since the first settlers reached the shores of Gulf St. Vincent, not knowing where to locate themselves. The territory on which they landed had never before been trodden by a white man. It was the abode of the kangaroo and the emu, and roamed over by tribes of wandering savages in quest of food; but the wilderness and solitary place have become glad, and Adelaide is now a flourishing city, possessed of the rights and responsibilities attaching to ecclesiastical and corporate power, and supporting four newspapers. The mud and water, however, in its streets during the rainy season, and the absence of lamps, render travelling about the city, especially at night, exceedingly irksome, and not without danger. I was told that some time ago an ox had been drowned in one of the streets, and that in another a waggon had been nearly engulfed.

The Colony of South Australia, of which Adelaide is the capital, comprises an area of 300,000 square miles, or 192,000,000 acres,

– being more than double the dimensions of the British Isles. Of this territory the greater part is, if not totally unexplored, at least very imperfectly known. It is not a mountainous district, though it has a sufficiency of hills and other inequalities of surface to redeem it from the character of flat monotony. The highest summits rise slightly above 3000 feet from the sea-level. The fertility of many parts of the country for arable purposes, the adaption of large tracts for sheep pasture, the abundance of mineral wealth, and the salubrity of the climate, are all admitted on the best evidence. We possess less satisfactory accounts respecting springs and water-courses. The white population in 1849 was 50,000, but has greatly increased, and the country will doubtlessly become very prosperous and attractive.

May 8th – Sabbath

And we sailed for Melbourne. We had service as usual, in the saloon; but I found it very difficult to engage the attention of the passengers, – the land of gold being manifestly the all-absorbing subject, and laying up treasure on earth a much more interesting concern than laying up treasure in heaven. In the evening, we had the finest sunset I ever witnessed. All the hues of the rainbow, delicately blended like dissolving views, were spread over the heavens.

May 10th

Early this morning we sighted the colony of Victoria; and as most of the passengers were to leave the vessel here, their joy on the occasion was unbounded, and showed itself in various frolics. Some, like so many schoolboys, chased each other along the deck, shouted, leaped, and seemed nearly frantic. Nor was this confined to young men in the heyday of life; but men of years, whose grey hairs might have guaranteed more control, were seen throwing up their hats, and attempting practical jokes of the most unmeaning character, and puns such as mortals had never previously heard. Most of them, if not all, saw a splendid fortune in the distance, which they hoped soon to realize, and return to England; but in many cases the bright vision will vanish, and they will see the land of their fathers no more.

As I was about to leave the *Adelaide*, I could not part with my fellow-passengers without considerable feeling. Earnestly prayed that after the voyage of life had been accomplished we might meet again in a happier world, where there shall be 'no more sea', 'neither shall there be any more pain, for the former things' will have 'passed away'.

IN MELBOURNE

May 11th

Entered the bay of Port Phillip. The entrance is scarcely two miles in width, and, from its numerous and powerful eddies and whirlpools, it forcibly reminded me of 'Hurlgates', near New-York. The haven is most capacious, having a breadth varying from 20 to 60 miles, and including an area of not less than 875 square miles of water, capable of holding in perfect safety the largest fleet of ships that ever went to sea. We came to anchor at 5 o'clock, off Williamstown. Soon after, a boat came off, and I availed myself of the opportunity of landing. It was quite dark when we reached the shore; and, as I was anxious to get forward to Melbourne, two miles and a half distant, I wished to engage a return cab that I met with; but when the driver refused to take me for less than 50s., I determined to walk. I did so; and, after plunging into sundry bogs, and walking into many a deep pool, I reached the Wesleyan Mission-House in Collins-street about 8 o'clock, thoroughly tired, and covered with mud. Undoubtedly my entrance into Melbourne would have been different had my friends known of my arrival.

May 12th

After an early breakfast, the Rev. W. Butters drove me through the city and its suburbs, showing me everything calculated to interest a stranger. The city stands upon undulating ground, favourable for draining, and from various points commands an extensive view of the splendid bay and the rich surrounding country. Many of its streets are wide, crossing each other at right angles, and a few are macadamized; but most of them, in wet weather, are covered with liquid mud of a frightful depth. This inconvenience, however, is capable of being remedied, and will doubtless soon be so.

In January, 1838, Melbourne consisted of a nucleus of huts, embowered in the forest foliage, and had much the appearance of an Indian village. Two wooden houses served the purpose of inns for the settlers who frequented the place. A small square wooden building, with an old ship's bell suspended from a tree, was used as a place of worship by various religious denominations; two or three so-called shops formed emporiums for the sale of every description of useful articles. The flesh of the kangaroo and varieties of wild-fowl was abundantly used, – for fresh mutton was still scarce, and beef seldom seen; and a manuscript newspaper was the organ of public opinion in the new colony. The progress of Melbourne during the ensuing six months was extraordinary. Brick buildings, some even of two or three stories high, were numerous; the inns were transformed into handsome and convenient hotels; the lines of streets had been cleared, marked, and were in some parts under a process of partial macadamization; many shops, warehouses, and agencies had been established; the population had quadrupled; branches of two Sydney banks were in active operation; and, in October, the *Port Phillip Gazette* was issued from the printing-office of Melbourne. The rapid growth of the capital received, in the years 1841–2, a severe but temporary check. Its subsequent progress, though less speedy, was steady; and, in 1850, it was said, 'Melbourne would do no discredit to a province of far older establishment and more developed resources'. Since 1850, the discovery of gold in Victoria having attracted to its shores multitudes of people, I found the population of its capital, including the immediate suburbs, estimated at not less than 80,000, of whom, however, 8000 were living in tents, in and about the city. The public buildings of Melbourne, though necessarily not very numerous, are of a respectable and even superior class. The different places of worship – belonging to the Episcopalians, Presbyterians, Roman Catholics, Independents, Baptists, and Wesleyans – are substantial edifices, and both externally and internally respectable in their appearance.

May 13th

Took breakfast this morning at the 'Wesleyan Immigrants' Home', and met with parties from Nova Scotia, the West Indies, Ireland, and most of the counties of England. The 'Home' will accommodate 150 persons, and is generally full. It was opened on December 6th, 1852, and in five months it had afforded shelter to 1026 persons. The position of immigrants, on their arrival, is in many cases distressing. At a public meeting in the city a gentleman said, 'Multitudes are daily arriving, and what is their reception? In many instances it is truly sad. They are landed in mud, – crammed to suffocation in uncomfortable abodes. Many without shelter, without friends, and without money, find nothing before them but an early grave. They bring with them the savings of many years, but in a few days they are penniless; and often is seen the poor immigrant's funeral, without a single mourner following him to the tomb.' Many of the newly-arrived immigrants, finding themselves unable to cope with the difficulties, get into a deep desponding state of mind, and the moment disease visits them, it generally assumes a typhoid form. In many cases the disease is more of the mind than the body, and the result is truly melancholy. One evening, about 2000 men, women, and children were landed from the bay. Darkness soon enveloped them, and, with but few exceptions, they had to sleep upon their luggage at the wharf during a wet and most uncomfortable night. Occurrences like these led the Wesleyans to provide an Immigrants' Home, an example which was soon followed by the city; and, to the honour of the people of Melbourne, they have prepared an Establishment, at an immense cost, to afford accommodation to those immigrants who may require it on their arrival at this port, and in other respects have exerted themselves to meet the wants of helpless strangers.

May 15th

Preached twice in the Wesleyan Chapel, Collins-street. It will seat 1000 persons, and although the day was wet more attended than could gain admittance. At both services three-fourths of the hearers, at least, were interesting young men, destined, no doubt, to exert a powerful influence upon this rising country, and should, on that account, as well as on account of their spiritual and eternal benefit, receive suitable pastoral attention. The word was manifestly with power, and I had hope that the result would be seen after many days. At the conclusion of each service I received many congratulations: some from parties who had, in different parts of England, been under my pastoral care; and others from individuals who had, in the West Indies and Nova Scotia, attended my ministry. In many cases the meeting was deeply affecting, especially where spiritual loss had been felt, or where a family circle had been broken by death.

May 16th

In the evening, the Missionary Meeting was held in Collins-street Chapel. The attendance was good; the spirit equal to anything I had seen in England; and the proceeds more than four times the amount of any previous anniversary.

May 22d – Sabbath

And preached twice in Collins-street Chapel. The crowd in the evening was immense; every aisle was full, and hundreds of persons could not gain admittance. It was a blessed day, and I hope profitable to many.

May 24th

This evening met a large and interesting party of friends at Mr. Powell's, who had all become wealthy since the discovery of gold, and evidently felt their responsibility. They were not unduly elated by their sudden worldly prosperity; but anxious to perform, with acceptance, the new duties devolving upon them. The evening was profitably spent. There was no foolish trifling, nor unedifying gossip, such as too often characterize evening parties; but important conversation as to their obligations to the Giver of all good, and how they could best promote the prosperity of religion throughout the colony. These topics were entered upon, with manifest zest, by both ladies and gentlemen; and I have seldom spent an evening with greater satisfaction to my own mind. I clearly saw that it was not money, but the '*love*' of it, that is the 'root of all evil'.

May 26th

Received calls from several persons recently arrived, and ascertained that their impressions respecting the country were various. Some thought it the best country in the world; others were not quite so enthusiastic in their expressions; and others declared themselves disgusted with it, and bitterly lamented that they had left the land of their birth. I observed, however, that these opinions had been greatly influenced by personal circumstances.

June 5th – Sabbath

In the morning I preached at Collingwood, and in the evening at Collins-street. Both chapels were crowded, and in the evening many hundreds were unable to find accommodation. Never did I witness more attentive congregations than those to whom I this day ministered the Word of Life. A solemn and deeply-interesting sacramental service terminated the labours of this blessed Sabbath.

June 7th

During my sojourn in Melbourne I endeavoured to make myself acquainted with its social and religious character, and left with a deep impression that it had been greatly misrepresented. The frightful stories of robberies and murders which had appeared in the papers, and led the passengers of the *Adelaide* to prepare their revolvers for action on the day of our arrival, had been greatly exaggerated. Some frightful cases of wickedness have undoubtedly occurred in Melbourne, a result which might fairly have been expected from the sudden influx of a tainted population from a neighbouring colony, on the discovery of gold; but that is now prevented by a prompt and effective administration of law. Besides, the arrival of vast numbers of highly respectable immigrants has, no doubt, exerted a corrective and highly beneficial influence upon the city. The religious state of the community, however, is far from being satisfactory. It is true, places of worship are numerous, and generally well attended, and the Sabbath is outwardly observed, and benevolent institutions liberally supported; yet the prevalence of intemperance and gambling is deeply affecting, and, if not checked, will ruin many a family, if not the city itself.

June 8th
Early this morning I left by the *Cleopatra* steamer for Sydney.

IN NEW SOUTH WALES

June 11th
About 12 o'clock we entered Port Jackson, the magnificent harbour of Sydney. Its length from 'the Heads' to the city is about five miles; and its deeply-indented shores are fringed with evergreens, whilst its placid bosom is decked with numerous islets of exquisite beauty. As the voyager proceeds, he perceives bays within bays, coves within coves, displaying on their gently-sloping banks sundry villas of matchless loveliness, and handsome cottages encircled with gardens and shrubberies of peculiar and fantastic form. Every minute a fresh vista opens on his view, each, as it seems, more lovely than the last, until the scene becomes perfectly enchanting. Whilst thus impressed and captivated with what I saw, the vessel came to anchor; and the Rev. W. B. Boyce, and other Ministers and friends, came off in a boat, recalled me from my reverie, and gave me a most hearty welcome to New South Wales. Mr. Boyce drove me to his residence at the Glebe, a

beautiful and sequestered spot, which was to be my home during my sojourn in the colony.

June 16th

Examined Sydney, the capital of New South Wales. It is built partly on a small promontory, and partly in a narrow ravine or valley. The formation on which it stands is a freestone rock, which passes inland for about two miles, in undulating and nearly parallel ridges, in a direction almost due south of that portion of Port Jackson generally known as the *stream* or *middle harbour*, which, with Sydney-Cove and Darling-Harbour, incloses the greater part of the city on three sides. The ridges decline as they recede from the middle harbour, until they terminate in the almost level plain, bounded on the south by a transverse range of elevated rocks, known as the Surrey-Hills, which comprise the southern suburb. The streets, generally, are laid out at right angles; 34 of them have each a carriage-road of not less than 36 feet wide, and a foot-path of about 12 feet. Their length varies from one to three miles. Many are well paved or macadamized, regularly cleansed, watered, and lighted with gas. George-street and Pitt-street have continuous ranges of handsome cut-stone or brick edifices, with shops that would do no discredit to Regent-street or Oxford-street, London. The new Government-House, which stands in a conspicuous position, overlooking Sydney-Cove, is a very handsome structure, built of white freestone, in the Elizabethan style of architecture, and forms a striking feature from the harbour, of which it commands a fine view. The contrast is very great between this princely mansion and the canvass house of the first Governor of New South Wales, or the wretched wooden tenement in use for several years. The different denominations of Christians have here their respective places of worship, many of which are spacious and highly ornamented; and the Jews have a Synagogue. There is nothing of a foreign aspect about the city. As I walked through its bustling streets I could hardly realize the fact that I was not in my native land. The houses, the shops, and other buildings bear the English impress; the carriages – including stage-coaches, waggons, cabs, and omnibuses – are all constructed as in England: the busy population, too, are all English, or thoroughly Anglicized; and so are the various customs of life. In the goods displayed in the shops, in the furniture found in the houses, in the grates with their coal-fires, and in the style of living and mode of cooking – you have

England, and England only. The population of this very interesting capital, including its immediate suburbs, is supposed to be about 70,000. It is rapidly increasing, and doubtless destined to become an exceeding great city.

June 22d

This evening I preached to a large congregation in York-street Chapel; and in the prayer-meeting held after the public service the spirit of intercession was poured out in a very remarkable manner, when several persons appeared under deep conviction for sin, and a few professed to obtain 'peace with God through our Lord Jesus Christ'.

Since my arrival in the country, so far as I had seen the Wesleyan churches in South Australia, Victoria, and New South Wales, I had been greatly delighted with their harmony, liberality, and evident desire for the revival and extension of religion, and could not but anticipate increasing prosperity. Upon their 'spiritual Jerusalem', especially, I hoped showers of blessing would descend, that, like Jerusalem of old, it might send forth streams of living water, and become the means of salvation to many people.

June 30th

Started with Mr. A. McArthur, for Windsor, a journey of 35 miles. I greatly enjoyed the drive. The road as far as Parramatta, a distance of 15 miles, is well macadamized, and passes over a gently undulating country. The primitive forest exists on either side, with here and there patches of cultivation; but the soil generally is very poor. There are, however, several cottages, some gentlemen's villas, and, I am sorry to say, many public-houses. We met a large number of persons on horseback, most of whom were riding at great speed, and, with hardly an exception, each rider had a short pipe in his mouth. In approaching Parramatta we passed a milkmaid-looking girl, driving a cart. She was perched on the front of the rude vehicle with the reins in one hand, and, although the day was bitterly cold, a parasol in the other, shading her face from the sun! On reaching the town, we halted a short time at an inn, to feed our horse; and the ostler having told me that he had been fourteen years in Australia, I asked him how he liked the country. He replied, that he did not at all like it, it was so stupid; and that he greatly delighted to see real life. 'What do you mean by seeing real life?' I inquired. He immediately replied, 'I mean broken heads and peeled skins.' I told him that I entertained a very different opinion. That to see real life – life in its highest and best form – was to see men devoted to God, doing good to their fellow-men, and preparing for heaven. He looked amazed, and seemed at a loss whether most to pity my ignorance or my want of taste.

July 9th

In the examination of several official documents, I met with a chronological record, illustrative of the rise and progress of the colony of New South Wales, of which the following is an abridgment.

In 1789, one year after the establishment of the colony, the first harvest was reaped (at Parramatta). In 1790, the first settler (a convict) took possession of the land allotted to him. In 1791, the first brick building was finished. In 1793, the first purchase of colonial grain, (1200 bushels) by Government, was made. In 1794, the first church was built. In 1800, the first copper-coin was circulated. In 1803, the first newspaper was printed. In 1805, the first colonial vessel was launched. In 1810, the first census was taken, and the Free-school, toll-gates, police, and Sydney market were established. In 1815, the first steam-engine began to work. In 1817, the Supreme Court, and first Bank were originated. In 1818, the Benevolent Society was formed. In 1819, the Orphan Institution was founded, and the first Wesleyan Chapel was opened. In 1820, the first spirits were distilled, and the first colonial tobacco was sold. In 1822, the freedom of the press was conceded, and the first Agricultural and Reading Societies were instituted. In 1824, the Charter of Justice was granted, the Legislative Council appointed by the Crown, and the first Court of Quarter Sessions was held. In 1826, the first criminal jury was empanneled, the first Archdeacon ordained, the first coroner appointed, and the first constitutional country-meeting held. In 1827, the first daily newspaper was issued. In 1829, the first Circuit Court was opened. In 1830, the first civil jury was empanneled, and the first college founded. In 1831, the first colonial steamboat was built. In 1832, the first Savings-bank was instituted. In 1833, the Mechanics' School of Arts was formed, and a monthly magazine was begun. In 1834, land sold in Sydney at £20,000 per acre. In 1835, the first Protestant Bishop of Australia was appointed. In 1840, sheep sold for 1s. 6d. each, and thousands were 'boiled down' for the sake of their tallow. In 1842, Sydney was incorporated, with a population of 40,000 citizens. In 1850, there were in the colony 12,000,000 sheep, 2,000,000 horned cattle, 150,000 horses, and 100,000 pigs.

The colonists themselves are not disposed to consider their fine country as a vast 'sheep-walk', or to restrict their energies to the multiplication of flocks and herds. The first steps in the progress from the pastoral to the agricultural state have been taken with most encouraging success. In 1850 the colony not only grew sufficient grain for the consumption of its own people, but exported a considerable quantity. To say nothing of its gold-fields, and its various mineral riches, it is capable of producing the vine, the olive, and the mulberry; cotton, sugar, tobacco, hemp, and timber, to an almost incalculable extent; all which products are in constant demand in Europe. Humanly speaking, therefore, the welfare of the colony rests on a sound basis, and, with the blessing of Divine Providence, its future greatness may seem as marvellous to our descendants as the position it has already attained appears to those whose lengthened space of life has enabled them to watch its progress from the infant, starving, struggling, penal-settlement at Sydney-Cove, to the present flourishing colony of New South Wales, with its precocious, energetic, and wealthy offspring Victoria.

But, whilst contemplating this prosperity, I met a wretched-looking native, whose unhappy condition originated a very different train of thought from that which I had been indulging. I remembered the unmitigated wrongs inflicted upon his people by the march of colonization; that the early settlers had from various motives cut them off, under circumstances of revolting cruelty, and apparently without remorse.

July 27th

By the kind invitation of the Attorney-General, and a member of the Legislative Council, I visited Cockatoo Island. It is situated in the harbour of Port Jackson, and is the only Convict Establishment in New South Wales. We found upwards of 300 convicts, who were generally employed in making a dock, 276 feet long by 76 wide, cut out of the solid rock, which will afford great accommodation when finished. The Superintendent took us through the whole establishment, which was beautifully clean, and apparently well regulated. The island is only about 20 acres in extent, and yet there is sufficient rain-water caught upon it to supply the whole of its population. Several convicts were in the hospital, and as one of them was said to be 'sinking fast', I spoke to him on the necessity of a preparation for another world: his heart became affected, – tears rolled down his deeply furrowed cheeks, – and with great emotion he said, 'God has heard my prayer; and I am not afraid to die.' This unexpected reply led me to institute an inquiry as to his views of the plan of salvation, and the foundation of his confidence and hope; when, to my increased surprise and delight, he replied that he had been a grievous sinner, and had no goodness of his own; but that Jesus had died for sinners, and his only trust and hope was in Him, whose blood cleanseth from all sin. This afforded me a good opportunity of speaking to others in the hospital.

August 21st

Preached this morning in York-street Chapel. A collection was made for the Wesleyan poor, especially to relieve those who had, as immigrants, recently arrived in the city, and required some assistance. The amount realized was very creditable to the congregation. The almost entire absence of copper was remarkable, especially as many working-people were present, and all appeared to give. In the evening I preached at Toxteth-park Chapel, which will accommodate 200 persons, and is quite a gem of its kind. It was built by George Allen, Esq., Member of the Legislative Council, and its worship is generally conducted by himself every Sabbath morning. He married Miss Bowden, the daughter of a gentleman who was the principal instrument of obtaining, in 1815, the appointment of a Wesleyan Missionary to this country. Since that period, what hath God wrought! In Sydney, and its immediate suburbs alone, we have six Ministers, and twelve Chapels which will comfortably accommodate 5000 persons.

The Sabbath, in Sydney, I found much more observed than I had expected. I saw no riot, nor disorder of any kind in the streets; neither did I see any shops open, save here and there a small fruit-shop; and, certainly I witnessed much less outward desecration of the Sabbath than is frequently seen in the towns and cities of Old England.

August 22d

To-day, as I walked through Sydney, the traffic, especially in Pitt-street and George-street, with the numerous omnibuses and coaches running to and fro, reminded me of some of the thronged and busy thoroughfares in London. It is doubtless designed to be a great commercial city. Its relative position is favourable; its harbour, for extent, convenience, and security, is unparalleled; and when railways shall be opened into the interior, as contemplated, and the country's resources rendered available, it will no doubt become one of the busiest marts in the world.

August 25th
The foundation-stone of the Sydney Exchange was laid by the Governor-General, Sir Charles Augustus Fitzroy. His Excellency was presented with a trowel made of Australian gold, beautifully executed, and bearing a suitable inscription. A prayer was read by the Archdeacon, in which was the following petition:– 'O Lord, we intreat Thee to preserve unto us the great privilege of our national Constitution; and suffer us not to be alienated from the United Kingdom, in which our fathers were taught to know, fear, and honour Thee . . .'. The day was beautiful, the crowd witnessing the ceremony was large and respectable, and the flags of nearly all the nations of the earth waved in lovely harmony over the site of the intended building. It was impossible to be present, without reviewing the past and anticipating the future. We were assembled on the very spot where the rude huts of the first settlers had been erected; and on which generations yet unborn would meet for purposes of commerce, and realize, in all probability, many a princely fortune.

[On August 30, 1853, Young embarked at Sydney for New Zealand and the South Sea Islands. From there he returned to Melbourne, via Sydney, in December, finding the weather 'greatly altered'. 'It was now summer – warm, but exhilarating.']

ON THE VICTORIAN GOLD-FIELDS

December 25th – Sunday
Christmas-day, and very cold. Yesterday the sun was so hot as to produce a blister on the back of my hand, but to-day I had to wear an overcoat, and a fire in the tent was necessary to prevent me from shivering. At 5 o'clock A.M., I attended a good prayer-meeting. Several appropriate Christmas carols were sung, and many fervent prayers offered. At 11 o'clock I preached, and again in the evening, to large and deeply interesting congregations. Several present had formerly been under my pastoral care; and our

meeting on Mount Alexander was therefore attended with peculiar feelings and many reminiscences. In this part of the gold-fields I found five Wesleyan Chapels, or tents; one capable of accommodating 700 persons, the others of smaller dimensions, all supplied by Mr. Currey and 14 local-preachers.

December 26th
Left Forest Creek for Bendigo, 35 miles distant, but another part of the Mount Alexander gold-fields. We started early, and, after travelling nine miles, called at the Porcupine Inn, and were told by the landlord's father that his son had been twelve months there, and having during that period realized a handsome fortune, was now about to retire. I greatly marvelled at this statement; but when our bill was presented, which showed we were charged 7s. 6d. for a feed of corn, and 6s. for a bottle of weak ale, the profit on which must have been at least 1000 per cent., I ceased to marvel, excepting at the flagrant extortion practised upon us.

We reached Bendigo at 1 o'clock. The valley through which this creek runs was for miles covered with tents, some of which formed streets and squares, bearing names familiar to those who have lived at the West end of London. The tents were of a superior description to those of Forest Creek; the stores more numerous, and better arranged; and the whole city-looking place presented a most imposing aspect, telling of both labour and reward.

The Rev. Thomas Raston, our Missionary, and several friends, gave us a hearty welcome. The Quarterly-Meeting of the Circuit being held in the afternoon, I availed myself of the opportunity of attending it, and was gratified with the spirit manifested, and the vigorous character of Methodism in that locality. Piety, intelligence, zeal, and liberality marked the character of the meeting.

I was kindly furnished with an apartment in a store for sleeping; but the heat was so intolerable, and the large flies so numerous, and so ferocious in their attacks upon the stranger that I hailed the morning dawn with grateful emotion, as it enabled me to escape from my tormentors.

After inspecting many of the diggings, I attended a tea-meeting in the afternoon at White Hills. It was held in our tent-chapel, and numerously attended, chiefly by Cornish people. I was grateful to find that so many of our people had remained faithful, and were prosecuting their religious duties with vigour and success. I also learned with much satisfaction that several persons at the diggings had found that which is more precious than gold, and were laying up treasure in heaven. Not fewer than a hundred conversions to God had taken place in connection with Bendigo, and the old members had been greatly quickened and invigorated. One person told me he had come in search of gold, and had found the 'pearl of great price'. But there were other individuals who had proved unfaithful, and become dissipated. The influence of the Christian Church is, in my judgment, the chief cause of the moral improvement which has taken place. Religion is everywhere respected, its Ministers honoured, and all places of worship are well attended. Christianity here does not merge itself – does not lose its identity. It stands out in bold relief and full expression, and the distinction between the man of God and the man of the world is so striking and manifest, and is so generally acknowledged and felt, that an ameliorating and moralizing influence is diffused among the community.

'About six months ago, there was a great revival of religion at White Hills: some hundreds were converted to God. The work alluded to was carried on entirely by the lay-members, there being then no Minister in the place. During the last four months there have been many additions to the Society, and many signal conversions to God: many have become members who had previously belonged to no branch of the Church of Christ. Not a week passes without conversions to God.'[1]

In reply to various inquiries relative to the Forest Creek gold-fields, I received from the Rev. W. C. Currey the following communication:

When the gold-fields were first discovered, a great number of prisoners from Van Diemen's Land made their way to them. Having obtained an abundance of wealth, they thought they had a right to spend it as they pleased. In consequence of the inducements offered, the police, with other Government employés, left their situations, and thus completely disorganized society. When I arrived in Melbourne, the city appeared to be in the possession of the mob, and every man did what seemed right in his own eyes. A change, however, has been effected.

The number of inhabitants on the principal gold-fields is about 80,000, – that is, about one-third of the population of the colony. The population of Mount Alexander, including Forest Creek and Bendigo, has generally been about the same in number: very great

[1]These words are a quotation from Thomas Raston.

fluctuations take place between the two places; sometimes the population in one place doubles that of the other, – Bendigo being preferred in winter, and Forest Creek in summer.

The people, upon the whole, have conducted themselves well. The reports in the public papers were, in many cases, untrue, and others greatly exaggerated. I never lived in any place with the same number of people, where there was so little disturbance, or where there was greater security of life and property. For eighteen months I did not see a fight or disturbance of any consequence. I have seen upwards of 700 diggers at once chasing a thief, or thieves. This absence of riot, so rife in other localities, I attribute in a great measure to the prohibition of the sale of intoxicating drinks: since the public-houses have been opened it is very different.

As a church we have accomplished much. We were the first to preach the Gospel in the gold-fields, erect chapels, commence Sunday-schools; and we have been made an abundant blessing. Mr. Symons commenced to labour there, in conjunction with Mr. Chapman, in the month of February, 1852. They had to submit to great privations, in common with the diggers. They had to perform all the domestic duties for themselves. I went to the diggings in August, 1852. Mr. Symons had left for Adelaide. I found one chapel, and now at Forest Creek alone we have five. We have also 14 Local-preachers with 7 Class-leaders, 107 full members, and I believe three times as many who are members elsewhere, and hope soon to return to their friends.

We have to endure hardships; but I have laid down this principle, that what any number of men can do for gold, I can do for Christ. We have had glorious manifestations of the Divine presence, – souls saved, believers comforted; and although we have been unfaithful, I hope that God has been glorified.

SOUTH AUSTRALIA AND FAREWELL

Having engaged a passage in the *Madras* for England, I left Melbourne on January the 30th, 1854, at 12 o'clock. At 2 o'clock we weighed anchor; friends shook hands and parted; the *Madras* steamed away with great rapidity; and the wonderful city of Melbourne soon faded from our view. Should my eyes never again be fixed upon its busy marts, nor my feet stand within the gates of its hallowed temples, for my brethren and companions' sakes, I will ever say, Peace be within thee.

February 2d, 1854

Arrived early this morning at Adelaide. The Rev. D. J. Draper came on board, requesting that I would take proper steps to send from England, as soon as possible, two additional Ministers for South Australia, the people paying, as in the other colonies, the expenses of outfit and passage.

Wesleyan Methodism in this colony has advanced with considerable rapidity. Amongst the first settlers that arrived were some Wesleyans, who very soon organized a church after the model of that with which they had been connected in their fatherland. Before the formal foundation of this colony by Governor Hindmarsh, the parties specified were accustomed to meet together for religious conversation and prayer. Two worthy men, still associated with the Wesleyan church in South Australia, Messrs. East and Boots, were fellow-labourers in Kangaroo Island, and in a carpenter's shop at Kingscoate Divine service was performed as early as the close of 1836.

In a little memorandum-book, the following interesting entry is found, which casts light upon the early efforts of Methodism in South Australia:–

'15th May, 1837. – At a meeting, held this night, at the dwelling-house of E. Stephens, Esq., (Adelaide,) for the purpose of establishing a religious Society, to be called the Wesleyan Methodist Society, the following persons gave in their names as desirous of becoming members.' After this comes a list of fifteen members. This was the first organized Christian Body in South Australia. The first Class-meeting was held by Mr. Abbott, on the 15th of May, in a rude hut on the banks of the Torrens. The first sermon was preached in the open air; but subsequently a reed-hut was obtained as a place of worship, and then the kitchen of Mr. E. Stephens. The infant cause greatly prospered, and the building of a commodious chapel was determined upon. This was commenced, and in March, 1838, the Hindley-street Chapel was opened. There were at this period 6 Local-preachers, 7 Class-leaders, about 50 members and 100 Sabbath-school children. The want of a shepherd was now greatly felt by the little flock. As individuals, they had prayed for the coming of a Pastor; but now they set apart seasons for special prayer, that the Great Shepherd would compassionate their case, and send some one to minister unto them. Their prayers were heard. An *accident*, as some would call it, – a *providence*, as the parties in question considered it, – brought them the aid they so earnestly desired.

The Rev. William Longbottom had for several years been labouring in India, but, his health being greatly impaired, he was appointed to Australia, in the hope that its more salubrious climate would soon recruit his strength. His appointment was Swan River, in Western Australia; but there being no vessel direct from India to that port, he sailed for Hobart-Town. Thence he took a passage in a small vessel of 40 tons called the *Fanny*, bound for Swan River. After some days, the vessel was wrecked in Encounter-Bay, on the 16th of June, 1838.

[Encounter-Bay was a desolate, uninhabited location and it was only after much difficulty and danger that the party reached Adelaide – an unintended destination at the outset of their voyage.]

Mr. Longbottom at once entered upon his work. To his astonishment he found a flourishing Society, with an interesting Sunday-school, and a substantial place of worship. The labours of Mr. Longbottom were successful; – the cause increased, so that a larger place of worship became necessary; and in June, 1839, another and much larger chapel was opened. Since that period the cause has still advanced; a more capacious and handsome chapel has been erected in Adelaide, and much good has been effected throughout the colony. The Wesleyan Church in South Australia has 27 chapels, 19 other preaching-places, 12 Missionaries, 3 Day-schools, 26 Sunday-schools, 1534 Scholars, 63 Local-preachers, 1122 church members, and 5000 members of congregations. In this colony the respective Denominations are entirely cast upon their own resources, there being now no State support afforded to any church in South Australia.

Australia is doubtless designed to occupy a prominent position in the world's future history, and to become the centre of light in the Southern Hemisphere. The Australian Wesleyans being aware of this, are evincing an earnest and noble solicitude to increase the number of their faithful Ministers, that Wesleyanism may take its full share in giving a Christian impress to the institutions, and in directing the destinies of this great country.

12

RECOVERY AND OPPOSITION IN SYDNEY DIOCESE

The Embarkation, Waterloo Docks, Liverpool

I

Frederic and Jane Barker

In 1839 Jane Harden, while visiting her clergyman brother, Joseph, in Liverpool, England, heard Frederic Barker preach on the occasion of his fourth anniversary in the parish of Edge Hill. Both in their early thirties, Jane and Frederic married the following year and she exchanged her much-loved country home for the bustle of an expanding city. Born at Brathy Hall, Ambleside, in 1807, Jane was the eldest in a family of three. If Liverpool was a contrast to the silence and beauty of Lake Windermere, her world of spiritual convictions remained unchanged. Since her conversion in the 1820's (an event blamed by Hartley Coleridge upon her Aunt Rankin, 'that incarnation of Calvinism') Jane was as committed to evangelical Christianity as her vicar, the Rev. William Hodgson, whose parsonage stood close to her home at Brathy. Hodgson, as Barker, was a product of the influence of Charles Simeon in Cambridge, an influence which gave primary place to the Word of God and to the necessity of spiritual life imparted by the Holy Spirit.

For nearly fourteen years Frederic and Jane Barker served the parish of Saint Mary's, Edge Hill, then a period of continued poor health led to his resignation in 1854 and to his acceptance of the rural living of Baslow, Derbyshire, 'virtually a position of semi-retirement'.[1] In Derbyshire they were scarcely unpacked and settled when Barker was offered the metropolitan See of Sydney. Others had declined this bishopric since the death of William Grant Broughton in 1853. Barker accepted. He was consecrated at Lambeth on St. Andrew's Day in November 1854, and they sailed from Liverpool on February 28, 1855.

[1] For this and other information I am indebted to *Mrs. Barker and her Diary*, K. J. Cable, Royal Australian Historical Society, vol. 54, part 1 and reprinted separately.

Jane Barker supposed herself able to endure three years in the strange world of the Antipodes. In fact, apart from two visits home, she was to remain until her death in 1876. Throughout this whole period abroad she maintained a series of 'journals' for her sister, Jessie, who had also married a clergyman, the Rev. John Clay, Vicar of Stapenhill, near Burton on Trent. Regrettably the only portion of these journals which survive run from March 26, 1855 – a month after the start of their voyage – to December 27, 1856. From this source the following extracts have been taken. Although they only cover the Barkers' first nineteen months in Sydney, they are, as Marcus Loane says, 'a mine of information, and her shrewd and pungent comments bring to life the problems which they encountered on their arrival'.[1] Jane Barker had her own ministries, in the management of an hospitable home, as a visitor among the young, the sick and the poor, and as the founder of the Clergy Daughters' School (St. Catherine's), but her colourful narrative is perhaps chiefly important for the way in which it reveals her husband's plans for the re-establishment of the evangelicalism pioneered by Johnson and Marsden and disfavoured in the days of Bishop Broughton. 'You may have a duly organized Church,' Barker was to say, 'a Church in which learning and respectability have their place, and piety being wanting, the whole system will be dry, sapless, withered and unfruitful'.

At many points Jane Barker's words are tinged with the homesickness and culture shock from which she suffered. Sydney was, at best, a 'head-quarters' and, at worst, 'banishment' rather than a home at the time when these journal pages were written. Had her later journals survived they would undoubtedly have revealed a different perspective. But, in her tears for Britain and her longings for her family, for a sight of Windermere and Edge Hill, Jane Barker also expresses something of the great sorrow arising from the tyranny of distance which nearly overwhelmed so many, and especially women, in their first years in Australia. It was sorrow which only found consolation as it rested upon assured faith in God.

[1] *Hewn From The Rock*, Marcus Loane, 1976, p. 71.

2

Jane Barker's Journal

30th May, 1855 (Government House, Sydney)
We did not preach on Sunday. We heard Mr. Riky in the morning.
He is a very clever preacher and clear in his doctrinal statements
but I should like a tone of greater love. He and his wife and child go
this week to Cooma – the clergyman there is leaving under painful
circumstances, but he is not suspended.

We were very comfortable with the Cowpers.[1] The Archdeacon
is such a dear old man and sometimes looked so like our precious
Father that it almost made me weep to observe him. He has been
46 years in the Colony and lately acted as Bishop's Commissary.
His joy and thankfulness now are quite unutterable at the answer
to his prayer for a 'godly Bishop'.

1st June, 1855
We have now been here a week and it looks like a month from the
variety compressed in it and the amount of work accomplished by
dear F.

On Monday we went with Sir Charles Nicholson in his carriage to
look at the site purchased for the Bishop's residence.[2] It was a
disagreeable day with a high wind and clouds of dust. The road led
through a poor suburb of the town to an eminence about a mile and a
half distant. Very barren, without trees, a plot of six acres railed
around, on the roads etc. The view extensive and bare, looking upon
the ugly side of Sydney. Not a glimpse of the beautiful harbour, in
short as undesirable a spot as could have been fixed upon and F. has
protested against it. Happily the land is valuable and will sell for

[1]They had stayed for a few days on their arrival with William Cowper and
his wife in Spring Street (see p. 86) before becoming temporary guests at
Government House.
[2]Near Grose Farm on the Newtown Road and adjacent to the grounds of the
new University of which Nicholson was the Provost.

£6000 and be exchanged for some more eligible spot. Everybody thinks as we do about it. We have not yet met with a house tho' several have been mentioned, and I fear we shall be obliged for a time to live at Parramatta in a large parsonage House which is unoccupied. It has been a painful thing to find ourselves thus homeless wanderers, and it is not very creditable to the authorities here that no accommodation of even a temporary kind should have been provided for the Bishop. The fact is there is no unity of action especially among the Clergy. We would rather be as we are than see a house waiting to receive us in the spot I have described to you. In a little time I doubt not that things will arrange themselves for our comfort and well being, under the merciful guidance of the Heavenly Friend who never forgets His people, and we *know* that when these earthly cares are ended, there is a 'mansion prepared', a house not made with hands, eternal in the heavens.

We walked in the Domain on Tuesday.[1] It was very beautiful, the sea quite still and reflecting every object. Little boats were skimming about and sometimes the ripple against an oar brought Bell Bay and Windermere to mind. We sat for a long time, thankful to be quiet, for I need hardly tell you that visitors have poured in upon us in an incessant stream and one clergyman after another has called to have an interview with dear F. It is amazing what a quantity has been done; the business habits of Liverpool come to dear F.'s aid.

2nd June, 1855

We have spent a few pleasant days at Government House. They are truly kind people and so plain and domestic and unspoiled by their high position that it is a source of thankfulness to us to have them. They have ten children and propose soon sending the two eldest boys to England for education. . . . Sir William Denison is a very manly person, a practical man of business, with a determination to do all the good in his power and reform abuses. They have prayers morning and evening and, when no chaplain is present, he reads a comment of his own.

The heat and mosquitoes are so bad now in 'December'[2] that

---

[1] The Park close to Government House and Sydney Harbour.

[2] The winter month of June was, of course, the southern hemisphere counter-part to December.

what they will be in summer I cannot think.

18th June, 1855

I am copying Lady Denison in my use of journal letters. She has been employing this method of writing home for eight years. F. has again asked Mr. Hodgson to come and take charge of a theological college (Moore's) within 20 miles of this place.[1] There is at present no place in operation for the training of young Colonials and so great is the demand for them that I trust some good and efficient Principal will be sent us by Him who has all hearts in His hand.

We have not got into our home at Miller's Point but hope to do so tomorrow or the next day. It begins to assume a very different appearance from what it did, with a little new paper and paint on the walls . . . our furniture is coming by the *Golden Era*.

19th June, 1855

This evening we are going to Mr. and Mrs. Kemp's extraordinary party of clergymen and churchwardens, with their wives.[2] One of the churchwardens is a horse dealer, and we heard that his wife has got a new headdress for the occasion. The amusement of the evening is to be Church Music with the organ, after which by the Bishop's wish he is to conduct family prayer. Supper concludes and I daresay we shall be rather late. You shall hear tomorrow how it answers my expectations. Sydney is like a large village where continual gossip goes on and reports are circulated that have little or slight foundation.

20th June, 1855

We were not home until after eleven last night. Such a queer party. An immense organ in a small room. I cannot describe the din made by the Hallelujah Chorus. There was one very pleasant half hour when dear F.'s calm voice was heard in reading Phil. 4 with an exposition and prayer. I felt for him surrounded by such a group, but the Lord was with him and there may have been hearts that were benefited. . . . I am packing up for a start to the 'Palace' –

---

[1]Thomas Moore (1762–1840) came to Sydney as a ship's carpenter in 1791, he rose to affluence and, dying childless, left his house and grounds at Liverpool for the education of young men of 'the Protestant persuasion'. William Hodgson, her former vicar at Brathy, was also well-known to Bishop Barker.

[2]Charles C. Kemp served the Newtown parish.

alias 7 Crown Street, Miller's Point.[1]

21st June, 1855

At Miller's Point on the 20th. On the same day I began my attendance as a Committee woman at the School of Industry. It contains fifty little girls and a weekly committee is held, besides a monthly one, to superintend its proceedings.

25th June, 1855

Paid a visit to the *Golden Era*. To the Bible Society in the evening. There is an account of the meeting in the newspapers. Dear F.'s speech is better reported than I ever knew any of his to be, though it yet contains many errors. The Society has been quite checked in its growth here, though dragging on a kind of existence for 38 years. The Bishop and clergy (with that one honourable exception of the Archdeacon) set themselves against it. But that day is past, let us hope not to return. As F. and I approached the room we met a stream of people. Way was of course made for the Bishop, and I held fast by his *apron strings* while we struggled through the press of people. His appearance was greeted with general applause, and I must say it was gratifying that his presence should thus be hailed by the *good* in the land, by the lovers of Truth and Gospel light. The Governor soon after entered and was of course applauded as he deserves to be. It was an excellent meeting, quite surpassing, Morgan says,[2] those of Liverpool (you need not believe that). The room only holds seven to eight hundred people, and I hope there will be 'ere long a larger one for such purposes. The speaking was very good.

27th June, 1855

F. and I went to pay visits in a cab. Began at 'the Glebe', so called because it was one time church property – 40 acres still belong to the Bishop, besides a corner including 6 acres set apart for a Church and parsonage. . . .

[1]They preferred to rent this house, on the western side of the promontory between Sydney Cove and Darling Harbour (looking down on the latter), to the unoccupied parsonage proposed for their temporary use at Parramatta. Lacking any garden and in a busy, dusty district, with 'a row of ugly offices on the wharf below us', the house was too accessible to callers. But Jane came to regard the view as 'a pretty scene, and very animated with the steamers and boats and craft of every kind going to and fro'.

[2]Morgan, one of their most trusted servants and their cab driver. Their household servants, including Ann and Emma, had come with them from England.

28th June, 1855

Crossed by ferry to Pyrmont, one of the many long peninsulas running into the harbour of Sydney. We wished to try this method of approaching the Glebe as, if practicable, it would be more pleasant than the long dusty suburb through which one has to walk or drive – but on reaching the other side of Pyrmont we found ourselves in 'Black-wattle swamp creek', across which there was no ferry boat. The Glebe looked nice, for it is not yet denuded of its trees – some of the oldest have been taken, but sufficient remain to give the place a character which is greatly wanting in the inhabited districts. There, almost every tree has been ruthlessly felled, leaving only stone or rock or patches of barren ground to look upon. A little taste and cultivation would have made Sydney a beautiful city, but there is no time to be spared from things of 'more importance' for such as these. . . . On our return to Miller's Point we found a shower of cards on the table. We try to get out daily at half past one, for fear of being kept in altogether. Had a nice quiet evening by ourselves.

29th June, 1855

Heard that a lady was coming to see me the first thing after breakfast, which kept me in a small fidget. However, it was twelve before she arrived. The hours for *working* are very short, it is really only light from 7 to 5,[1] and you cannot calculate upon having more than three in the house, for all you want to cram into it, of reading, writing, unpacking and housekeeping. I am in a delightful state of untidiness upstairs – a dozen half-unpacked boxes, without drawers to hold their contents, but still I could arrange them in some measure had I but time. The maids are washing and ironing from morning to night, having a laudable ambition to get through the mountain of clothes we brought off the voyage. Ann is to have a new kitchen range, the one we found here being worn out. Dearest F. looks only middling. He has some things to worry him, and *nobody* to consult.

30th June, 1855

A happy day for us, in bringing sixteen letters, all from those we dearly love, by the *Marco Polo*. This is our one pleasure here and we thank you for dealing it out, beloved friends, with so liberal a hand: our gratitude consists also in the hope of favours *yet to come*,

[1]i.e., in mid-winter.

[223]

so you will I know keep that in mind. I read yours and one or two others and then deposited the precious bundle in my reticule, to be read on the way to Parramatta, feeling very like a boy that had a large piece of plum cake wrapped up in his handkerchief – to be devoured in some quiet corner. We were very busy, of course, just leaving home, and accordingly started by the one o'clock steamer, leaving the servants with sundry instructions about cleaning. . . . Once on board our feast began, nothing was seen or heard all the way on our one and a half hour's passage, but the dear letters, one loved handwriting after another. . . . I do lament your being such a weary time without letters from us. If the *British Empire* proved true, you ought about this time to receive what we sent by her, otherwise it will be nearly the end of August before you hear, enough to make the heart sick with hope deferred. But the first news you get will be followed by many more, please God, an unceasing tide, until we again see each other face to face.

2nd July 1855 (Parramatta)

The object of our visit here was that dear F. might open St. John's, the Parish Church, which has been rebuilt. It was first raised by Marsden of missionary fame, and three years ago nearly fell down, and was again founded by his son-in-law Mr. Bobart.[1] It is a beautiful Norman church of the pure simple style I admire so much. The seats are not yet placed there, but a large supply of forms and chairs made up the deficiency.

We were received by Mr. and Mrs. King and while dear F. was engaged in visiting the Gaol and Lunatic Asylum, I walked with the 'Ks' to Colonel McArthur's house, and once beautiful garden.[2] It is now a tangled wilderness but in one part we found camellias growing abundantly and gathered a bouquet. There were trees yellow with oranges, also cypresses, English oaks, blue gum trees, Chinese elms, white cedar, the last three very different from what their names indicate. The cedar is more like an acacia or very delicate ash than anything, and at this season has a pale yellow leaf. The vegetation now daily becomes more verdant, and I have

[1]H. H. Bobart, Marsden's successor, died in 1854 and was followed by Robert L. King who was to become one of the closest of Frederic Barker's friends.

[2]Elizabeth Farm House, built 1793 as the home of John and Elizabeth Macarthur. Denuded of most of its garden it remains open to the public today.

already seen many luxuriant creepers including the passion flower which appears wild here. In a few weeks it will doubtless be prettier still.

3rd July, 1855

Paid a few visits and shopped. The Bishop of Newcastle arrived and took up his abode at the Archdeacon's. . . .

4th July, 1855

F. longs for more labourers of the right kind, and wants a few superior men to have ready for important situations. He has not *one* whom he would like to succeed to the Archdeaconry whenever it pleases God to remove our reverend friend. The Bishop of Newcastle's companionship for a little while will be a comfort to dearest F., for though not exactly his kind of man (*far* from it) he is yet open and sensible and straightforward and can sympathize and advise. There is nobody here, lay or clerical – save our good Governor – to whom F. could say, 'what would you advize?'. It is indeed a lamentable state of things, and makes us feel wofully isolated after the *luxury* of friendship that has been ours.

The Bishop of Newcastle is awfully brown in his tinge – but I suppose we must come to the same complexion by and bye. He is to dine here tomorrow off the dressing tables! We are much patronized by the Dissenting Ministers here. Mr. Salmon of the Free Church is greatly respected[1] and Mr. Beazley the Independent is really a superior man.

7th July, 1855

I was hindered yesterday from going out by the arrival of the furniture and so busy a day we had unpacking that I declined seeing visitors. Dear Mary and Allen and Jessie and Aunty all came forth to smile upon us – previous visions of past happy intercourse. All the old furniture looked as if it would have said 'what business have I here' and these beloved all – of Brawshay, Ilkewite etc. – how carefully shall they be guarded to return, please God, to their native land, to be prized hereafter by those who have been taught to care for them.

16th July, 1855

. . . Many mornings have been so cold that I could not keep warm

---

[1]Alex Salmon, Free Church of Scotland, had arrived in 1849 and served a congregation which had broken away from Scots Church. His work was so successful that in 1855 the people moved to a new building which could sit 800 in Macquarie Street (subsequently known as St. Stephen's).

even with a fire; but on going out the sun is so hot that a muslin dress would be warm enough.

Our servants go on very happily together. Emma has £25 and is a real comfort to us and has not, I think, any idea of leaving. Indeed they would not easily get higher wages elsewhere, for these are falling gradually owing to the concourse of immigrants who arrive week after week.

F. keeps well upon the whole, I am thankful to say, and if we had a quieter abode he would not be overdone with his amount of work: as things are now he is interrupted from morning till night. Our dinner parties are come to an end, we dine only once out next week – at Government House in a quiet way, which is always agreeable. They are very friendly kind worthy people, really desirous of doing their duty. Their eldest daughter was confirmed on Monday. I like hearing dear F. address the young. He is always at home then, and is *generally* more so now than he has been in preaching. It is lamentable, I think, how they have systematically been brought up for the world. There is one clergyman here, the Principal of the University, who even says it is as much a *duty* in the upper classes to attend balls and such places as for doctors to visit the sick. He has influenced some young clergy by such arguments to go to balls etc. May our gracious God pour out His spirit upon this colony and cause a revival to take place among the dry bones, and above all keep us and ours to Himself, ever drinking at the pure fountain of His word and obtaining strength at His footstool, for all our needs.

Mr. Clarke, a nice clergyman on the North Shore, told me that the tendency of people here was to degenerate very rapidly and he did not know what the next generation would be; that if a person came out straight and true and good he was in a year or two no better than all around him!

19th July, 1855

Have you found any clergymen for us? We want superior men to fill vacancies in Sydney – none other ought to be placed in them and plenty of means will be found when they appear. Dear F. is going to make an appeal to the public before long on behalf of endowments for the Church, and for the erection of six churches in Sydney.

21st July, 1855

A fine day. Very cold it always is in the mornings in the house, but out in the sun as warm as midsummer. Some very interesting letters from Mr. Riky. He has a comprehensive mind and gives an excellent idea of what is required in the country parts. He says that two or three sawyers and splitters going through the country to build 'slab' or wooden parsonage houses and churches would be doing more for the Church of England than Her Majesty's Ecclesiastical Commissioners sitting at Whitehall.

27th July, 1855

A very busy afternoon with callers. We got out however about half past eleven for a long drive, first to a district called Waverley to call on the Inspector of Police Captain Mayne. Found Mrs. Mayne and her family living in what was erected as the stable for a castle to be called 'Waverley Honour'. He began and was unable to finish and the entire castle remains in the air. Mrs. Mayne took us to a mound, which commanded a very fine view of the Ocean 'road to England', in a small bay called Nelson's Bay below, we saw the late abode of Mr. Robert Lowe, an enviable looking secluded spot. The tenth commandment is often in danger of being broken in these localities where people are favoured in possessing a house.

We were to have visited some government land near 'Big Coodgee' with a view to the building of a house, but the gentleman who was to have met us failed in doing so. We proceeded to the South Head and returned by Vaucluse. We were late home and Mrs. Hayden was tired.[1] Nevertheless we had a small party at tea – the Ashwins, Messrs. Rich and Goodman and the young Cowpers and good Mr. Unwin.[2] A very pleasant hour was passed in reading Phil. 3 and conversing upon it, like the good old times. I daresay such meetings will be repeated monthly in this house. Dear F. said it was the pleasantest evening he had had since he came here.

25th August, 1855

Yesterday dearest F. held a Confirmation at Darling Point. The church is quite in pattern style of architecture and other things and is really very pretty and its position most exquisite – but the candlestick wants light! F.'s address to the young people and his whole demeanour would have quite satisfied his Edge Hill friends. Indeed I fear he must never be their Bishop as they would certainly

[1]Thomas Hayden and his wife, recruited by Barker, had just arrived from England and were staying with them prior to taking up church work in the Darlinghurst district of Sydney.

[2]Young evangelical clergy and their wives.

make him into a golden calf. I do wish you could see and hear him on these occasions. The people here are not given to idolatry; on the contrary some of them have difficulty in being civil to him – some of the clergy I mean. With the laity he makes sure and steady progress and occasionally a pleasant expression comes across unknown faces that we meet in the roads. Every body expected an explosion between F. and the Clergy who with one exception were all High Church, but he did not indulge them, keeping on the even tenor of his way which eventually will no doubt carry the day. All new openings will be occupied by clergy of his own selection, as far as he is able to procure them.

25th August, 1855

. . . Dearest F. sometimes gives a deep sigh, so deep, so full, it goes to my heart and I assure you one of my principal endeavours is to cheer and keep him up. We want more good men *so* much. The poor people in the country are sadly lost for want of a shepherd.

[From August 28, 1855 to November 2, Jane Barker's journals are occupied with their first visit into 'the bush' and the vast diocese for which her husband was responsible. They travelled west across the Blue Mountains in their two-wheeled Lansdowne carriage, their luggage containing 'a supply of Ryle's tracts . . . in order to scatter good seed by the wayside'. By October 5, when they reached Yass, Morgan had driven them 654 miles. There were some encouraging meetings with a few clergy, including Robert Cartwright who came out in 1809 and 'like the good old Archdeacon has stood up for Evangelical truth amid many adverse elements', but their principal impression was of the vast need of those in danger of 'entirely forgetting God and His day'. At one place, near Goulburn, they found a couple, aged 96 and 101, who were responsible for a small wooden church building without any preacher: 'They lamented feelingly over the absence of the "Word of God" and said there had been no service since last Christmas day'. Out of this first visit to the bush came Jane Barker's commitment to start a school which would educate the daughters of country clergy.]

7th November, 1855

I feel greatly benefited by our trip both in mind and body. The depressing weight seems thro' God's mercy much lightened if not removed. I never felt very well before going away. We are now getting a circle of our own English friends (the recent arrivals)

[228]

among us, and they gave us such an unfeignedly warm welcome
back that it was cheering. Our nice well-conducted servants did
the same and the house seemed to show such evident symptoms of
care and labour that we could not but.praise them. The pretty
chintz I brought together with muslin curtains has made the
drawing room look very English and nice.

9th November, 1855
I sat up twelve o'clock on Tuesday finishing our home packet but I
could not write all I wished. Now it is Friday and I have not much
to relate. Sydney is Sydney. A most 'wonderful', most beautiful
city, with the finest harbour in the world whose deep blue waters
afford room for vessels close to the shore etc. etc. etc., but
——————! Today we have a real hot wind, which may be
described to you best, by begging you to imagine yourself before
Jane Holmes' oven, with a fierce wind blowing its heat upon you.

10th November, 1855
I hope we shall have a Prayer Meeting on St. Andrew's Day,
perhaps it will be in this house, to which we may invite all 'our
own' people . . . While doing our best to set an efficient agency to
work, we must not forget to implore the blessing of the Good Spirit
who can alone put life into the machinery, or cause the dry bones to
live. Good Mr. Unwin has a prayer meeting of his own every week,
attended by six or seven men. He has also a meeting in a room on
Sunday evenings which began with nine and numbers sixty. We
look for Mr. Gurney next month and Mr. Wilson, recommended
by Mr. Maurice Day and Mr. Venn, the month after, and are told
that Mr. Champneys has three young men to be ordained at
Christmas to come out. I hope our friends will not cease to pour
Evangelical labourers in upon us – as soon as the Colony is
thoroughly stocked with them we may perhaps be allowed to think
that dear F.'s work is done!!!! What a change will come by and bye
in the face of society. God grant the beginning of this may soon
appear, for it has been truly depressing to witness the absence of
vital Christianity, and the whole city given to idolatry of the god of
this world in one shape or another. A new evil has appeared since
our departure which causes a sad amount of Sabbath desecration,
viz the opening of the railway to Parramatta.

. . . Lady Dowling is going home . . . She wants us to take her
house, but it is not good enough for a permanent Episcopal
residence and is I think too much *among* the gay folks of

Woolloomoolloo from whom we should never be free. We are considered out of the world where we are and had perhaps better remain until some place three or four miles from Sydney can be found.

11th November, 1855
The wind still is most vehement – a boat was upset yesterday with three men, but they were rescued. Dear F. was to have gone to Cockatoo Island to preach to the prisoners as he did last Sunday, but dear Walter not being quite well he agreed to take his duty at St. Phillip's and send Mr. Cuthbert (the last arrived, a Scripture Reader) to Cockatoo. F. preached a sweet sermon this morning on 'in his favour is life'. He is quite at home in St. Phillip's – the atmosphere is not a 'musical' one, but of the good old English kind. He will take also the evening service. We had a dreadful walk back – clouds not of dust only but gravel, very like being pelted with sharp particles. The wind usually subsides with the sun, so we may have it quiet for our evening walk.

12th November, 1855
I went to sleep last night thinking that dear John and dear Joseph were just beginning their sermons.[1] The wind ceased not and we had another 'pelting' walk. This is 'severe weather' in the Antipodean sense. Today it blows as hard [as] ever and the Bush fires on the opposite shore have been raging furiously for two days. The flames on the horizon extended for miles and were fearful to behold.

14th November, 1855
Began to read McCheyne's life which dear Matilda gave me. How much our thoughts meet and our prayers ascend for one another in reading our daily portions [of Scripture].[2]

16th November, 1855
I hope dinner parties are over for this year, except for such as we must have in according to invitation . . . We had a *small* affair, Captain and Mrs. King, their nice daughter and Miss Manning

---

[1]Her brother-in-law and brother, Sydney being nine hours ahead of England.

[2]The 'portions' were probably those of McCheyne's calendar for reading through the Bible in a year. She enjoyed the memoir, quoting later to her sister words written by McCheyne on his journey to Israel; 'A foreign land draws us nearer to God. He is the only one whom we know here'. *R. M. McCheyne, Memoir and Remains*, 1844 (Banner of Truth Trust, 1966, p. 90).

(their guest) dined with us at three o'clock.[1] The Kings are really good people, and keep more aloof from the world than anybody else we know of here. I pity them in losing their daughter who is the *only* lovable young person I have met with – piety is a rare plant and to it she adds a sweet face . . . and a nice manner. She is going home to marry a Mr. Prior who is a Barrister at Eltham near Greenwich.

17th November, 1855

The weather seems now to be that of settled heat; one can bear it well enough sitting still in the house, but exposure in the sun is not agreeable. A sea breeze certainly springs up now and then which is an alleviation.

Mr Pearce called yesterday with a map of the environs for F. We are puzzled about the site, and should be glad when it is fixed. It seems useless to find a house ready to our hand, though you may fancy with how little *heart* we should undertake to build; but for the heat I would rather live like Abram in his tent, in this land of our pilgrimage, that all might be in character with that which is felt within.

The *Emma* is long overdue, which happens so often that it will be a comfort indeed to have steam communication again.

20th November 1855

Had a long visit yesterday to the Infirmary, the first I remember to have been in. It is well managed and the poor patients very kindly treated. The chief complaints are consumption and rheumatism and among the men scurvy. There are more men than women, and generally it is soon after their landing that they go there. One poor young girl in decline told me she came from 'The Meeting of the Waters' in Wicklow and left Father and Mother and brothers and sisters. 'Ah, ma'am if I'd known what I was coming to I'd never have left them'.

The day has been cool, not to say rather cold, and last night we should actually have liked a fire. It is a very changeable climate, and the dust of Sydney is such as to make you dread leaving the house if there is any wind.

23rd November, 1855

In the afternoon F. drove me to Randwick to look at some Crown

[1]Captain Phillip Parker King was a son of Governor King, and Robert King, serving St John's, Parramatta, was one of his seven sons. There was only one daughter.

lands that he might possibly get in exchange for the five acres at Grose Farm.[1] We got out and strolled over a beautiful portion of country looking down upon Great Coogee Bay and Gordon's Bay adjoining that in which the Lowes lived. A fine open sea view with an eastern aspect, the best here. The ground contained a good site, plenty of water, stone for building, a gully in which tropical fruits might be grown, suitable spots for gardens, gravel for roads, in short everything and what to us was better than the rest, retirement and nature while still only four miles from Sydney. We scrambled down to Gordon's Bay, a pretty little inlet and most enjoyable retreat, with the purest of salt water rippling up on the sandy beach at our feet. I have seen nothing so pretty since our arrival.[2]

24th November, 1855

I called on Mrs. Unwin and did a little shopping, while Frederic went to speak to the Governor about the land at Coogee. A violent wind sprang up from the North just before I reached head-quarters, a hot wind, and at this moment I am resting on my bed writing to my darling sister, while the thunder peals over my head and shakes the house under me, and very forked lightning flashes before my eyes.

26th November, 1855

. . . Yesterday was Sunday. We were at St. Andrew's . . . Many thoughts of home, it was six months since our arrival in Sydney. Time begins to go more rapidly, and the pleasure of hearing from our precious friends keeps our hearts up. There is nothing worth being here for except to do good, and promote the Lord's work with all the diligence in our power. May we have strength given us to do that.

F. had a Confirmation at Cook's River six miles off. Meanwhile I visited the School of Industry and heard a class read Matt. 11, on the verse 'come unto me . . . and I will give you rest'. I asked who it was that promised to give us rest, and one girl answered 'God' and another 'the Bishop', which gives you a fair specimen of

---

[1]i.e., the land at Newtown which they had earlier viewed unfavourably as reported in the journal for *1st June, 1855* above.

[2]This district, which Jane also refers to as Waverley Grange, was to be their future home. By the end of the year the government confirmed a grant of 59 acres on the northern slopes of the gully behind Coogee beach for a 'Bishopscourt'.

colonial school teaching. The poor children are taught like parrots to repeat, but their minds are wholly unexercised and I really doubt whether their mistress could have answered the question better.

27th November 1855

An interesting letter from Mr. Macarthur about the Australian section at the Paris Exhibition – the wheat, wool and wine all gaining prizes, also the woods and marbles and ores much praised. It is amusing to see the indignation of the people here about the ignorance of Australian geography shewn in England. They forget that it is not so very long since 'New South Wales – capital Botany Bay' was all that was known of the great Continent in an old world.

29th November, 1855

Dearest F. better, but had some disagreeables to bear of a clerical kind. Frederic is beginning to know what the Clergy really are, and it is often different from what they seem. He has something to encourage and much to pain him, so that St. Andrew's Day will find us with some ground of hope and a good deal for humiliation.

30th November, 1855

St. Andrew's Day! How many thoughts are with you this day as yours with us as I well know. We went to Church. Dearest F. preached an excellent sermon on 'follow me, and I will make you fishers of men'. There were about twenty clergy there, and a good congregation. I thought of Lambeth and sitting between you and dear Mary, and near the other loved ones. It has been a dark year to me. I hope the next will be different and find me a more cheerful fellow helper of my dear Husband. He dear fellow was much cast down in thinking of the absent, beginning with dear Arundel. 'Oh I wish he would come, I wish *somebody* would come!' A burst of tears followed this. Then he fell asleep on my bed and a friendly cup of tea came to refresh him.

At half past six o'clock Mr. and Mrs. Hayden, Mr. and Mrs. Ashwin, Messrs. Hulton King, Richardson, Goodman, Gurney and Unwin appeared to spend the evening with us.[1] I had a 'strong tea' ready in the dining room, and when that meal was cheerily devoured we adjourned to the drawing room. It was intended as a kind of little prayer meeting in remembrance of the day. We sang a hymn sitting, 'Come ye that love the Lord' – then we read Ezek.

[1]All evangelicals who had come on Barker's encouragement.

37 and F. made some remarks and elicited a few from others, and offered up a prayer, in which as you may suppose everybody and everything was remembered. Then another hymn, 'Come Holy Spirit, heavenly Dove', following by reading the prayer of St. Paul in the 1st and 3rd Ephesians, and a prayer by good Mr. Unwin. Then there was half an hour for conversation. The servants joined with us in singing 'Rock of Ages' and Mr. H. King prayed, and after supper our little company dispersed. It was a comforting service and seemed to bring the promise of a blessing. The influence of the Holy Spirit being the thing dwelt upon, that which can alone put life into the skeleton form of outward observance, that surrounds us. We were all of one mind, and felt safe from Jesuitism. In order to begin something fresh on this day, it was proposed to have a similar meeting to this the last Friday in each month, and all seemed to rejoice in the arrangement.

5th December, 1855

. . . F. is well and enabled to possess his soul in patience in the midst of this 'crooked' generation. He begins to tell me that *I am too good* for this place, which shews the bad opinion he has of it. I always thought *he* was, and now more than ever. A ruder man with Evangelical principles and plenty of impudence would have suited better. Dear F.'s gentleness and forbearance are abused, and you know how Tractarian clergymen can treat and speak of a Bishop or Archbishop whose sentiments they dislike . . .

11th December, 1855

This morning we attended a Confirmation at Christ Church, the High Church par excellence here, Mr. Walsh being the clergyman . . . We are not yet sure of *one* family belonging to the Church of England, except the Archdeacon's, who on principle separate from the world.[1]

3rd January, 1856

I am up early, half past five a.m., an hour sooner than I intended, but we were disturbed by the mosquitoes so often that I thought I would get away from them. Dearest Frederic shews as much patience with them as he does with his clergy! though in a different way, for in one case it ends in mercy and in the other in murder. Our nights are very broken; you are startled out of a sound sleep by

[1]'The world' here has reference to the universal attendance of balls and theatre. The Rev. W. H. Walsh was the leader of the 'Sydney clique' of Tractarian clergy and he was to be a centre of opposition.

the bloodthirsty little imps blowing their horn in your ear –
probably not until they have committed a robbery on your person,
or at any rate with an intention of doing so. You cannot rest until
the enemy is discovered and it often takes nearly half an hour to
find him and catch him. By the time this is done you are tolerably
wide awake, let the hour be what it may, and the scene is repeated
two or three times during the night, I think our net is too open and
intend to get another for it seems probable they penetrate the
openings. The chimney and open door give them free admission
and as it is after sunset that they swarm into the house it is most
difficult to see them.

The water looks so beautiful this morning with soft shadows
under each promontory.

5th January, 1856

I send you one of our Prospectuses of the School, but do not want
any English money for it.[1] It will shew you what we are about. We
have got about £300 in donations and £200 in subscriptions.
School apparatus we should be thankful for from home, books etc.
but I don't exactly know what.

30th January, 1856

The longer we are here the more entirely F. is becoming separated from the clergy he found in Sydney, excepting the
Archdeacon and Mr. King of St. Andrew's; that is there is no
open rupture, on the contrary civility, and we intend occasionally
to invite all of them to dine with us. But confidence is gone and
the attempt quite given up to attempt to work with them. I am
very thankful for it, as it only led to continually fresh annoyance
and disappointments.

Dearest F. has been more cheerful since the last letters from
home. In general he is more depressed than I am, indeed I am
generally more cheerful now, though with many a good crying fit
about Jessie and her pets and my other treasures. There is not that
constant burden there used to be, and it is a mercy for which I may
be thankful. How much of it do I owe to your prayers my dear
ones.

[1]Jane Barker was now giving much time to the commencement of the
Clergy Daughters' School. She already had a 'Superintendent' (Miss Loftus),
and with a house temporarily rented on Point Piper Road, two teachers and
'Scotch women of the Free Church' engaged as servants, the school opened on
March 5, 1856.

14th February, 1856

In the afternoon I drove with F. in the Lansdown to Bishops-court and fixed with him where to place the Entrance Gate and Lodge, and how to wind the approach, all preliminary work to the building of the house. The land has not yet been made over to F. It may be made very pretty, and I hope we shall see it transformed before long from a wilderness of Bush and 'scrub' into a Park-like Demesne, with gardens etc. bringing forth fruit for the use of man. I want to make it fit for somebody else! But how much more earnestly do we desire to see this great moral and spiritual wilderness fertilized by showers of divine grace and yielding fruit a hundred fold to the glory of God. I have no doubt it will do so, in His own time, and think a crisis is not far off when the powers of light and darkness will be seen in mortal conflict in this very town of Sydney. The darkness will be headed by Popery, for no longer can it be allowed to be the predominant influence at work here – it must yield when once the Sword of the Spirit is fairly brought to bear against it. Dearest Frederic has shewn by his actions that he will have no fellowship with it, as others have had, Clergy and Laity alike appearing to be on terms of cordiality with certain Romanists here, and their Archbishop.[1] F. keeps quietly aloof, declining their hospitalities, which the Chief Justice says is a 'fatal mistake', and more than once mentioning the errors of Popery from the pulpit. On Sunday last indeed it was explained to be one of those works of the devil (yea, his masterpiece) which 'the Son of God was manifested that He might destroy'. The Sydney University is another thing he will have nothing to say to, which makes them rather sore, but the Bishop is not a person to go with the times, and must adhere to his own principles if good is to be done.

18th February, 1856 [Private note to Jessie Clay]

F. is better this day or two, but he does not look as well as he used to do. Dear creature, his spirit is often bowed down. I often long for one of those light-hearted peals of laughter which you remember, but where are they! Care, care and worry are his lot, but blessings are interspersed which makes us feel that God is with us.

19th February, 1856

The heat of yesterday was intense but about sunset it cooled

[1] J. B. Polding, an English Benedictine, came to Australia as its first Roman Catholic bishop in 1835, and remained active for over forty-two years.

somewhat and F. and I took a walk on the Flagstaff Hill near this [house]. The moon soon came forth in her brightness, more like another sun than you can imagine. We thought and spoke of home and our loved ones there. Then came home to tea and the mosquitoes. F. had eight gentlemen to visit him in the afternoon – each one going out just as another came in.

28th February, 1856

A year today my Jessie since our last fond embrace. You will not forget it, and may the God who comforteth those who are cast down be present with you and pour His sweet peace into your heart. . . . But after all, we have only been separated a year, and such things have happened before when but few miles comparatively lay between us, and the period of exile may be shorter than we think it. I wish I could take more comfort from the assurance that we shall dwell forever in blessed union above, without fear of any evil, any sorrow or shade of sin. I know it will be greater happiness than any to be found here. But I am so little attuned to this prospect thro' the earthliness of my heart that England too generally forms the horizon of my landscape. . . . Surely I required some sharp process to wean me from resting on and being satisfied with anything that earth could afford, and I must not complain of being dealt with as a child.

Dearest Frederic is not looking any better than he was, and feels the heat very much. He has still occasional troubles and many hindrances through the want of principle and efficiency here. But amongst his own all goes well, with one painful exception, and in looking back to the nine months that have elapsed, there is every reason to praise God for the great accession of help He has sent us. The Word faithfully preached by these excellent young clergymen will, by God's blessing, soon produce an effect upon the city of Sydney.

10th March, 1856

F. . . . is preparing to preach at St. James' for the Diocesan Society, a venerable society which is at the meeting tomorrow evening to be voted into its grave, and a new one called the Sydney Church Society to take its place. This is an epoch in Church matters here which we hope will promote the spread of the Gospel.

12th March, 1856

I am most thankful that the Diocesan sermon and meeting are over. They were a great weight beforehand, but we have reason to

[237]

feel that a merciful God was mindful of us and sent His angel to help my precious Husband. It is quite a turning point, and the one to fix it is another meeting to establish the new Society [at] the end of April. There are a few clergymen here who are I am sure writhing under an Evangelical Bishop. . . . Expediency carries the day and to be in favour with the powers that be!

13th March, 1856

A pupil for the Clergy Daughters' School, Miss Gunther, from Mudgee, came this morning, and owing to the election we could not get a cab for her, so the useful Lansdown was put in requisition. I heard of a new mode of punishment yesterday occasionally used in the School of Industry, viz. to put the offender into the prison room and feed her on bread and water and have her head shaved! . . . It is a part and remains of the convict system, eminently calculated to make the heart ten times harder than before and I think fifty girls might easily be managed by wisdom and love.

21st March, 1856

How fondly our heart turned homeward today. Edge Hill has been uppermost, for this season was ever a marked one there, and has found a very wretched imitation in this far off land . . . We have no flock here and I feel myself put upon the top shelf quite out of every body's reach and covered with a thick layer of dust and rust.

I told you we were at Bishopcourt on St. Patrick's Day. F. and I went again yesterday. It is becoming quite a *sort* of Ullswater to us, and a pleasant retreat from the Sydney world. The little room that is to be ours is getting on nicely.[1] It has a window at one side and a glass door at another. The wooden walls have to be lined with calico and papered.

26th March 1856

Easter Sunday (23rd) was a day to make the heart glad if it was in a right state. F. preached at St. James' in the morning, John 11:23, 24, and at St. Phillip's in the evening, John 11:25, 26 – the latter was a beautiful sermon, he feels at home in the good man's pulpit. It was the Archdeacon's last service in the oldest Sydney Church; the new St. Phillip's is to be consecrated tomorrow. Dear F. made an affecting allusion to the circumstance and will again tomorrow.

[1]In addition to the church land acquired for the episcopal residence the Barkers purchased some adjacent ground for themselves and put up a two-roomed hut named 'Rock Cottage'.

15. *Hell Gate, Tasmania*

26. *The Scots' Church, Collins Street, Melbourne, 1886*
This building, the fruit of the early labours of such preachers as James Forbes and Irving Hetherington, marked the end of an era. With a decay in preaching the era which such churches represented was to end and the large congregations of earlier years began to dwindle.

He has been making his first *quite new* sermon for the occasion, and we have invited five and twenty clergymen here to luncheon after the service, rather a business but Ann is so good a cook that I have no fears about it, and Mrs. Bloxsome has sent me a pile of grapes and figs to cover the table with.

29th March, 1856

You heard of the new Church Society here. Dear F. has been making out the statistics of the Diocese very carefully in order to lay its wants before the public. He finds that no less than 30 stationary clergymen with 30 churches, as well as ten missionary clergymen, are required to meet the present wants of his See. For this a large sum and a large income will be needed, and I hope obtained. What a blessed thing it would be to pour in such a band of faithful ones to evangelize the land. It is well to look the difficulty in the face and get people if possible to rise to the emergency of such a state of things.

On Friday evening (28th) we had as usual our prayer meeting. I being the only lady sat in the corner at my work, a little bit that made no noise. F. spoke beautifully on 2 Cor. 6, it was a real pouring out of his heart.

2nd April, 1856

Began a class at the School of Industry and afterwards attended the committee there. F. paid his first Pastoral visit to the Clergy Daughters' School.

[From April 9, 1856 to May 2, the Barkers combined a holiday on the Illawarra coast with a further exploration of the diocese, Wollongong, Kiama, Dapto etc. It was their first real break since arriving in Australia. To her sister Jane wrote: 'F. is much altered in appearance since we came here, as no doubt I am. But I could often weep when I look upon my precious Husband's grey hair and faded looks'. Relaxation included a swim in the Pacific.]

12th May, 1856

I have had two rides with dearest F. through the streets of Sydney and Hyde Park which unfortunately must be traversed, making about two miles from this before the country is attained. I thought of you when I was dressing for my first ride, and fancied myself like you in my habit. The weather is become so bracing and beautiful (tho' very cold in the mornings) that I am beginning to take long walks. Today I walked more than half the distance to the CD School and all the way back, which was five or six miles.

Autumn was always my strong time and May is Autumn in this perverse land.

13th May, 1856

My riding day but a violent West wind, which is the same as *our* East wind, set in and prevented me. I only had a short walk instead, and a Bathurst clergyman and his wife Mr. and Mrs. Lisle dined with us to meet the Foxes. The F.s are destined for Bathurst, and got a few hints from them. They brought a daughter to the CD School. That institution flourishes but I must have another round of begging and we think of begging or buying five acres of land near Waverley, on which to build CDS, a Church, Parsonage and village school. Would not that be a nice little missionary settlement? It is half a mile from our little place.[1]

25th May, 1856

Before going to bed I must have a word with you on the anniversary of our arrival in this land of our banishment. Dear F. and I were reading yesterday 1 Pet. 4 and were impressed with verses 12, 13, 14 as illustrating our case. A part of our blessed Lord's sufferings in which we are now partakers is the banishment from our Father's house, to dwell among those who have no love of God. It makes us feel indeed strangers and pilgrims and constitutes our chief trial. What must His have been. If He ever rejoiced in spirit it was because some ray of heavenly light gilded the darkness and so it is here. The arrival of a Christian labourer, the communion which we have occasionally with such, are gleams from our Father's presence to illumine the dreary melancholy world in which we live. Let us be thankful for these and diligent in prayer that God will rend the heavens and come down and bless the means used.

30th May, 1856 (the 'Woolpack', Parramatta)

(On) Wednesday *28th* we were to have come to Parramatta in the Lansdown, but finding it was the day of the 'Home Bush' races, we declined the honour of being seen in the road. So Henry was sent hither with a couple of horses, and we came by the Steamer, leaving Sydney at four o'clock. Henry told us the road was as crowded as he had ever seen it between London and Epsom, and with clouds of dust. We came to the Woolpack, a very poor imitation of the original, though a respectable hotel.[2]

[1] i.e. Rock Cottage at Coogee.

[2] Originally the Freemasons' Arms it was renamed in 1821 and finally sold in 1887. The present Court House stands on the site.

(On) Thursday *29th* dear Frederic rode to Liverpool after breakfast and had some conversation with Mr. W. Cowper the Principal (at present) of Moore College. He and his three young men seem to be going on very nicely. There is a Benevolent Asylum containing some hundreds of men, where they visit three times a week. It is capital training for the ministry, and it is a pity more are not in it. It is wonderful how this college has been excavated by dearest F. and how Mr. Cowper was brought to occupy the ground with his pupils all ready for him from the Diocese of Newcastle.[1]

9th June, 1856

I had a very exhilarating ride with F. to Waverley Grange. We followed the fencing now in progress around Bishopscourt. It is a huge piece of land which will come in very useful by and by but where are the funds for an episcopal residence to come from? They amount to about £3000 at the present time, and we do not intend to help it out of our own pockets which have enough to do to erect the cottage at Waverley and other demands. It is not a thing one can beg for and our operations in that way promise to be pretty considerable. A Clergy Daughters' school I am *bent* upon erecting and I shall spare neither friend nor foe in the attempt . . . I care nothing for the Palace in comparison and expect never to live in it. Our own cottage will be more snug and is in a finer situation.

In the afternoon I went into my district and met a Wesleyan who said he had thrice heard the Bishop and liked him far better than any clergyman of the Church of England he had ever heard. *He did* preach conversion in a plain way – indeed, he was almost like a Wesleyan Minister!

23rd June, 1856

F. is trying to organize a plan whereby we may borrow money from the Church Society here to invest in books – it is done very successfully on a large scale by the Bishop of Newcastle and is the only way to keep up a supply of what we really want. Ryle's tracts will be a large item in our first order.

---

[1]Hodgson after 'a hard struggle' had decided to respond to Barker's call for his aid as first Principal of Moore College. William Macquarie Cowper, the son of the old rector of St. Phillip's, wishing to leave the Diocese of Newcastle for Sydney, had become the acting Principal when the College opened in Moore's old home on March 1, 1856.

25th June, 1856

The Archdeacon has had a letter from Mr. Venn in which he expresses a hope 'that the Bishop is making a bold stand for the truth'. I should have been obliged if he had expressed a word of sympathy with his trials and difficulties. There are not many here who know how to sympathize.

27th June, 1856

I have been looking into Mrs. Winslow's Life which is to be my next book.[1] She seems to have been such a *decided* Christian, and doubtless influenced others powerfully. I feel it very difficult here to be openly Christian, but hope that lending books will help me on. I try to do this especially in cases of sorrow with a few kind words, which is calculated to pave the way for further attempts.

27th July, 1856

I am seldom very unhappy now except when sorrow comes over the sea. F. is doing well. A year or so equally successful with the last fourteen months will give an impress to this land and implant the Gospel seed effectually.

Wickedness and forgetfulness of God abound in this city and country. The children who swarm wherever you go are so badly brought up that it gives poor hope for the future, unless something can be done to improve the system. However, that something may be accomplished this session, and if the government will aid scriptural schools we may at once send home for a band of efficient and if possible Christian teachers. Mr. Burke is for the present appointed Inspector of Schools and assistant to Mr. Clarke, North Shore.[2] He is quiet and sensible and good but not strong – he looks very delicate.

28th July, 1856

F. has been to see the Premier who is afraid of making a move about education on account of the Roman Catholics.

A letter in the 'Herald' signed Philo Maynooth which F. intends to answer. . . . The gauntlet has been thrown down. . . . We are as busy here with the Sabbath question as you are at home and F. has twice met the Heads of other denominations to consult about what can be done. We have thorough Gallios in the Cabinet here, who are afraid to do right lest they should offend any party.

[1] *Life in Jesus, A Memoir of Mrs. Mary Winslow*, Octavius Winslow, 1855.
[2] The Rev. J. Burke, one of Barker's twelve new men, referred to later this year by Mrs. Barker as 'our clergy'.

Railway travelling is the particular grievance here and likely to become worse and worse unless some check is now put upon it.

F. is going to Ryde and Parramatta to set up Church Society branches there. It is wonderful how the plan is taking among the middle classes. Some of them are quite impatient because their clergy delay forming a branch and bringing their contributions to the vestry.

F. had a Committee Meeting with the Dissenting 'Heads' about the Sabbath. What a dreadful Bishop!

[In a postscript to the journal of 31st July, 1856 Bishop Barker sends some comment on his wife to her sister-in-law. She looks well, he reports, is the bright figure at dinner parties and 'so much liked by the people in the country that they complain when he goes on visits without her. She is much happier than she was and enjoys our puritanical gatherings on the last Friday in the month and is a mother to the young wives and a confessor to the young clergy. Her counsel is of great use to me, only sometimes I am obliged to say, "My dear, I allow you to go so far but this is a little too far" when some *very decided* step is recommended.']

13th August, 1856

We spent the day at Waverley Grange. The delicious air and retirement of the place quickly raised our spirits and though we had taken poetry, drawing, newspapers and Macaulay to beguile the hours, very few of them were spent within doors. We rambled about from Carr's Tent in Bishopscourt Bush, where his good wife has made a place for a pig and some ducks, onward to the proposed site and round by the fence of our own estate (how grand we are). We had luncheon on sandwiches, and rice, and some of your strawberries out of 'the Jug'. We also boiled a couple of eggs and not having anything to hold them made cups of our pocket handkerchiefs. Afterwards Mr. Pearce[1] came and we set out with him to inspect *my* bit of land, which turns out to be the cheapest and prettiest lot of the whole, with a lovely view towards the Pacific. Then we proceeded to the Clergy Daughters' piece, which is really a noble donation of 3½ acres in a choice place. I am quite in spirits about it and devizing all kinds of things when I can raise a little money. Below it is the spot for a parochial school, church and parsonage but the 'Daughters' will crown the hill and command the pre-eminence.

[1]Samuel Pearce, the local Crown Lands Commissioner.

The Hodgsons have not yet arrived. I am less glad to think of their coming than of any previous arrival. The sacrifice was so great and they had so much to leave. This cannot be said of any others who have come except ourselves. . . . I feel that having them will greatly tend to increase the interest felt at home about Sydney and New South Wales generally. It is another strong link between us and home. Personally they will be our *greatest comfort*, though not near enough for constant intercourse.

17th August, 1856

F. read me the Report of the C.M.S. meeting in London of 7th May. How pleasant it was to hear the different speakers. We are struck with the greater union with Dissenting brethren that is insisted upon. It is what we are beginning to practise here, and I am sure that where the two great enemies of Popery and Infidelity have to be withstood it is our wisdom, and in accordance with the Spirit's teaching, that we should heartily co-operate with other Christians, though they may be dressed in a different uniform.

18th August, 1856

We have met our home friends but I will go back and tell you about yesterday. Went in the morning to Paddington where F. preached for the Church Society in Mr. Wilson's Schoolhouse. It was very full and the Clergy Daughters made a good appearance. We returned home and often looked wistfully from the windows before and behind for signs of the *Telegraph* steamer. At last the signal was up and we saw the vessel pass under our windows. F. and I waved our handkerchiefs from the verandah and were answered in the same manner. Morgan had been despatched to the pier and before long the cab appeared which brought our poor friends. We had a tearful meeting, and found it difficult to realize the nature of it. At last we began to do so, and today we seem to settle down after the excitement.

Dear F. preached on Babel, and Mr. Hodgson and I walked to hear him, leaving Mrs. H. with little Elizabeth. I could hardly sleep after all this. This morning Mr. H. went down for his luggage, and made all comfortable. I took them a drive to see the Botanical Gardens and Domain and other parts of interest, and they were warm in their admiration of the Harbour. F. meanwhile attended three different meetings at three, four and five o'clock and is now gone to a seven o'clock one for the Church Society at St. Phillip's School – hard work, you will say; indeed he has too much

[244]

to do now, and work increases upon him. Mrs. H. and I have remained in case . . . Mrs. H. looks ill and Mr. H. grey. She says I am grown *stouter* and the Bishop *taller*! It is so nice to talk with her about persons and places long known and loved and most refreshing to meet again with decidedly Christian people. They will be a great blessing in this dark cold land.

[For their first four weeks the Hodgsons stayed with the Barkers as they prepared to take up their work. A brief early visit to Moore College at Liverpool saw them return disappointed, not least among the problems being the evident hostility of the local clergyman, Charles Priddle, a strong Tractarian. Visiting the College at this same period Jane Barker narrowly escaped serious injury when she was thrown on her head from the Lansdown as it overturned on hitting a tree-stump.]

15th September, 1856

F. was not able to come down to breakfast, but *I* was, for the first time since my accident. The sultry heat of yesterday or a Beefsteak pie disturbed many of the household – not of much consequence or to a great extent. After breakfast Mr. Hodgson set off to make a finish in George Street about his furniture. I had my Doctor who took leave of me and said the head was so nearly well, he would not come again. Then I prepared my circulars, 'Mrs. B. returns thanks for the favour of kind enquiries', and saw one or two persons for Frederic. Then Mr. Hodgson came in and we had an early dinner, so as to let them go by the half past one train to Liverpool. Poor things, they thanked us so very much for the month's abode they had had here. Their disappointed feelings have been a great trial to us, and I charge you never to *urge* anybody to come to our help – it is paying a great price and seems to bring back all our personal griefs in leaving home and country. But I hope the worst is over for them, though it has given a sort of damper to our feelings in regard to their coming very different from what we had expected.[1]

[1]The Hodgsons had the added trial of having left children in England but they soon began to share the Barkers' vision for the College. By the time that ill-health brought his resignation in 1868 seventy-six more men had been ordained and Moore College had become, in the words of Marcus Loane, 'the key to the spiritual strength and well-being of the Diocese of Sydney'. 'I have endeavoured,' said Hodgson in 1868, 'to guard those within the sphere of my influence alike from ritualistic innovations and from the old and oft-refuted objections of rationalistic infidelity'. Returning to an English parish in Westmorland he died there the following year at the age of 59. The words of a

A new Bishop will we suppose ere long be named for the Northern part of New S. Wales, as it is to be placed under a separate Government – I mean the Moreton Bay District. It is a very much warmer climate than Sydney, and immensely extensive.

15th October, 1856

F. is this evening at Chippendale, forming a Church Society Association. Mr. Alfred Stephen is the Clergyman. He has been under the powerful influence of Mr. Walsh and not able tho' apparently willing to throw it off. Mr. Walsh saddled him with two ultra-puseyite Church Wardens, whose yoke is tolerably severe, but he is beginning to emerge from his thraldom and to come out more decidedly on the right side. They were very angry at his having a meeting for the Lord's Day Observance [Society] in his schoolroom and threatened him with the dissatisfaction of the whole parish. He came to consult his Bishop who comforted him by promising to go and take the chair. There were Dissenting Ministers there of course which was the chief ground of offence, but the people generally attended and were stirred up to do so by the behaviour of the Church Wardens. F. was invited to preach there last Sunday evening by Mr. Stephen and a third Church Warden who is more amiably disposed, and public notice was given of the sermon, the collection being for the Church Society. After F. had left the Vestry Mr. Stephen begged that the money might be forwarded to the Society, but the evil minded Church Warden said, 'No, indeed. It shall not go there, except with the consent of the Church Wardens. It is contrary to all rule', and swept the money off the table into his own receptacle! Peculiar incidents these, but Mr. Stephen said the same gentleman had been heard to complain grievously at the Bishop getting so much money to send home 'for clergymen to come out and *swamp* the Church'. Poor man, if he had said *save* the Church, it would have been more correct, for under the sway of such as he, it was fast

---

correspondent in the *Australia Churchman*, Dec. 28, 1868, were to prove true: 'His influence will continue to be felt long after he will have left these shores to return no more'. The College was relocated and reopened in Newtown, Sydney, in 1891. See *A Centenary History of Moore College*, Marcus Loane, 1955.

melting away. I suppose the aforesaid collection will find it's now the only parish in Sydney without a branch. I wish the men were as easy to obtain as the money, but let us be thankful for what we have and may our God make them more and more efficient and successful in winning souls to Him.

Sydney is a godless place, full of temptations to idle amusements and sin, and from its little size you see all that goes on.

[From mid-September 1856 the Barkers made another journey in the diocese, beginning with a 240 mile voyage in rain and heavy seas to Eden, a southerly point on the NSW coastline. Once more they saw the necessity for both evangelical preachers and literature. With regard to the former, she wrote to her sister: 'Young men and single are decidedly the best, unless they have paragons of wives. Nobody that is turned forty should come unless it be to a charge in or near Sydney, and even then youth and spirit are preferable'. Meeting individual Christians – 'the Lord's "hidden ones"' – in isolated places, she comments: 'Who can tell the influence their prayers have had in bringing the Gospel to this dark corner of the earth?' Her husband continuing his visitation on horse-back, Jane returned to Sydney on October 9. 'It is a huge concern to get into working order this great Diocese,' she wrote to her sister, 'and my poor F.'s brain is kept continually on the stretch'.]

12th December, 1856

Today we have had the examination at the CDS. Lady Denison was there all the time and Sir William came in likewise, with two other gentlemen. A few parents were there also. It went off very fairly; the sixteen girls looked very nice, and much improved since March when the school opened. I have got £250 towards the new house. I want to call it St. Catherine's.

Dearest F. looks worn and worked and has almost daily engagements up to the middle of January . . .

Dearest Frederic left me on Tuesday morning (*16th*) [and] my hands [are] rather full, for a brother of Mrs. Smith's took up his abode with me, and in the evening I had a working party for the first time of eight ladies. It was rather formidable, and not very successful. I read Mr. Cobbold's account of his Missionary journey, and we all worked a certain amount. I hope it did some little good and that it may lead to more. Walter came in later and acted as Chaplain for us very nicely. I had my Edge Hill table cover and sorely wished for some of the hands and hearts that had concocted it. What a difference it makes when you know you are speaking to those who sympathize in your sentiments and love yourself! A sort of Paradise that would not always be good for Zion's pilgrims, and therefore am I put here awhile away from such rich pasture, to crop the scanty herbage in this dreary desert. May it make me small in my own eyes, as I am in the sight of all here and in the sight of my God, and then the lesson will not have been in vain.

21st December, 1856

To St. Phillip's morning and afternoon. We heard the Archdeacon, and Mr. Synge, the latter on 'The end of all things is at hand, be ye sober and watch unto prayer'. It was a very delightful sermon chiefly on prayer, very experimental. I felt it really *good* to listen to this dear servant of God.

[With two more entries, for December 22 and 23, the second volume of Jane Barker's journal closes.]

SEQUEL, 1876

On March 10, 1876, Frederic Barker wrote to his wife's sister, Jessie Clay:

The greatest earthly sorrow has befallen me and it will come with almost equal force on the bereaved sister. The Lord enable us both to bear it. Dearest Jane is with the Lord. She died last night after one week's illness from erysipelas and fever.

I send you the last letter, the last writing of hers except a memorandum in her pocket book, which she regularly filled in for your letters.

This letter and others which followed gave more details. The previous week she had become ill with a high pulse rate and diarrhoea. On the Sunday she appeared somewhat better. After Frederic prayed with her before leaving for church 'she took up the prayer and asked for her dear husband that he might be able to speak so as to exalt the Saviour and lead sinners to Him'. That afternoon, on his return, they both spoke much together: 'She said she had only one earthly wish ungratified – the wish to see her dear sister. She observed we had had a very happy life, so unlike the lot of many. . . . Thinking she was better I felt relieved and she observed it and said, "You look very happy". . . . She said she did not know what the end of this world would be, but that she was in the hands of the Lord, that from the age of sixteen she had given herself to Him and knew that all was well.'

The next day, Monday, a swelling in the head began and increased, along with the onset of fever on Tuesday. On Wednesday her condition worsened:

When the Doctors had left the room she beckoned to me and said, 'Come over. I want you', and put both her arms around my neck and drew my face to hers and kissed me saying, 'What do the doctors say?' I told her they thought her very weak and low but hoped to stay the fever and raise her up. She smiled and said it was all well – she was in the hands of the dear Lord and He would do what was right.

It was only now at intervals that her mind was lucid. Wednesday evening and night passed without sleep but

she was generally speaking. . . . She named many of the clergy and her friends and acquaintances, particularly the poor woman she had visited. . . .

She was much set upon our return to England and as our General Synod is not to be held this year she thought we might go in November next and I promised to try and do this. She often reverted to this in her wanderings and it made her happy for the time. I used sometimes to say to her, 'my dear, we little know what may happen before the Lambeth Conference is held, the Lord may interfere in some way we cannot mistake and settle the question for us.' But in saying this I had more thought of my own removal than of hers, dear thing – but I sometimes felt that this great desire to return to England might be disappointed. The day but one before she died she said, 'If I leave you you must go home, I could not bear to think of you living here without me.'

On Thursday morning the doctors despaired of her life and friends and servants gathered in her room for the last time. 'Though her mind was not under control and she wandered from one subject to another she never said anything irrational or different from what she would have spoken in health – kind, sensible and earnest for the good of souls'. With her sight and hearing nearly gone, someone said to her towards the end, 'It is the Bishop, do you know him?' 'Yes, I know him, you may trust him, he is a true man'.

[249]

Jane Barker died at 10.20 that same evening, in perfect peace and was buried at Randwick on the Saturday afternoon.

'Oh! My desolate home!' Barker exclaimed in his letter to Jessie, 'A very Paradise for me to return to evening by evening and now a desert. Of our loss dearest Jessie I can hardly venture to think. Often have dear Mary's words come to my heart when we were first engaged. "You little know what a treasure you have won."'

Broken in health, Bishop Barker sailed for England in 1881 and died at St. Remo on April 6th, 1882. His recovery of evangelicalism for the Church of England in the Diocese of Sydney was the greatest work of his life. In his episcopate the number of clergy had increased from 54 to 127.

13

IRVING HETHERINGTON: 'THE POOR MAN'S MINISTER'

Irving Hetherington

Irving Hetherington: 'The Poor Man's Minister'

Irving Hetherington, the first evangelical minister of Singleton, New South Wales, and subsequently of the Scots' Church, Melbourne, was born in Ruthwell, Dumfriesshire, Scotland, on July 23, 1809. In this parish one of his friends of youth was Robert M. McCheyne, who, being a relative of the minister, frequently spent his summer holidays in the Ruthwell district. After nine years at College in Edinburgh, Hetherington was licensed to preach in the Church of Scotland in 1835 and, the following year, he became a missionary in the poor eastern suburbs of Edinburgh. While engaged in this field of labour, and with evident signs of the help of the Spirit of God, Hetherington read Dr. Lang's appeal for preachers in New South Wales. Lang's words came to him as a divine call even though he knew it could mean the refusal of his fiancée, Jessie Carr, to accompany him. But there was no refusal – 'Where *you* wish to take me, *there* I wish to go' – and immediately upon their marriage they travelled to Dundee to embark on the *John Barry* for Sydney. Their last Sunday, before sailing, they spent at St. Peter's Church, Dundee, hearing R. M. McCheyne. 'It seemed as if God had directed them there, to hear the Saviour's last command: "Go ye into all the world and preach the gospel to every creature".'[1]

The *John Barry* sailed on March 24, 1837, with nearly 400 people on board, more than 100 being children. By Sunday, April 19, they were at St. Jago, in the Cape de Verde Islands, and Jessie Hetherington wrote to her sister of the 'confused and unchristian-like Sabbath'. The British Consul and three Roman

---

[1] For this and all the following material we are dependent on the *Memoir of the Rev. Irving Hetherington*, F. R. M. Wilson, Melbourne, 1876.

Catholic Portuguese gentlemen had come on board at breakfast-time and remained all day:

Our sailors were employed in getting water into the ship; and many of the emigrants, who had been on shore the preceding day, were suffering from the effects of intemperance. The noise of the sailors prevented our having divine service in the morning; therefore Irving and I spent most of the time in our little cabin. In the afternoon the people were collected on the quarter-deck, and worship was performed. Our Catholic strangers were very attentive; and the Consul, who is a Protestant, expressed himself highly pleased. In the evening we had a prayer meeting between decks, which was numerously attended. O that God may give efficacy to His own word, and that the seed sown may hereafter appear, for His own glory!

On May 4 Jessie Hetherington began a letter to her mother but it was never finished. The next day she took ill with a sore throat which, in a few hours, was followed by fever (the next symptom of dreaded scarlet fever). A few minutes after midnight the following Thursday she died and was buried at sea in the morning. In his subsequent prostration of body and spirit, Hetherington himself caught a fever and, in the delirium of the fever, he rose from his cabin, went up on deck and 'was at the very point of casting himself into the sea, when he heard a voice, as though from heaven, restraining him'. Some passage of Scripture, says his biographer, came to him as command from God with such vivid force 'that even in the delirium he at once obeyed. When he came to himself, and remembered the circumstance, though he did not think it was actually a voice from heaven, he did think it was virtually such, and he thanked God most fervently, to the very end of his life, for this merciful interposition of providence'.

As no ship heading for England passed them throughout the entire voyage to Sydney, it was not until two months later that he could complete his wife's letter to her mother. After describing the week which preceded Jessie's death, he proceeded:

And now, my beloved mother, having got over the account of her disease – many tears it has cost me to write it; how shall it be read to you? – you will expect me to give you other information regarding my lamented darling's illness, no less interesting – how she looked, and what she said; and, were I now with you, it is possible that I could describe every look, and repeat the few words she spoke. I say few, for, her throat being affected, it caused her much pain to speak, though she had little pain when not speaking. Were I with you, I could do this; but I feel I cannot on paper. I write now in Sydney, for, during our whole voyage, we met no opportunity to England; yet is my Jessie's every look and every tone as distinctly engraved on my memory – as fully remembered, as they were two months ago. O yes! I never can forget. And in particular will you be anxious to know what was her experience in the prospect of eternity. It was of the serenity of heaven. Let me die the death of the righteous, and let my last end be like hers. O, it was the most perfect peace! On the surgeon apprising me on Tuesday of her extreme danger, I thought it right to communicate this to her. She was quite collected at the time; and was looking at me in the affectionate manner that was so usual to her, and which will, I think, never cease to haunt my dreams. I said to her that Mr. Thomson did not give us reason to expect her recovery. 'It is the Lord's will, and we must submit, Irving,' she quietly answered. 'And have you no fear then, of death, Jessie?' 'No, dear.' 'And how is it that you are not afraid to die?' 'I have long taken Christ for my portion, and set my hopes on Him.' I could but weep. Afterwards I asked her what word of God it was that then gave her most comfort. 'Come unto me, all ye that labour and are heavy laden, and I will give you rest,' she replied, with much eagerness; and, after I had made some remarks on this, she bade me repeat some of those scriptures in which salvation by grace is offered to sinners. This I continued to do, when I thought she was in a state of consciousness; and prayed with her day and night. Her spirit ascended as I was commending her to the God of grace. As assured do I feel of her blessedness, yea, as confident that she is now with the God for whom she gave up so much, as I could be were an angel to bring to me tidings of her mingling with the choir above. To her, death was indeed unspeakable gain. But what a loss have I sustained!

Arriving in Sydney on July 13, 1837, the *John Barry* and all her passengers were held in quarantine in Spring Cove for about six weeks, a number of other passengers having also died of scarlet fever. On his landing, the Sydney Presbytery appointed Hetherington to Singleton, a little town on the bank of the Hunter river, 123 miles to the north. Here, covering a district 50 miles long by 30 broad, he was to remain for nine years. His out-stations included Patrick's Plain, Jerry's Plains and Muswellbrook. A letter, written to a ministerial friend in England in 1838, gives some account of his situation and advises against emigration: 'In addition to the Sabbath services I give an occasional sermon at the houses of the settlers for the sake of their servants; and I do assure you that if I wanted an attentive auditory I should almost prefer a convict one. The poor wretches seem to swallow every word; and every appeal seems to be strongly felt. I lament my district is so extensive, and my weekly rides so long, that I cannot get this other part of my duty so fully cared for as I devoutly wish I could. I trust, however, that ere many years pass I shall be relieved of my more distant connections, and be thus enabled to concentrate my efforts on one sphere. Meanwhile I must do my best to manage what is committed to me. The families in connection with me are the most respectable in the district, and are very wealthy; and I can number not a few carriages and phaetons and gigs at my stations every Sabbath. I have therefore, beyond what is enjoyed in most of our Scottish parishes, the advantage of good society – a literary society I may term them; for having much leisure all read a great deal. And perhaps you would infer, as another advantage, a good revenue for the support of the tabernacle. But of this I cannot boast, for truly my stipend is not oppressive. Through a law passed some time ago, I have from Government an allowance of £100 a year to aid my people's contributions. That allowance has, however, been all I have received. This is not the land for a voluntary church, for, as far as my own experience goes, it does not seem to form one of the maxims of Australians to give anything to their ministers. But, notwithstanding, I am content. For me the £100 is abundance; I am thankful for it. The law by reason of which this salary is enjoyed is this:– When a hundred people above fourteen years of age, male or female, bond or free, agree to attend the ministrations of a clergyman at any one station where he officiates, there is given one hundred pounds; where two hundred adults attend, there is issued £150; and when three hundred adults, £200. Now, my district yields me but the lowest rate at present; though it is not impossible that in a few years it may yield the second. Yet, as I said, were that all my income, it would suffice. And most enlightened and praiseworthy was the enactment of the legislature, whereby the ministers of our church were admitted to such a boon. The law noticed applies to the three denominations alike: there is here no established church, properly speaking. There is, however, one palpable flaw in this Act; it is not permitted in it to combine two districts in making up the aggregate of our people, when suing for the salary. Suppose – as is nearly correct – I have two stations twenty miles apart, where ninety-nine adults do agree severally to convene for worship, and that I do, by dint of hard riding, regularly every Sabbath preach to both congregations; nevertheless, were I to fail in making one of the ninety-nine one more, that is, a hundred, I should be held to have no people at all, though in reality a hundred and ninety-eight. That is very hard. . . . But notwithstanding, I thank the Government for so much. Through this aid the ordinance of the ministry will still be kept in the country; and it is not a vain hope that, when this ordinance has been for a time possessed, men will learn to appreciate it, and of their superfluity to give unto those who spend themselves in seeking their good. . . .

'But how have I been wearying you, I fear I should say, by these egotistical representations! You will forgive me, my dear friend, when I tell you how it is I have been so tedious about my own affairs. I have almost fancied myself again in William street, and I have written as though we were still sitting over the drawing-room fire, and you were still inviting me to say everything to you that at all interested myself. Very delightful to me were those evenings! When I think of happiness tasted by me from earthly sources, I think of them. You were then a patient listener, and hence I have taken for granted that you are a diligent and patient reader. And besides, it is a mournful but much valued gratification to me to write to you; and I could keep writing to you without ceasing: While I write, distance seems, as it were, withdrawn; and my heart, which I thought sorrow had chilled entirely, is again warmed by renewals of my dearest associations. But I must not indulge too far at your expense.

'I would thank you for your affectionate letter, though it was a bitter sight to me. And very gladly would I now say to you – accept of Dr. Lang's invitation, and join us here, as you mention in your letter he had urged; but I dare not advise that you should accept it, though it would be a new life to me to see you and your dear family in this land of my pilgrimages. If you were here just now, I would yield Jerry's Plains to you, where you would have the Government salary of £100; but that, I fear, would be the whole of your income; for the number of resident proprietors is small, and neither would they give liberally, nor would they build a house for you – as is being done at Patrick's Plains – where you might have a school, so as to add materially to the Government allowance. Were it the case, indeed, that here we lacked laborers for the vineyard, I should certainly say – Come. For on £100 a year you could at least subsist; and souls are perishing, for whose sake you are bound to reduce yourself to a bare subsistence, if need were. But neither can I say this. In truth, many allege that there are more ministers here than, humanly speaking, can be supported, or rather, will be supported. And if I chose to limit myself to Patrick's Plains at present, where I have not eight families, – which I would do for you – I have only to signify as much to two or three ministers, to secure them to it. Now this I will not do at present for any but you. There are at this time in the colony nineteen Presbyterian ministers holding ordination, and three licentiates unordained – a full force, considering the amount of the Presbyterian population. Wherefore I do dissuade you from coming; and the more, that you have such a field of usefulness in actual possession. O, my dear friend! Be thankful for a church-going people. Be thankful that you live where the Sabbath is in some degree honoured, and where men profess – at least, profess – some respect for spiritual things; and that you have the satisfaction of speaking to some who not only understand, but have a taste for such realities. What a relief it would be to me if I could meet with a man or woman in my district who – [The rest is wanting].'

Hetherington's biographer, giving an account of the 'hard and rough work' which his subject faced, writes: 'He once mentioned to the writer a few facts in connection with the convict element in his district. He was appealed to sometimes by the convict servants, to use his influence to protect them from unkindness and tyranny. For although tyrannical treatment was certainly exceptional in his district, there were stations on which cases of it did occur. He mentioned one case specially. The man was an unusually civil and industrious servant, a very superior man. For some trivial fault he was sent off to the police quarters where, of course, he would get a flogging. And the floggings of convicts in those days were severe. Mr. Hetherington pled for the poor fellow most compassionately, but in vain. The man was marched off to the whipping-post, and the lash unsparingly laid upon his back; and Mr. Hetherington heard the blows, and, at length, the cries of tortured nature, that haunted his memory long after. The poor fellow never forgot Mr. Hetherington's kindness and sympathy.

'The long rides which Mr. Hetherington had to take in all weathers, conjoined with the mental work required in the preparation of a young minister's discourses, and, at first, the care of the school, which he superintended for several years, were trying enough. At that time he wrote out his sermons in long hand; and carefully were they prepared. Much of his studying, however, he was compelled to do on horseback; and when a thought struck him, he would dismount and note it down, and then remount and pursue his journey. At one time a drought of long continuance had so bared the pastures as to weaken the horses, and make them useless. He had, therefore, to perform his journeys on foot, and generally during the night, so as to avoid the heat of the day. One Saturday night he had to walk thirty miles; and, after climbing a hill, and while resting on a log at the summit, the idea of ministers in Scotland complaining of being Mondayish after two services, and without other fatigue, struck him as so ludicrous that he could not help bursting out into a loud "guffaw" of laughter, which sounded strange in the darkness and loneliness of the bush. On one occasion, long after he had left New South Wales, and when he was travelling with the writer in a wild part of the bush in Heytesbury, in Victoria, it was suggested, as the night came on, and the roads were bad and somewhat dangerous, that we had better camp out for the night. "Did you ever camp out for the night?" asked Mr. Hetherington. "No," was the answer. "I have," quoth he decidedly; "press on." Still, trying as his work sometimes was – and he never spared himself – it was useful work, and to him it was congenial work. After his removal to Melbourne, he often said – while staying now and then for a week or so with a minister in the country, and assisting in his labors – "The bush is the place after all."

'While minister at Patrick's Plains, Mr. Hetherington was brought unpleasantly into contact with the Church of England clergyman; whose lofty assumption of priestly dignity as a direct successor to the Apostles, and his supercilious treatment of the dissenting preacher, and his public assertion of extreme high-church views, stirred up Mr. Hetherington to deliver a series of lectures on Presbyterianism, and otherwise to defend his position as a minister of the Gospel. The remembrance of this passage in his life, and the research involved in getting up the lectures, gave that definiteness to his views, and that firmness to his expression of them, from which we reap the benefit in the Presbyterian Catechism, drawn up by him not long before his death.'

There is no record of the spiritual results of Hetherington's work in his first Australian parish but, on his accepting a call to Melbourne, Victoria, in 1847, the inscription in some theological volumes reveals the warmth with which some viewed him:

Presented to the Rev. Irving Hetherington by the inhabitants of Singleton and Patrick's Plains, as a mark of their esteem and affection for his talents as a preacher and kindness as a friend, during the period of nine years he laboured among them . . .

Hetherington had remarried in 1842 and, with three children, the removal to Melbourne was a considerable undertaking (as well as costing him £30). As the second minister of the Scots' Church (founded 1838) he was to labour in the town which became the capital of Victoria until his death on July 5, 1875. In his latter years (from 1867) his congregation called a young colleague to lighten his labours, the Rev. P. S. Menzies. Menzies was proved to be a very popular preacher, but his theology was not that of the first Presbyterian settlers. F. R. M. Wilson writes:

Mr. Hetherington, sympathizing as he did so deeply with evangelical views, was much exercised in mind by the preaching of his young friend. It was a subject of anxious thought with him, and many prayers; and he felt called upon to preach the doctrine of the atonement of Christ for sinners with even more earnestness and fulness and frequency than ever.

One day when Mr. Hetherington and Mr. Menzies were dining together at the house of one of the people, a gentleman from a neighbouring colony was present – a man of piety and of singular dignity and impressiveness of manner. The conversation turned upon theology, and Mr. Menzies made some rather brusque remarks reflecting upon the doctrine of the vicarious atonement. The gentleman, speaking with quiet earnestness and almost judicial dignity, said – 'If you take away from me the doctrine of the atonement for sins by the death of Christ, you leave me nothing peculiar to Christianity within the boards of the Bible which I care to retain.' Mr. Menzies was much struck with the remark, and with the manner in which it was uttered. And Mr. Hetherington noticed that he never again heard from Mr. Menzies the same tone of observation with regard to that doctrine.

It would appear that, aided by his older colleague, Menzies became increasingly evangelical. Instead of succeeding Hetherington he was to die at the age of 35, and his colleague, in a funeral sermon, reminded the church 'how he agonized for our salvation'.

The necessity of being sure of a saving relationship to Christ was an emphasis particularly apparent in Hetherington's latter years. An illness in 1874, says his biographer,

brought before his mind the whole subject of personal religion, and studied it anew from the foundation as though he had never studied it before, studying it now in the immediate prospect of eternity. He thought upon the nature and character of that God before whom he was soon to stand, and upon his own relation to God by nature as one conscious of sins against God: He thought what must be the demands of justice on account of his sins against such a Being: He considered anxiously how he might escape from these demands: And he came again to the assured belief that only through the atoning blood of the divine Redeemer is there ground of hope for a sinner. He studied carefully the plan of salvation as revealed in scripture; – the substitution of Christ for the sinner, and the imputation of Christ's righteousness to those who believe in Him. With all his heart he committed himself to the Lord Jesus Christ, whose blood cleanseth from all sin; and in this faith waited for His salvation.

It was also noticed how, in his later years, he lost some of that Scottish reserve which disinclined many to speak of their spiritual feelings and experiences. His biographer has recorded some of his friend's testimony, which would sometimes be spoken at the fireside at night when the rest of the household had gone to rest. The feelings he expressed, says Wilson, 'were evidently deepened and softened by the various trials which God sent him'. One of these trials had been his inability to return to Scotland to see his father who was still alive in 1865, another was the sudden death of his wife in 1870. The following words, recorded by Wilson, reveal his spirit:

I now realize how it is that men can postpone preparation for eternity, even when they have attained to old age – even when they have one foot in the grave: we never feel old. However it may be with the body, the mind never grows old. At least, I don't feel one bit older than when I was a boy. I am not so active as I once was, and a smaller amount of work fatigues me now. Sometimes, when I have been in the town, and have made a few calls, I am so tired when I return that I can scarcely lift my foot to come up the steps; but my spirit is still as young as ever. The most notable symptom of declining vigor that I experience is the loss of recuperative power. When I am attacked by illness, I find that I do not recover so readily as I was wont when a younger man. But you may note it as a fact that a man never feels old.

It is a merciful provision of Providence, this gradual taking down of the tabernacle piece by piece – taking out a pin here, and loosening a cord there – giving warning to secure, now if ever, eternal habitations.

O, what a blessed hope is set before us through Christ! Life and immortality brought to light through the gospel! We know not what we shall be; but when He appeareth, we shall be like Him; for we shall see Him as He is.

I am conscious that I have been an unworthy servant, and that my ministry has been in many respects a failure; and though I have been most mercifully preserved from many grievous sins, yet I have much to answer for – opportunities unimproved, time misspent, souls unwarned. O, I have much to answer for! But the blood of Jesus Christ cleanseth from all sin.

Irving Hetherington preached almost until his death. On June 20, 1875, he preached in the morning on, 'It is finished' and in the evening on, 'Put on the whole armour of God'. The following Friday evening he was writing until late at night, 'as he very generally did', when an illness came on which prevented him the next day from travelling to Geelong for Sunday services at which he was expected. Nonetheless, at 4 a.m. Sunday morning he struggled to get up, thinking it was the hour to leave for Geelong. His sickness and weakness increased until in the early morning of the following Friday 'he sat up without help (which he had not done for some days), and when his daughter asked him, "What do you want father?" he said, "Get pen and ink". "What for?" "I want you – to record – no rebellion in me".' These were among his last audible words.

Much was said by way of tribute upon his death, 'He was a true man of God'; 'he was pre-eminently the poor man's minister'; 'his endowments were marked by a richness and fulness which have left a stamp upon his young community'; 'his Christian character was a power, no one could know him without his giving the impression that he was walking with God'. A funeral sermon, preached by Dr. Macdonald in the Scots' Church, included a paragraph which is a fitting summary of his life as a servant of Christ:

Mr. Hetherington also shrank perhaps too much from all revelation of his own inner life. He did not wear his heart on his sleeve. It was only on rare occasions that you found that his soul was much with God, and especially when he engaged in prayer you heard breathings of spirit and wrestlings which brought you into the inner sanctuary, and into the very presence-chamber of Jehovah. As a preacher he had many excellencies, including, of course, the chief that he himself believed. He preached in a way that I am afraid is going out of fashion now – logically, doctrinally, evangelically. His sermons were full of marrow, founded on the first of all gospel doctrines – atonement by blood, Christ crucified; and no man mourned more than he over the loose preaching which is becoming popular now-a-days, which does not convince of sin, and in which sound doctrine and godly experience are dropping out of sight.[1]

[1]This testimony to Hetherington as a preacher is borne out by the three sermons which are appended to his *Memoir*.

14

AN ASSESSMENT OF PRIORITIES

Moorabool Street from Myers Street, Geelong, 1857

I

Introduction

The first article in this chapter was written as an editorial article in *The Presbyterian*: A Record of Religious, Literary and Ecclesiastical Intelligence; Conducted by Members of the Presbyterian Church of New South Wales, February, 1872. This 22-page monthly commenced under the Editorship of the Rev. Colin McCulloch in April, 1871, in Sydney. In his 'Introductory Remarks' to the first issue of this magazine McCulloch wrote: 'Oh, the mighty change were the Spirit of the Lord awakening here in power! What sighings for this visitation there are in some lonely hearts! Why not in all?' In August 1871, when McCulloch was translated from Balmain (Sydney) to Wickham Terrace (Queensland), his name ceased to appear on the title page of *The Presbyterian*.

Another contemporary recognition of the necessity of the Holy Spirit was the pamphlet on *Revivals of Religion*, Their Place and Power in the Christian Church, by the Rev. Archibald N. Mackray of Ashfield Presbyterian Church, Sydney, 1871.

It would be a serious mistake to regard revivals in Australia in the last century as a purely Methodist phenomenon. In the opinion of J. Campbell Robinson, 'one of the most remarkable awakenings of the Spirit of God that we know in Australian history' occurred in Presbyterian congregations under the preaching of the Rev. Allan McIntyre on the Manning River in New South Wales in 1860. At one service, when the preacher spoke for two hours from the words of Zechariah 12:10, 'I will pour upon the house of David and the inhabitants of Jerusalem the Spirit of grace and supplication . . .', it was said that 'there were not three pairs of dry eyes within the walls'.[1] Similar scenes were witnessed under other Presbyerian

[1] *The Free Presbyterian Church of Australia*, J. Campbell Robinson, 1947, p. 88.

preaching at this period. Robinson recalls a service where he was present as a youth on March 20, 1870, when another McIntyre was preaching:

The writer has seen as hard-headed Highlanders as he ever met pulling out their handkerchiefs in a very hurried manner as if they had held out as long as they could against showing their emotion, but had to give in at last. . . . You see that honest-faced Celt. That is not the face of a novice, tanned and browned as it is by many an Australian summer. It bears the marks of shrewdness which men of strong understanding acquire by the rough probation through which they have often to pass amid the shifting scenes of colonial life. Yet it is an open and honest face, and if the preacher has to wipe the streams of perspiration from his face, that sturdy Highlander makes no secret of taking his handkerchief and wiping both his eyes. He has never heard the like of this before. It had been his lot in Scotland to be in a district where moderation flourished. In the arrangements of Providence it was reserved for him to hear the Gospel preached after this fashion in the wilds of Australia.[1]

The second article in this chapter is a large extract from The Annual Address of the Australasian Wesleyan Conference in 1859. It gives a fine statement of what were then considered the priorities if churches were to prosper.

[1] *The Rev. Alexander McIntyre*, J. Campbell Robinson, 1929, p. 29.

2

Church Progress

The Presbyterian

At times a degree of enthusiasm takes possession of congregations in favour of their prosperity. They are anxious to get out of the jog-trot, half-dead, half-alive condition in which they think they find themselves. Possibly they are not quite so bad as they imagine; but they think that something is wrong, or that things might be at least somewhat better than they are. Perhaps the psalmody is rather below the medium; indeed, may be wretched. By it they may be reminded of anything save 'the sweet, solemn sound'. Perhaps the old Psalms are not sufficiently appreciated by a non-Scottish race. Perhaps the church is out of repair, the walls wretchedly dirty, and the whole aspect of the place anything but comfortable and respectable. And hence a degree of enthusiasm springs up in favour of rectifying what is out of order.

But, however commendable zeal in external matters may be, we should not forget that the cause of all true congregational prosperity lies in having the Divine blessing. Prosperity lies in the conversion of souls and in the edification of the members of Christ. Everything connected with the building and with the externalism of public worship may be such as the best friend of the church could wish, and yet death of the deepest character may prevail. Life from God is what we need; and this Life we must have, if we are to make progress in this land. Our wants go deeper than those which affect the principles of mere outward order. They belong to the spiritualities, which, when existing in due measure, raise the church to the highest moral power.

It would be a token for good if we found the members of our congregations seeking the spiritual welfare of their own souls and the conversion of others. It would be the precursor of the richest blessings if we saw our people directing their thoughts towards the

[269]

spiritual state of their congregations. It would be an 'earnest' of days of prosperity if we found our people earnest in prayer for the Divine blessing upon the ministrations of the sanctuary. How many attend public worship with the mind directed towards God and with prayer for His grace? How many remember the congregation to which they belong when they appear for themselves at a throne of grace?

We pride ourselves on having the most perfect ecclesiastical organization. We boast of our Presbyterianism. We delight to speak of our *post*-Reformation martyrs, and of the sublime heroism which led our forefathers to the mountains and caves of the earth, in order that they might transmit to us a pure form of faith and church order. But, of what avail is our pure faith, our Scriptural organization, and our heroic history, if we have not the Spirit of God, the conversion of souls, and the increase of the body of Christ? We should look to externals; we should do what we can in order to avoid giving offence to the taste and culture of the age; we should do what we can to make our churches and our services attractive. But we forget our character and our profession; we forget the high obligation laid upon us and the momentous interests committed to our care, if we overlook the fact that we as a church exist for the conversion of sinners and for the edification of saints.

Those who know the value of prayer should seriously consider our present condition. We need prayer. Every congregation and every minister stands in need of prayer on the part of those who know what prayer is. How can we expect the Divine blessing to rest upon our congregations and upon the Gospel preached to them, if the praying portion of our people have so little interest in their congregations and in the increase of the body of Christ as to neglect prayer on their behalf?

The preaching of the Gospel among us has not that power in it which it ought to have. If we search for reasons several will be found in ourselves, in our own character and conduct, and in neglect of known duty. How is the congregational prayer-meeting attended? Looking at the insignificant numbers who attend these meetings one would be disposed to say that few have any desire for the Divine blessing either for themselves or others. People can find time for lectures, for gossip, and for visiting their friends and attending places of amusement, but they cannot afford time during which they may seek the sanctuary and unite in prayer. The whole aspect of our churches on the week-day service tells how dead and unconcerned we are. It is in this direction that we must look, in order that we may discover our source of weakness, and be prompted to seek the strength which commands success.

It is not in intellectual power, nor in social influence, nor in political stratagem, that the strength of the church is found. Our strength lies in the possession of the Divine Presence, and in that Presence being felt in the conversion of souls and in the nourishment of the faithful. In this lies the source of all prosperity and power. With this Presence we can do everything; without this Presence, nothing. We have abundance of preaching; but where is the power which renders this preaching the wisdom of God for the salvation of souls? Ministers preach and pray, but where are the fruits? Where are those who pass from death to life, and who become the strength of the church? The Gospel is the same as ever; the Divine promises are still the same as of old; but where are the effects which should attend the preaching of the Gospel?

Want of faithfulness must exist somewhere – perhaps in more directions than one. But this is certain, that our people have not that spirit of prayer for a blessing upon the ministrations of the sanctuary which they ought to have, and which they must have before they can find that measure of congregational prosperity which all would delight to witness.

The pious members of our congregations should lay these suggestions to heart. Upon them depends the offering of prayer for an outpouring of the Holy Ghost. We cannot expect the prayerless portion of our people to enter the Divine Presence, and plead for a manifestation of power; but we have a right to expect the prayers of those who value prayer. We expect their sympathy in the cause of Christ. We look for their compassion on behalf of the lost. They have it in their power to do more for our church in this land than all that can be done in the way of order and external beauty. Let us have their prayers, their constant, earnest, 'faint not' prayers. Let us have them in earnest about the spiritual prosperity of their own congregations; let us have them seeking the good not only of the exterior form but of the glorious inner temple of living souls. Let us have all this, and we know the results – a living church, mighty in word and in deed; mighty because of the indwelling of the Almighty, without whom we are not more than 'sounding brass' and 'tinkling cymbal', which may suffice to keep souls asleep; but can never lead them from darkness to light.

We ought to have the special prayers of our pious people. It is their duty to seek the prosperity of their church in the conversion of souls. They are unfaithful in withholding their prayers. They cannot expect to prosper in their own souls if they fail in that which their own professional character as well as the claims of Christ demand. If they who know the truth care so little for the progress of truth as to neglect prayer on its behalf, how can they expect the congregation with which they are connected to prosper?

The eyes of the people appear to be fixed on the minister, not on God. They look to the minister for that which may please, not to God for that which may profit them. They act as critics on the matter and manner of the preacher, not as prayerful listeners anxious for a message from God. We do not mean to say that the preacher is nothing; that his qualifications are matters of indifference; and that he should never be in the thoughts and affections of his people. We mean that the preacher should not be allowed to absorb the attention to the exclusion of prayer for the Divine blessing. The minister is the messenger, not the Master. He is the servant, not the Lord. And the more that he and his work are made the subjects of prayer, the more shall he have a place in the affections of his people, and the more effectually prove himself the messenger of God to their souls. If you desire to love your minister, pray for him. If you would have him be a messenger of peace to your own souls and the souls of others, pray for him. If you would have your congregation prosper, pray for your minister and his work. The best way by which to forget him as *the* man of the religious service, and to remember God, is to pray for him and his work. The best way by which to avoid the character of mere sermon critics (a despicable race) and to cut off the 'itching ears', is to take advantage of the services of the sanctuary as a means of grace to the soul.

3

The Annual Conference
Letter, 1859[1]

Dearly Beloved Brethren,

We, the united pastorate of the Wesleyan Methodist Church in Australasia and Polynesia, assembled in our Annual Conference to watch over and direct the work of God entrusted to our care, 'send greeting unto the brethren' who belong to the Church 'over which the Holy Ghost hath made us overseers'. 'Ye are our glory and joy . . .'

We proceed, dear brethren, to offer you a few general counsels that our experience and observation have suggested as appropriate to the present circumstances of our Church.

We affectionately remind you that we do not exist as a religious body for any merely political or party purposes, neither can our objects be accomplished by the maintenance and prevalence of any peculiar doctrinal or ecclesiastical principles. Party has its uses in the political world. Doctrine and Church polity have an important province in the Church of God. But the great and paramount purpose of your association with us in Christian fellowship is your *personal salvation*. Permit us, therefore, to urge the Apostolic injunction, 'Examine yourselves, whether ye be in the faith; prove your own selves'. – 2 *Cor.* 13:5. If you 'stand fast in the liberty wherewith Christ' did 'make you free', you will not lack consolatory assurances of your acceptance with God. 'The Spirit itself beareth witness with our spirit, that we are the children of God', and 'Because ye are sons, God hath sent forth the spirit of his Son into your hearts, crying, Abba, Father'. This is your *present* and *abiding* privilege, as the sons of God. And in proportion to the distinctness and power with which this divine testimony is borne

[1]*The Christian Advocate and Wesleyan Record*, vol. 1.

to your souls, will be the *life*, and *joy*, and *hope* of your personal piety. We warn you against living in a state of doubtfulness on this most vital point. You would thus be bereft of peace, and shorn of strength, and become weak as other men. O take care that the manifested love of God continually inflames your heart with a growing filial devotion, then will your peace be 'as a river', and your 'righteousness as the waves of the sea'.

As means for the promotion of this great end of your being, we affectionately urge your diligent and earnest use of the various ordinances of the Church of your choice. They have been fully proved to be eminently adapted to promote personal holiness. The memorials of thousands of the dead in Christ, and the consistent testimony of tens of thousands yet alive, bear witness to the value of these ordinances. Be regular and punctual in your attendance upon public worship, and strive with your might to enter into its spirit. *Hear* the word of God. It is the *bread of life*. Frequent the table of the Lord, and thus solemnly renew your covenant engagements with him. And let not your religious duties be confined to the Sabbath. The week-night preaching, and the weekly class and prayer meeting, are all needful and helpful to your spiritual prosperity. If you neglect these, you will not live in the spirit of your duty as Wesleyan Methodists. It is matter of regret that some of you do not so fully appreciate these means of grace, as you did in the days of your first love. O brethren! we are jealous of you with a godly jealousy. We cannot but fear that you have suffered loss. We exhort you to 'consider one another, to provoke unto love and good works; not forsaking the assembling of yourselves together, as the manner of some is; but exhorting one another: and so much the more, as ye see the day approaching'.

Some of you, to whom God has given leisure and understanding that fit you for posts of honor and influence in the Church of God, are in great danger of unfitting yourselves for such service by your neglect of the more private and spiritual means of grace. Men of an unspiritual mind are sometimes ambitious of office, and impatient of disappointment. Such persons frequently leave our Church because they think they are not allowed a just influence. If you so use the Weekly Class Meeting and Prayer Meeting as that your godly profiting shall appear unto your brethren, you will have all the influence in the Wesleyan Church that your hearts desire; and if you neglect these, it may be doubted whether any influence in the Church of God can be safely committed to you.

We are grateful to God for the peace and unity which prevail within our borders, and we beseech you to 'let brotherly love continue'. Avoid contention and strife, for they 'eat as doth a canker'. 'Be kindly affectioned one to another with brotherly love; in honor preferring one another'. – *Rom.* 12:10. We also commend to your practical regard the apostolic exhortation to the Thessalonian Church, 'We beseech you brethren, to know them which labor among you, and are over you in the Lord, and admonish you and to esteem them very highly in love, for their works' sake'. – 1 *Thess.* 5:12, 13. If you do not esteem your Ministers you will not profit by their ministrations, and you will be in danger of injuring their influence with your families and others, and so damaging the work of God. The indulgence of a disrespectful and hypercritical spirit towards ministers, by christian parents, has not unfrequently cursed whole families with alienation from the ministry and Church of their fathers. If you wish your children to follow in your path, and swell the ranks of the Church of your choice, O, beware that you do not by word or deed teach them to despise the ambassadors of Christ!

We exhort you brethren to seek and cherish a burning charity towards all mankind. The souls of men in multitudes are perishing around you, and hundreds of millions of the human race are going down to the pit. O let your souls realize and feel this sad truth, that you may be influenced by a self-consuming zeal for the salvation of men! If this spirit dwell in you, you will be eager to enter every open door of usefulness, and ready to become all things to all men, if by any means you may save some. Your Church affords you ample opportunity to employ your gifts and means for the extension of the work of God, both at home and abroad, and we beseech you, by your obligation and love to Christ, and by your charity to men, to consecrate yourselves to this highest service of mankind.

As one means of promoting your usefulness seek an enlightened attachment, and cherish a loyal devotion to the Church with which you are identified. Make all its interests your own. Wed yourselves to it, and, as your spouse, love it and provide for its wants. Be jealous of its *honor*. Call to mind its history. Remember how your noble ancestry nursed and defended it in its infancy. Think of its mighty growth, and of the beneficent influences it has shed upon the wide world. And determine that its glory shall not be tarnished in your keeping. It demands your *sustenance* as well as your love. Deal not with a niggardly hand. 'Freely ye have received, freely give.' And let not your contributions be fitful and irregular, made under the influence of uncertain impulses, but let them be the spontaneous and well considered offerings of duty. The system of weekly payments for the support of the cause of God, which has been observed as a rule in the Wesleyan Church from the beginning, is sanctioned by inspired precept, and the example of apostolic times, and it has proved highly advantageous. Other Churches have admired it, and been astonished at its power for good. There is great need in this new country, where your numbers are few, and ministerial labourers need to be multiplied, that you should adhere to the plan of regular weekly contributions for the support of the ministry. Otherwise you will most assuredly cripple the Methodist work of God, and involve your hitherto progressive Church in comparative feebleness and defeat. A word to the wise is sufficient; and we make these suggestions to awaken and help your meditations on a subject, which a little thoughtfulness will convince you is of great practical importance to the kingdom of Christ.

Need we remind you that without God, 'nothing is wise, or holy, or strong', therefore, be instant 'in prayer' for the divine blessing upon all you do for Him. The divine spirit in you, the divine wisdom guiding you, and the divine power helping you are all absolutely essential to the efficient fulfilment of your mission as disciples of Christ. These things must be sought in *prayer*, – in your closet and at the family altar, as well as in the house of God. Guard against a cold and formal discharge of this duty. Deadness in your closet will curse you as with a blight. Deadness at your family altar, if you be heads of families, will be a curse to those you most tenderly love; and your want of earnest prayerfulness will stay the gracious rain of heaven upon the Church of God. O then give yourselves to prayer! Let nothing turn you from this duty, or rob you of this great privilege. What higher honor or joy could be given to man than this, that he should be permitted to plead and prevail with God! Prove me now herewith, saith the Lord of Hosts, if I will not open you the windows of heaven and pour out a blessing that there shall not be room enough to receive it. – *Mal.* 3:10.

[276]

We trust you will bear with us, dear brethren, if we put you upon your guard against the seductions of the world. There is a spirit abroad which would remove the ancient landmarks, both in faith and practice. We affectionately warn you against this, and entreat you to cherish a reverential regard for the truths and institutions of religion, and to abstain from all appearance of evil. Particularly, we commend to your reverent and godly observance the holy Sabbath of the Lord. We believe the loose notions that prevail respecting this most beneficent and sacred divine institution are infidel and immoral, and subversive of the highest interests of men, as well as the honor of God. Beware, therefore, of the sophistries that would lessen your religious esteem for the Lord's day, and 'call the Sabbath a delight, the holy of the Lord, honorable, and honor him, not doing your own ways, nor finding your own pleasure, nor speaking your own words'. – *Isa.* 58:13. We also earnestly caution you against the fashionable amusements of the present times, which do not tend to godly edifying. Perhaps there never was a period when sin was so deceitful as it is now. It *affects* to be clothed even with moral charms. It calls to its aid intelligence, politeness, and philanthropy, in order that it may, if possible, 'deceive the elect'. O, remember that you are called to 'come out from the world', to 'be separate', to 'touch not the unclean thing'. 'Know ye not that the friendship of the world is enmity with God'. 'Let your conversation be as becometh the gospel of Christ', and 'adorn the doctrine of God your Saviour in all things'. Finally, brethren, farewell. 'Be perfect, be of good comfort, be of one mind, live in peace, and the God of love and peace shall be with you'. – 2 *Cor.* 13:11.

Signed on behalf and by order of the Conference,

DANIEL J. DRAPER, *President.*
STEPHEN RABONE, *Secretary.*

15

SUNDAY

The old Presbyterian Church at Wahroonga, NSW

I

Sundays in Kiama in the 1860's[1]

Kiama has not undergone many changes, so far as its physical features are concerned, since the days of my boyhood there in the early and middle sixties of last century. There are still the hills and dales, the meandering streams, the picturesque mountain range forming a background in which the artist and the tourist may find unending delight; and 'the ever-restless sea'. What district is there in all Australia that can rival Illawarra for variety and affluence of natural beauty?

But, from another point of view, great changes have occurred within that circuit since the days of which I speak. The veterans have passed away, and with them the heroic chapters in South Coast Methodism appear to be closed. The sanctuaries are larger, more substantial, and more comfortable, than those of which I have recollections in Kiama, Jamberoo, Gerringong, Shellharbour, and Foxground. The roads throughout the district are now good; in those days they were proverbial for their roughness and discomfort. Now, the train carries its passengers in ease and comfort from Sydney to Kiama, or vice-versa. Then, it was a case of taking the steamer on one of her tri-weekly trips, and travelling amid such noisome smells as exuded from pigs, calves, cheese, bacon, butter, and other *olla podrida* that a dairying district yielded up to the Metropolitan market. But there were compensations. The district was more self-contained. It was out of the whirl and swirl of things. The church and its services counted for more in daily life. Existence was more simple; it was more patriarchal – more pious. What a sight it was on Sundays to see the roads lined with horsemen and horsewomen, with an occasional gig or spring-cart to vary the scene, all wending their way to the

[1] From *Memories of an Australian Ministry*, 1868 to 1921, J. E. Carruthers, 1922, pp. 27–28.

churches and chapels; and at the hour of service to note the grounds surrounding the places of worship filled with horses and vehicles! The people were a church-going sort in those days. What prayer-meetings there used to be! Eighty or a hundred or more would regularly assemble on Monday evening in the Kiama (old) chapel; and class-meetings were an inspiration and a joy. Similarly, cottage services were regularly held on Sunday evening at Fountaindale, Old Place, and Gerringong House, and the trouble was to find room for all who wished to get in, and not infrequently doors and windows had to be left open to permit those who were crowded out to get the benefit, although compelled to remain in the open air.

2

Sunday in 1886[1]

It is a pleasant thing to attend a rural service on a typical Australian
day, when the sun is hot and the sky cloudless, and the whole
landscape steeped in peace and quiet. Driving along the road, we
see the sheep couched in the grass, or we pass a clearing where
wheat and oats are growing among the blackened stumps of fallen
trees; and nothing disturbs the stillness of the scene save, perhaps,
the lazy motion of a crow, or the rush of a startled native bear, a
sleepy, gentle, little animal, an enlarged edition of the opossum.
The church stands a little apart from the few houses that form the
infant township. It is generally built of wood, and surrounded by
tall gum-trees, which, however, afford a very scanty shade from
the burning heat. Here is gathered on the Sunday morning a
collection of buggies and horses, for the people come long
distances, and it is necessary in Australia to drive or ride. The
congregation stand in groups before the door, chatting over the
week's news, and waiting for the clergyman to arrive. The Day of
Rest is the only day in the week in which they have an opportunity
of meeting, and many come early and loiter with their neighbours
till the service begins. They are all browned and tanned by
scorching suns, but they speak with the self-same accent that they
learnt at home. There are Scotchmen of whom, to judge by their
speech and appearance, it is hard to believe that they have not very
recently left their native glens, and Irishmen whose brogue is
wholly uncorrupted by change of climate. Most of them, however,
have been settled for many years on the land, retaining their old
customs in the solitude of the bush, and among the rest a due
regard for the worship of God. The children have caught, to some
extent, the tone of their parents, and one could almost imagine

[1]From *Australian Pictures*, Howard Willoughby, 1886, pp. 32–34.

[283]

oneself in a remote parish of Britain. The service itself heightens the illusion. The hymn-tunes are old and familiar, and sung very slowly to the accompaniment of a harmonium. The exhortation of the preacher is brief, telling the old and yet ever new story of the Saviour's love, and it is listened to with evident attention. One hour suffices for the whole worship, and the audience contentedly disperse, and turn their faces towards their lonely homes.

In the towns the organization of the different Churches is effective. Their agencies are at work in the poorer quarters of the large cities, where the evils that exist in the Old World are showing themselves on a smaller scale. They have stood out strenuously for the observance of the Lord's Day, and with marked success. Sunday observance, if not so strict as it is in Scotland, is more general than in England. There is no postal delivery. Trains are not run on the main lines, and a limited suburban traffic is alone allowed. All movements for restricting labour on the Sunday meet with cordial sympathy and practical support.

Sunday-schools flourish in every part of the country. The total number of children attending them is returned in Victoria as 73½ per cent of the whole who are at the school age, and the average is not much less in any other colony. When allowance is made for the children who are kept at home by parents that prefer to give their own instruction, and for those in the country who cannot well attend a Sunday-school, it is evident that there are comparatively few who receive no religious education at all.

3

Sunday Among the Methodists[1]

The only written material a preacher took into the pulpit was his thumb-marked Bible and his sermon notes or manuscript. His prayer, the 'long prayer' after the first hymn, was supposed to be 'free' or 'extempore'. Although he might have given some thought to its content beforehand, the words were expected to flow as the Spirit moved him. It is safe to say that, apart from the set prayers in a baptismal or communion service, no Methodist preacher in the 1880s would have dared to read a prayer.

Most churches, apart from very small ones in the country, had two services a Sunday. Even Inkerman, the little church on the road to Port Wakefield, had one in the morning and another in the evening. The Gawler Bible Christian circuit had eight churches with 12 Sunday services, and the Primitive Methodist circuit based on Moonta Mines had ten services in five churches. Most of these services had to be taken by local preachers, who acquired that status after a period of study, a trial sermon, and an oral examination before a local preachers' meeting. In the words of the Bible Christians, local preachers had to be 'soundly converted, deeply pious, possessing much scriptural knowledge, or good reputation and established with grace'.

Sermons were long (up to 40 minutes was common) in nineteenth-century Methodism. Both the Primitive Methodists and Bible Christians sought to curb the loquacity of their preachers by prescribing the length of services as an hour and a half in the evening and an hour and a quarter in the morning. A Primitive Methodist minister, as distinct from a local preacher, could be fined ten shillings (no mean sum in those days) for breaking these rules, except under certain conditions. One of these

[1]From *This Side of Heaven, A History of Methodism in South Australia*, Arnold D. Hunt, 1985, pp. 150–51.

was 'when sinners are falling down under his word'. . . . Services could be prolonged if there were signs, in the Bible Christian phrase, that there were people under 'serious impressions'.

The evening service in many churches was followed by a prayer meeting, but this became less common as the decades passed. Most circuit plans for the 1880s show that each church also had a weeknight service taken by the minister. In some places this might take the form of a prayer meeting, or, where they still existed, that of a class meeting. A good Methodist could spend up to ten or twelve hours a week within the walls of his local church. On Sunday morning he might attend a prayer meeting or, after the growth of the movement from the 1890s, the Christian Endeavour Society. Then came the morning service. If he were a Sunday-school teacher, this work would occupy most of the afternoon. Then after tea there would be the evening service and prayer meeting. He could also be at his church on two or three evenings during the week.

Ministers in the various Methodist churches exercised considerable liberty in the administration of the two sacraments of Baptism and the Lord's Supper. There were set orders in each church, but whether or not these were followed depended entirely on the discretion of the minister. Communion was seldom celebrated more than once a month; in small churches, it could be quarterly.

Methodists in later generations were inclined to say that their church practised 'open communion', and often the invitation to share in the service was issued 'to all who love the Lord Jesus Christ'. Traditionally, the door had not been as open as these words suggest. In all branches of nineteenth-century Methodism the sacrament was intended primarily for members only, and, as Wesleyan law put it, a non-member could not 'statedly' (an archaic word for 'regularly') partake of the Supper without first receiving the sanction of the minister. The confining of this sacrament to members explains why the custom developed of having it as an appendage to the preaching service rather than a communion service in its own right.[1]

[1]This disciplined administration of the Lord's Supper reflects the high (biblical) view of church membership then existing.

[286]

4

The Biblical Basis for the Lord's Day[1]

1. *In seeking for Scriptural directions for the observance of the Sabbath, we must distinguish carefully between the commandments of the moral law, and those of the political and ceremonial law of the Jews.* What was moral was perpetual, what was ceremonial was temporary, and is done away in Christ.

2. *From the teachings of our Lord we learn that works of piety, necessity, and mercy are perfectly compatible with the due observance of the day*; *e.g.*, the labours of the priest in the temple (Matt. 12:5); the leading of cattle from the stall to watering (Matt. 12:11; Luke 13:15, 14:5); the circumcizing of a man child, and, *à fortiori*, the healing of the sick and infirm among men (John 7:22–24); the doing of good (Matt. 12:12); and the satisfying of hunger. (Luke 6:1–5) These are obviously specimens, rather than a perfect catalogue, of permitted works.

3. *But the Sabbath is a day of sanctity.* 'God blessed it and sanctified it' (Gen. 2:3); pronounced it holy, set it apart for himself; and dedicated it to holy purposes. *There must, therefore, be the laying aside of everything that may impede the spiritual observance*: (1.) All secular business and toil (Exod. 20:8–11), from which the servant-man is to abstain as well as the master-man, the maid as well as her mistress. (Deut. 5:14.) Except the works of necessity and mercy, there should be one unbroken and universal repose. (2.) Frivolities and amusements. (Isa. 58:13) (3.) Conversation upon subjects that are unconnected with and opposed to spirituality of thought. (Isa. 58:13.) *And there must be the observance of*

[1]From *A Handbook of Christian Theology*, Benjamin Field, 1885. An Australian Methodist, Field's statements are a summary of the convictions of all Protestant evangelicals of that period.

whatever would promote the highest interests of our being: (1.) Attendance on the public worship of God (Heb. 10:25), which must be regular, punctual, and devout; for it is a day of 'holy convocation'. (2.) Performance of the relative and private duties of religion. In this way 'call the Sabbath a delight, the holy of the Lord, honourable'.

16

DAYS OF REVIVAL

A Village on Darling Downs

I

Introduction

There has already been given, above, information on the origin of the Wesleyan Methodist Church in South Australia. The growth of this denomination, among others, illustrates how the spread of Christian belief and convictions kept pace with the growth of the population. The number of residents in South Australia rose from 22,460 in 1845 to 83,550 in 1854. Against a figure of 390 for accredited church members among the Wesleyans in 1847, the figure in 1855 was 1506 and, for 1858, 2477. Those 'on trial for membership' in 1842 were 24 and, in 1855, 226, while numbers in attendance at public worship over the same years rose from 2200 to 9380. *The Christian Advocate and Wesleyan Record* for July 21, 1858 reported its belief 'that the proportion of Methodists to population is very much greater in South Australia than in any other of the Colonies'.

The most influential of the Wesleyan ministers in South Australia at this period seems to have been Daniel James Draper, who, in his nine years from 1846 to 1855, saw thirty new churches built and a tenfold increase in membership. Immigration, of course, contributed a significant part to the rise in membership, but the vital factor in the sustained growth was the spiritual life of the churches themselves. Draper's diary for the years 1852–53 contains such entries as: 'Stirring prayer meetings'; 'a very solemn service'; 'Prayer meeting in the evening. A very good time'; 'In several places very gracious outpourings of the Holy Spirit have been vouchsafed and many have sought and found the "pearl of great price".'[1]

That local revivals in South Australia occurred for many years after this is clear from other records. We restrict ourselves to one

---

[1] *Life of Daniel James Draper*, John C. Symons, 1870, pp. 112–120.

extract taken from the Life of John Watsford who was appointed
to South Adelaide by the Methodist Conference of 1862.

★   ★   ★

The remainder of the material in this chapter is from the pen of
William George Taylor. Born in January 1845 at Knayton, near
Thirsk, in the North Riding of Yorkshire, Taylor was still an
infant when his Methodist parents removed to London in their
struggle to make a living. When he was ten years old the family
returned to Yorkshire and two years later, after earnest seeking, he
came to assurance of salvation. Devotion to Christ, to prayer and
to good books marked his teenage years. At seventeen, convinced
of his calling to the gospel ministry, he preached from a pulpit for
the first time in the village of Marton – the birthplace of Captain
Cook. He little knew that after two years at Richmond College,
London (1868–70), he was to be asked to repeat Cook's journey
and serve in Australia.

Firmly trusting the Word of God, and coming, as he said, from a
district of England 'saturated with the blessed revival influences
that, in those days at least, were the joy of our Methodist folk',
Taylor believed that he would see the power of Christ in Australia.
As the following extracts from his autobiography reveal, he was
not disappointed. We restrict our extracts to the earlier part of his
ministry. The greater part of his working life was to be spent in
Sydney where he was used to restore spiritual prosperity to 'Old
York Street' (opened 1839) and to build what became the Central
Methodist Mission – a powerful evangelistic force in the centre of
the city. In this work he laboured from 1884 to 1913.

William Taylor's autobiography, *The Life-story of an Australian
Evangelist*[1] first published in 1920, went through six editions in
five years. It is a book of outstanding interest and value and gives
penetrating insight into the causes of the decline of evangelical
influences at the end of the last century.

[1] The printings intended for sale in Britain bore the title, *Taylor from Down
Under*.

2

South Australia

John Watsford

I felt very much in leaving New South Wales. But, fully believing that the Lord had sent me to South Australia, I went in His name. I had not only to follow a great and successful ministry, but, having been appointed Chairman of the District, a heavier responsibility was laid upon me than I had ever borne before; but the Lord was my helper. The principal church in the Circuit, in Pirie Street, is a fine building that will accommodate about one thousand three hundred people. We had it crowded Sunday after Sunday, and the Lord heard prayer, and in a very remarkable manner poured out His Spirit. We had soon to carry on our meetings night after night for weeks together, and every night sinners were converted. Our midday prayer-meeting was continued for six months: sometimes as many as one hundred and fifty and two hundred were present, and each meeting was a time of great power. The local preachers, leaders, and Sabbath-school teachers were all baptized with the Holy Spirit, and heartily entered into the work. It was delightful to see our local preachers going out in different directions on a Sunday morning, all full of love for souls, and longing to bring them to Jesus.

Some of the cases of conversion were very striking. A young man, a stone-cutter, was brought under deep conviction of sin, and came to the meetings in great distress night after night, but could not find comfort. He was indeed heavy laden. It affected his health; he was pale, wasted, and sorrowful. We tried in every way to show him the simple plan of salvation, and, many a time, we unitedly prayed for him; but his trouble remained. One Sunday afternoon, as I was returning from an appointment, a local preacher being in my buggy with me, about a mile from Adelaide we saw someone coming toward us. As he drew near I said, 'Why, that is P——; where can he be going?' When he was near enough for me to see his face distinctly, I said, 'Depend upon it, P—— is saved; look at his face.' There was no mistaking that; all the sadness and despair were gone. His face now shone with a brightness that told of joy. Soon he cried, 'Glory be to God! I'm saved! I'm saved! I could not wait. I had to hurry out to tell you.'

One fine young fellow was convinced of sin at one of our meetings, and soon found the Saviour. A few weeks after, he sickened and died. His sufferings at the last were very great, but his faith was firm, and his end most triumphant. After his death, entries like the following were found in his diary:– 'Last night I dreamed that I was in heaven; and so real did it seem, that when I awoke I felt the wall of my room to make sure that I was still on earth.'

Among those converted were many young men. No sooner were they saved than they began to seek others. One band of twelve were distinguished by their earnest zeal for Christ. By distributing tracts, inviting others to God's house, 'and speaking to people about their souls, they were made a great blessing. Twelve or fifteen years after the revival, this band met again in Adelaide. They were not all present. One or two had removed to other lands, and two or three were in heaven; but the rest were still faithful to God. They sent me a telegram the day they met, and I greatly rejoiced with them.

The work was not confined to our meetings. Many in their homes, and at their business, were arrested and began to seek God. One evening about eight o'clock a young man came running to my house, and said, 'Come away, sir, and see my brother and his wife; they have been on the floor all night crying for mercy.' I ran with him, and found them in great trouble. I pointed out to them the simple plan of salvation by faith in Jesus, urged them then and there to accept Christ, and then went to prayer. Their sorrow was soon turned to joy. One afternoon a man well known in the city, a coachbuilder, rushing into my yard without his hat, cried, 'Oh, Mr. Watsford, come and pray for me, a poor, guilty, wretched sinner.' Nor was the work confined to the city, but spread into the suburbs, where many were added to the Lord.

In this as in most revivals there were some whose goodness was as the morning cloud and the early dew: it passed away. But this, surely, cannot be, as some affirm, a strong objection against revivals. Many who are brought to God in a quiet way, without excitement, fall away also; so that the objection, if it has any force, can be used as well against this kind of conversion. Many, again, in affliction begin to weep and pray, and are greatly concerned about their souls' salvation; but when the crisis is past, and health is returning, they forget the vows made in trouble, and 'rise to sin anew'. We had a very painful case of this nature in Adelaide. The doctors had said that there was no hope, and the sick man, knowing he was altogether unprepared to die, was filled with fear. He begged his friends to send for me. With our city missionary I visited him. We were encouraged to hope that he was sincerely seeking the Lord. Day after day we visited him; and most glad was he to see us, and most heartily he seemed to join in our prayers. One day we were told that we could not see him. We asked the reason. Was he worse? Had the doctors forbidden us? No, but he was better: the doctor had said the danger was past, and he did not want us now. No doubt there are other cases like that; but everyone knows that many who have been brought under conviction in affliction, when death seemed to stare them in the face, have, when raised up again, lived holy, consecrated lives, and have had to say, 'It was good for me that I was afflicted.' So in revivals, while many backslide, many stand fast. I venture to say that if we went through our Church to day, we should find that the majority of our members were converted in revivals. 'What is the chaff to the wheat?' No doubt great care is necessary in times of revival to guard against mere excitement, – to watch, and firmly, yet very tenderly, suppress all mere wildfire; but at the same time members of the Church, however much they may desire what is quiet and orderly, must be careful lest, in speaking against and opposing revivals, in connection with which there is some excitement, they should be found 'fighting against God'.

3

Queensland and New South Wales

William G. Taylor

ON THE TABLELANDS OF QUEENSLAND

On Wednesday, October 26, [1870] we bade farewell to all our
dear ones. Oh, these partings! How they do tug at the heart-
strings! At 6.15 o'clock next morning, Thursday, October 27, the
good ship slipped away from Gravesend, and our voyage had
begun.

A lengthened diary of the voyage lies before me. It is full of
interesting detail. Seventy-six days out of sight of land; the horrors
of sea-sickness; becalmed under a blazing equatorial sun; among
the icebergs in southern latitudes; Father Neptune's official visit,
with all its attendant horrors; the vagaries of the ship's table,
without milk, vegetables, or fresh meat for two months and a half;
an ideal opportunity for the studying of poor fallen human nature;
religious services under difficulties; the making of lifelong friendships; original methods of sermon-making; the blessings of
monotony – all a blessed preparation time for a life's work.

January 18, 1871 – the day of our arrival in the beautiful harbour
of Port Jackson – will always stand forth as one of the red-letter
days of one's life. The brilliant sunshine overhead, the deep blue of
the waters beneath, and the charming scenery of the innumerable
headlands and inlets around us – it was glorious. As we dropped
anchor in Neutral Bay, a boat ladened with clerical-looking
gentlemen approached. They were leading divines of the city come
out to offer welcome to their two young brethren. Then again it
was my twenty-sixth birthday. And such a birthday present as I
found awaiting me – a big bundle of letters from the loved ones in
England! At the moment my foot first touched Australian soil at
the Royal Steps, Circular Quay, I found myself involuntarily

offering the prayer, 'Lord, use me in this land to lead many souls to Thee'.

We spent a busy month in Sydney, preaching in its various pulpits, addressing missionary meetings and the like, meanwhile being almost hospitalized to death by an over-generous people. At the end of the month Rodd and I separated after an intimate companionship of nearly three years, he going to the Braidwater Circuit, and I to board the paddle-steamer *Lady Young* for Brisbane, there to commence my ministry in the historic Albert Street Church.

I soon found that I was called to labour in congenial soil. Two of the happiest years of my ministry were those I spent in Brisbane with the Rev. Wm. Fletcher, BA, of Fijian fame, as my superintendent – the only 'super', by the way, that I have had. During those two years the debts on both the circuit and churches were wiped out, and the circuit placed upon a healthy financial basis.

Better still, we were permitted to witness a truly remarkable revival, that extended to every part of the circuit. It broke out in the ordinary course of our ministry. No outside missioner was invited, but every Sunday, and frequently at week-night meetings, the power of God came upon us in a remarkable manner. My first Queensland converts were given me at Albert Street within a few weeks of arrival. I had preached from our Lord's words, 'If any man serve me, let him follow me; and where I am, there shall also my servant be; if any man serve me, him will my Father honour'. The spell of God was on the people, and ere we separated five persons were led into the joy of conscious pardon. Side by side knelt two women, one a fallen woman from the street, the other the wife of a well-known merchant of the city. Although a Presbyterian, she had been led out of curiosity to come to hear the new 'chum' preacher.[1]

Gradually the work spread. At South Brisbane the communion-rail was filled with penitents at almost every Sunday-night service. The meetings were frequently marked by a truly pentecostal influence. There was no attempt to 'get up' a revival; it simply 'came down', and in such a fashion that people from far and near came 'to see Jesus'. Albert Street and then Fortitude Valley, the

[1]Her husband was also subsequently converted and became one of Queensland's representatives in the Commonwealth Parliament.

only other Methodist church in the city, soon caught the flame. It mattered little who was the preacher, 'the power of God was present to heal'. Necessity compelled our arranging for extended meetings, which went on week after week for nearly four months. We had no outside help, but the three ministers of the city, William Fletcher, Matthew Henry Parkinson, and myself, pegged away, and soon had the joy of seeing over four hundred who had professed faith in Jesus Christ. All my life I have lived in the midst of revival work, but never have I witnessed a more scriptural, more deep, more permanent work of God than this.

Probably the most remarkable instance of the power of the grace of God witnessed was that of an ex-convict, eighty-four years of age. When a mere lad, working in a Yorkshire factory, he married, and within a week of his marriage was cruelly transported for life on the charge of stealing 8s. 6d. and a silk handkerchief. He was sent out either to Botany Bay or to Port Arthur, where, exasperated by the iniquitous sentence, all the devil that was in him came to the surface. Again and again he sought to escape, and suffered the severest punishment in consequence. When it was decided to establish a penal settlement at Moreton Bay, Queensland, the worst men in the southern settlements were drafted north. This man was among them. He was entered as one of the most incorrigible men in the gang. Several times he again sought to escape; and during the long years of his convict life received 1731 lashes on his back for acts of insubordination. When an old man he received the Queen's conditional pardon. For over sixty years he had never heard a line from wife or friends. A lonely, broken old profligate, he one Sunday night, in the Albert Street Church, tottered up to the communion-rail, and took his place among the seekers. His conversion was as thorough as it was remarkable. Up to the day of his death he witnessed a good confession before all with whom he came in contact.

I have already spoken of the wealth of affection showered upon me in this my first circuit. I was as happy and jovial as a sandboy – living in my study in the mornings, in the saddle, at work amongst my people, in the afternoons, and almost every night conducting services in or around the city. In the midst of this blessed work, in order partly to help keep my own heart right with God, and also to aid the many young converts in their growth in grace, I published a pastoral letter, containing, in extended form, 'Morning's Resolves', and evening 'Heads of Self-examination'. A copy is before me. It smells of the Puritanism of Fuller or of Rutherford, together with the introspection of a David Stoner or a Bramwell. I wonder at the temerity that rendered such a production possible, and yet I have the feeling that it would not, in these times, hurt our good people were a little more of this kind of thing brought under their notice.

At the end of two years' service in the Albert Street Circuit, Brisbane, I was unexpectedly removed, to make room for a second married minister, rendered possible as the result of the gracious revival with which the circuit had been visited. The next six years were spent upon the famous Darling Downs, one of the richest and healthiest, and since become one of the most prosperous, districts in Australia. In my early days Methodism in all this territory was worked from two centres, Warwick and Toowoomba.

Warwick was established as a circuit in 1859, when Queensland was still a portion of the colony of New South Wales. The Rev. William Fidler was its first minister, there being but three Wesleyan ministers and a supernumerary in the whole of what is now the State of Queensland.[1] For a number of years progress was so slow that in 1873 – the year of my appointment – there were only 35 members and 320 persons as adherents of the church in the entire circuit. The now beautiful and thriving town of Warwick was then a sleepy little township of less than 2000 inhabitants. Methodism was in a bad way there: no Sunday school, only eighteen members of Society, and party feeling crushing out what life still remained. The average Sunday-evening congregation numbered thirty, whilst the old slab building in which they worshipped was of so nondescript a character as to lead a witty visiting minister to say of it that you might fall down and worship it without breaking any one of the Ten Commandments, for it was made after the likeness of nothing that was in heaven above, or the earth beneath, or the waters under the earth.

I can never adequately express my gratitude to God for the manner in which He Himself solved the depressing problems that I found awaiting me, by the immediate outpouring of His Holy Spirit. At the first Sunday-evening service a remarkable influence

[1] By 1870 the number had risen to 9 ministers, who were over-seeing 26 churches with 373 members and 1600 adherents. By 1915 the number of members (in 303 churches) was 10,434 and adherents 19,309.

settled down upon the congregation. Many were bathed in tears, and ere we separated eleven persons came forward as seekers of salvation, amongst these being the two circuit stewards – between whom for several years there had been a painful estrangement – and several other leading members of the church. This was a new thing in Warwick, and naturally caused much comment. At once the little slab church began to fill. Within a short period we were compelled to take our Sunday-night congregation to the town-hall, which in turn was soon filled to the doors. Meanwhile a truly remarkable work of God had broken out, the influence of which affected the whole district.

I have before me a list of the converts of that time of wonderful visitation. It contains the names of quite a number of the leading people of the district, many of whom have since put their impress upon the religious life of the community. After forty years that list greets me with the names of many who are still at the forefront of things political, commercial, and religious. I can furnish no finer answer than this to the quibbles of doubters as to the permanent character of the results of revival work. Out of that list of 127 names, quite a number are to-day Christian stalwarts, scattered all over Australia, but still true to the stand for God they took in that old slab church. They include the father and mother of the first missionary sent by our Church in Australia to the mission-field of India, one who was for years a member of the Queensland Upper House of Parliament, three brothers and a sister connected with leading Irish Methodist families, several who are to-day local preachers, and others who have achieved success in the commercial world.

The soul-saving work compelled us to face a building scheme. For years the little band of members had longed to be able to build, and had prepared plans for a small brick church to cost £600. This blessed work of God altered all that, and with a joyous heart the people set to work to erect a commodious church. All through my life I have demonstrated this fact: given a real live spiritual church, built upon evangelistic lines, and you need never worry about matters of £ s. d. The money will come when the right atmosphere has been created. Before this Warwick revival the officials were perplexed to find money with which to pay the stipend of a probationer. After the revival I was paid £10 per quarter over the minimum, the furniture for the parsonage was paid for, on my marriage I was presented with a beautiful cut-under buggy, and on leaving the circuit with a cheque for £60 – all this in addition to the building schemes of which I have written. Would that far and wide it could but be ingrained into the very soul of the Church that God's order is this: First, a spiritual church; secondly, an aggressive missionary spirit; thirdly, financial prosperity. A curious document lies before me, giving a summarized account of my work in the Warwick Circuit for three years. From this I venture to take the following: Sermons preached, 465; prayer- and class-meetings held, 428; sundry meetings, 188 – making an average of between seven and eight per week; distance travelled, 11,532 miles, an average of 76 per week; baptisms, 83; marriages, 26; funerals, 11.

★   ★   ★

At the Conference of 1876 we were appointed to Toowoomba. On our arrival we were welcomed by a congregation of lovely people – intelligent, well-to-do, and, alas, contented. For years they had worshipped in a brick church that seated just eighty people, placed right in the heart of a rapidly growing town, with already 6000 people in it. They had a sweet little organ, and a select little choir, and a beautiful little carved pulpit; and they were as happy and contented as could be, too contented by far.

But I was restless. You see, I was little more than a lad, and a lad full of enthusiasm that would persist in finding voice. For the life of me I could not rest content with those lovely family services when I knew that, could my people be persuaded to move, we might easily multiply our congregation four or fivefold. The Quarterly Meeting came round, and now, thought I, is my chance. Gradually plans were prepared and presented to that lilliputian gathering of really godly men, who smiled and wanted to pass on to the next business. But I was persistent, and pleaded all I knew how, but pleaded in vain. At last in desperation I cried, 'Anyway, meet me thus far. As an experiment let us take the School of Arts for just one Sunday'. To end the discussion they agreed to this compromise. The School of Arts was engaged, the finest hall in the town. On Sunday morning we had a congregation of 300, and at night the building was filled by at least 500 people. Our own people were amazed; and when it was seen that the collections had more than doubled, even the circuit stewards were converted. *We never went back to the little church*, but here for eighteen months forgathered for worship; and in that hall many signs and wonders were wrought.

Ere long the question of a new church was motioned, but with little hope of success, until, as in the case of Warwick, the Lord took the matter into His own hands, and by a gracious and wonderful visitation of the Holy Spirit a blessed revival swept the town; and as the immediate result of that revival our present lordly church was built. In every sense that was a remarkable spiritual movement. It represented Toowoomba's first baptism of fire. Spontaneous in its outbreak; natural, though rapid, in its development, its results were abiding. On my study-table there lies before me a list of 135 persons who, within a few short days, were brought to God. I read that list to-day with a strange thrill of gladness. It contains the names of leading men and women of the town, who later on became buttresses of the church. Every section of the Church was enriched. Our own membership was increased almost threefold, and at once Methodism took its stand as one of the leading forces of the Darling Downs.

The work began, where all genuine revivals should begin, within the church itself. At Pentecost the Holy Spirit came upon the infant Church, and then followed the gathering in, under one sermon, of 3000 converts. It has ever been thus. Would that, at this writing, I could reach the ear of every minister and every church member in Australia, and elsewhere! It would be with an earnest cry for the Church itself to awake and put on its strength. It would pay us a magnificent dividend to cease for one twelve months all our aggressive evangelistic agencies, and to give ourselves to the one task of bringing back the Church itself on to Apostolic lines. No wonder that failure has so often to be written across our evangelistic efforts! With the Church itself formal and self-contained, we lack the foundation elements of successful evangelism. In Toowoomba the work began silently, slowly, amongst our own people. No special missioner was invited; no unusual efforts were put forth to awaken public interest. The work grew from within, and a fire was gradually kindled that went on burning in connexion with the ordinary ministries of the church.

I always think with gratitude of one case that at the time gave me special joy. It was that of a humble servant-maid, named Rhoda

[302]

Bidgood, who at one of the services was deeply convinced of sin. With streaming face she cried to God for salvation, but no light came. 'Go home,' I said to her, 'and upon your knees to-night read the third chapter of John.' In the middle of the night that girl wrestled in prayer; at last, whilst, by her bedside, reading that *vade mecum* of the soul, the light of God flashed into her heart. A hundred times since, on platform and in pulpit, I have spoken of that girl. Without the slightest approach to ostentation she set to work to lead her friends to Christ. Her home was at a rough and primitive settlement among the mountains, thirty miles away. At once she went to her people to tell them what great things the Lord had done for her. Within a week she had won her mother for Christ. Soon a work broke out amongst her farmer neighbours. One of the leading men of the district told me the following story: 'One day Rhoda came to my house to tell me how anxious she was that the children of the settlement should be gathered into a Sunday school. With strange tenderness she pleaded with me to become its superintendent. I refused, as well I might, for I was not a Christian. But Rhoda had not long left my house ere I found myself kneeling behind a log in one of my paddocks, crying to God for mercy. Soon, thank God, I found the pearl of great price.' That school was at once started, its newly converted superintendent became a local preacher, and within six months nearly one half the residents of that settlement had made profession of Christ, and this in a place that I had regularly visited, where I had conducted many services, but never seen the slightest movement amongst the people. Truly 'a little child shall lead them'.

Not long was I permitted to enjoy the fruits of our labours here, as within a few months my three years were at an end, and the Methodist policeman – our august Conference – ordered us to 'move on'. The pains and penalties of the itinerant system galled our flesh deeply. We loved our work, souls were being saved, financially the circuit was prosperous, and we were surrounded by friends connected with every Church. But, from the Methodist standpoint, our work was done; and so with a big effort we girded the loins of our mind, and tore ourselves away from a sphere of labour which my wife and I still look upon as one of the happiest of our life.

ON THE MANNING RIVER, NEW SOUTH WALES

My wife, three little children, and I left Toowoomba on April 2, 1879, reaching Taree – our new home – exactly three weeks afterwards. Our luggage was subjected to seven separate handlings, whilst we, poor things, were tossed about from pillar to post: a hundred miles by train, delay in Brisbane, waiting for our steamer, then several days of misery as the old *Elemang* tore her way through 500 miles of furious storm, the worst the captain had ever experienced on this coast. At times we were in danger of foundering. Owing to the continued roughness of the sea we were detained in Sydney for over a week, and ultimately started on our last lap on board a wretched little cockle-boat named the *Diamentina*. What we suffered must not be told here. But after three weeks of buffeting we reached our new circuit.

'Rain, rain, rain,' so says my journal, 'for the first month. There are fourteen places in this circuit, covering an area as broad and wide as an English county. I have no colleague, not even a circuit missionary, and but half-a-dozen local preachers. The circuit spiritually in a very sad way; can see an enormous amount of work ahead among the 6000 people living on this river. The whole district teems with young men and women. Oh for a copious outpouring of the Holy Spirit! We have had a special circuit-meeting from which arrangements have matured for a spiritual advance movement. I am trying to live for a revival.'

Everything in those days was primitive. The farmers were heroically facing their early struggles. Many of the homes were of the humblest; the parsonage itself was a ramshackle place, damp to the point of danger. We were 120 miles away from the nearest doctor. Once, when our eldest boy, only six years of age, was threatened with a serious illness, I had to take him in an open buggy all that weary journey to Maitland, occupying six days going and returning. There was one place I visited about once a month, to reach which meant over twenty miles of saddle work through thick forest, followed by eighteen miles of hard pulling in a rowing-boat.

In one part of my circuit I had a very heavy cross to carry. Many of the settlers had been farm-labourers in the old country. One such told me how in Berkshire he had brought up a family of fourteen, and had never received more than from eight to ten shillings per week. 'Such was our poverty,' said he, 'that we were only able to buy half an ounce of tea once a fortnight as a great luxury.' Many such had emigrated to Australia, and quite a number had settled in this district. My trouble with not a few of them was to get them to realize their responsibility to support the ordinances of religion. Though their circumstances had vastly improved, their giving continued that of their earlier days. Stingy Christians! Yes, I have met with many of them, there and elsewhere; and they have always been to me as the irritating presence of a thorn in one's side. In one place the nine collections for a quarter amounted to 14s. 6d. The congregations numbered 150, and there were forty members of the church. Thank God, a spiritual revival altered all that, and soon £20 averaged their contributions to the Quarterly Meeting. I was preaching one hot Sunday afternoon in another place to a congregation of eighty, mostly fairly well-to-do farmers and their families. The collection amounted to eighteen pence.

Within three months of our arrival in the circuit everything pointed to the speedy coming of a time of spiritual quickening. Much prayer was made to God by the faithful few, and soon we welcomed the droppings of a shower. Arrangements were carefully matured for 'a protracted meeting', and for nearly a fortnight meetings for prayer and others for preaching were held. My journal will give details of this, the most remarkable work of God that had ever been witnessed in that river district:

'*Sunday, May 25, 1879.* – After making prudential preparations we this day commence a series of special services. Our hope is in the God of Israel. For want of room in the church I preached at night in the Protestant Hall, the largest building in the district. The place was crowded, and there were two decisions. The spirit of expectancy is abroad . . . *Monday.* – Church full. Text, Luke 9:61. Nine persons came forward as seekers. *Tuesday.* – Mothers' Meeting at three. Hard conflict at night meeting. Church crowded. A glorious victory. Five persons went home rejoicing in their Saviour. *Wednesday.* – Children's service at three. At night preached on 'Saving Faith'. Seven persons professed faith in Christ as their Saviour. *Thursday.* – A glorious meeting! Never nearer heaven. Church crammed with people; and, better still, filled with the glory of God. Text, 2 Cor. 6:2. Thirty-two persons rose asking for the prayers of the congregation. Nearly all found the blessing of forgiveness. The interest deepens as we advance. The entire town is moved. *Friday.* – Another victory. Preached from Rev. 3:20. Seven souls slain and brought into the new life, amongst them an old man of seventy and an ex-local preacher. *Sunday.* – Three services. At night the most remarkable meeting ever held in the town; the large hall packed, and many standing outside. Six found peace. *Monday.* – One seeker. Church full. Had unusual liberty speaking from Luke 15:10. But it is easy to preach when one is surrounded by men of faith. *Tuesday.* – To-night I sang the gospel to the packed congregation. A time never to be forgotten. At times our voices could scarcely be heard; suppressed sobs, and cries of 'Glory!' were heard all around. Five persons came forward seeking Christ. *Thursday.* – Fellowship meeting. Between thirty and forty new converts spoke, sweetly and pointedly. Gave an address of encouragement to the eighty or ninety who during these meetings had professed conversion, and then six others came forward literally yearning for liberty. The poor body suffers, but, oh, I am happy! Tell me, is there any luxury in this world equal to that of pointing sinners to Christ?'

Thus commenced a genuine work that soon spread to other parts of the circuit, and ere long we were able to record the names of 180 persons who during this gracious visitation had yielded themselves to God. I was kept hard at work almost night and day. With no help from outside, my strength began to give out. My journal begins to tell of weariness and much pain, of difficulty in reaching home from distant appointments, &c.; but I simply had to keep going and at high pressure, the result being that the whole circuit was soon raised to a higher level, the membership more than doubled, finances lifted out of the bog, new congregations started, and three new churches erected. I confess that after all these years I read with devout gratitude the record of advance lying before me, knowing as I do what the circuit was and what it became, *absolutely as the result of the outpouring of the Holy Spirit.*

Before saying farewell to the Manning River I venture to emphasize the remark previously made that more than ever I believe to-day that the Church's short cut to financial strength and to general material prosperity is to be found along the line of spiritual power and blessing. To run a church successfully that is spiritually dead is like making bricks without straw; but given a church throbbing with spiritual life, and you may dare great things for God. The beautiful church standing to-day on probably the finest site in Taree furnishes another illustration of the truth of this. But for the remarkable revival throughout that circuit such a church building would have been an impossibility. . . . I tremble as I feel impelled thus to place upon paper the ever-deepening convictions that God's design in calling me into this ministry was that my life-story should point, with constantly added emphasis, to that central teaching of the Sermon on the Mount, '*Seek ye first the kingdom of God and His righteousness, and all these things shall be added unto you.*' And, as the perusal of these pages will testify, in each sphere of service God has been pleased to direct my imperfect efforts to point to this much-neglected scriptural fact, that the one way to secure material success in the Church of God is to put the spiritual where it always ought to be, right out in the front of everything. I am humbled this day as I am led to see how along this line the gracious Spirit has been pleased to direct me, one of the least worthy of His children. In Brisbane and Warwick, in Toowoomba and on the Manning River, in each case it has been the same – a gracious spiritual revival, manifestly, in every case, the work of the Spirit of God, preparing the way for permanent material advancement such as could never have been but for this wonderful leading of the Holy Ghost. When will our beloved Methodism, when will the Church of God generally, awake to this paramount fact? We are too often found making a serious mistake – creating machinery vast and varied, but not obtaining the necessary power with which to run it; putting more energy into the erection of elaborate ecclesiastical scaffolding than we are into the infinitely more important work of building the spiritual temple. This, as it seems to me, is the crying weakness of all our church systems to-day.

17

DAYS OF REVIVAL IN VICTORIA

Approach to Geelong, from the Bay, 1856

The Testimony of
Alexander R. Edgar

Alexander Robert Edgar, born in Tipperary, Ireland, in 1850, came to Victoria at the age of four and grew up at St. Arnaud, 160 miles north of Melbourne. There he attended the Anglican church with his parents but in the late 1860's under the preaching of a Methodist minister 'a gracious revival of religion' occurred in the neighbourhood, 'numbers of people, old and young, being converted to God'.[1] Alexander Edgar was awakened and arrested by this preaching. His conversion he relates as follows: 'The Lord called me and I answered, and sought, and found His salvation, in the month of June, 1869. Since that time my feet have run in the way of His commandments, His service being perfect freedom, and His will my delight. Almost immediately after my conversion the decision, which with a greater or less measure of force had been in my mind during many years, came to me with great energy. I felt that I was called to preach the Gospel, and for the first time this feeling was accompanied with one of great unworthiness, leading me to shrink back from the very thought. I determined to do what I could for the glory of my blessed Lord, but I dared not presume for a moment that I should ever preach the Word of Life'.

Edgar left home in 1870, with thirty shillings in his pocket, to find work at Stawell about 40 miles away. On this journey he spent a night in the open air, sleeping beside a large log, and it was while he was in prayer at this spot that he received a larger and glorious assurance of his salvation. It was from this time, according to his biographer, that 'he saw that there was a deeper and fuller experience of God to be enjoyed'. Settled at Stawell he became

[1]For all material quoted in this section I am dependent on *A. R. Edgar: A Methodist Greatheart*, W. J. Palamountain, 1933.

fully identified with the Methodists: 'I joined the Church immediately after going to Stawell, meeting in Mr. Sussex's class, a man of the right stamp. I shall never forget the blessed seasons I enjoyed in that class. It was composed for the most part of Christians who had been walking in the way of holiness for a great many years. I delighted to hear them give expression to their confidence in the power and grace of God which had kept them and guided them for so long.

'Several of the brethren were local preachers of great worth; in fact, two of them were the best lay preachers I have ever heard. They were men of great ability, natural and acquired, and, above all, men of sterling quality. I felt my littleness in such company, and fairly trembled when called upon to relate my experience before them. By some means or other I gained their esteem (as I afterwards learned), and very often have I been encouraged to persevere by a kind look, a cheerful word, or a pat on the shoulder.

'I became a teacher in the Sabbath School – a work in which my soul found delight, and I laboured hard to make the lessons interesting to the boys. I think I succeeded pretty well. I also laboured diligently to cultivate my mind, and, as it was inconvenient for me to study at night, I used to get up about 3.30 a.m. – never much later than 4 a.m. – for the purpose of studying. This I did for several months, but, owing to the long hours (ten per day) and hard work in the mine, I was compelled, though reluctantly, to relinquish my long morning's exercise. I felt that my mind was expanding, and my soul prospering, and I delighted in prayer.

'In the month of July of this year I was called out to preach the Gospel. My first sermon was preached at a little place named Concongella Creek, on Sunday afternoon, 18th July. Brother Makepeace, a worthy man, and a local preacher in the circuit, undertook to lead me and take me in hand. I managed to pull through, though I was exceedingly nervous. On the way home Brother Makepeace remarked that some day I would be called upon to devote myself wholly to the work of preaching the Gospel, a prediction since fulfilled, but which at the time spoken seemed a downright impossibility.'

The conviction that Edgar was called to preach was soon shared by many members of the circuit and at their urging he offered himself for the work to the Methodist Conference in January 1872. This led to his going to the Provisional Theological Institute at

Wesley College, Melbourne. Included in Edgar's account of his subsequent student days are these words:

'I entered on my student career in April, 1872, at the age of 22. There were ten theological students during my first year. We got on well together, and all felt the importance of making the very best use of our time and privileges. I look back on this period of my life with great pleasure. The Rev. J. S. Waugh, DD, the theological tutor, was all that we could wish – kind, considerate and good. He seemed to be intensely anxious for our welfare and improvement. I shall never forget the earnestness which he displayed many a time while speaking to us of the greatness of the work to which we were called. He would have us throw ourselves wholly into it, and labour faithfully in dependence on the aid of the Holy Ghost.

'I achieved a great victory over my temper while in college. I had given way for some years to great depression of mind, rendering me miserable in myself and very miserable and unpleasant to others. I sought the help of God's Spirit, and by watchfulness combined with prayer I overcame, and God's grace has been sufficient for me ever since. I profited very much mentally and spiritually by intercourse with the other students in our class meetings, and in our prayer meetings. We often held conversations with each other about our souls' concerns, seeking thereby to help each other and to stimulate each other to energy and prayer.

'I well remember one evening, while together in the "reception room" engaging in prayer. We were visited with the power of the Spirit, and it was in the highest sense of the term "good to be there". We continued praying for a long time, and when we rose to leave we felt as though we could not, and fell to prayer again. This was repeated twice or thrice'.

Edgar commenced his ministry at Kangaroo Flat, near Bendigo, Victoria, in 1874. At this time he also began to keep a diary and his entries give a clear idea of the spirit in which he laboured:

27th July, 1875 – Throughout this day I have been very much drawn out in prayer for the baptism of the Holy Ghost.[1] I am thirsting for all

[1]This language was once common among evangelicals with reference to the anointing of the Holy Spirit in larger measure and it should not be confused with later Pentecostal teaching. See, for example, the Presbyterian author, George Smeaton, *The Doctrine of the Holy Spirit* (1882), Banner of Truth Trust reprint, 1958, p. 47.

the fullness of God. I have made an entire consecration of all I have, and am, to God. I have taken Jesus as my all, and in all, and I wait His guiding hand. I desire to do nothing without His direction. My heart cries out: 'Now, O my God, fulfil my heart's desire, and come in Thy great glory'.

I visited a poor woman in the hospital this morning, and was enabled to speak words of comfort. The whole of the afternoon has been spent in visiting from house to house. My soul was blessed while preaching Jesus to the people. This evening I met nine persons in class, and we all felt the presence and fullness of God. I believe in the communion of saints, and I love it.

10th August. – Since making the last entry I have had a run up to St. Arnaud to see my dear family. Found but little alteration, but my parents are beginning to show signs of old age. The younger members of the family are shooting up, and if I am spared a few more years will find them grown into men and women. My father and sister, Eliza, are walking in the fear of God, and have felt the renewing power of God's Spirit. I preached in the old place last Sunday week (1st inst.). There were many old faces to be seen of men and women who a few years ago I knew as boys and girls.

My heart was filled with gratitude to God for all He had done for me, for the way He had led me. I had a good time in preaching, both morning and evening, from Matt. 15:22, and John 12:21. I preached again on Thursday evening to a good audience from Job 1:22. Left home on Saturday morning and reached my circuit at 11 p.m. I felt weary next day, and had a poor time in consequence.

11th August. – Visited during the afternoon. My thoughts have been towards God for a revival of His work. Oh, when shall the time be when this place will feel the glory and power of God. I am waiting for the power of the Holy Ghost. 'Oh, that it now from heaven might fall!'

29th November. – I am still pressing onward. The fear of God is before my eyes, and I am longing for all His fullness. Since my last entry I have not seen that fruit to my labours I have so greatly desired. I have been blessed in my soul, and I have reason to believe that good has been done. My people stand by me, pray for me, and hold up my hands, but O, my God, where is the power, the influence of the Holy Ghost, that awakening which leads sinners to cry aloud for mercy? I had a profitable time in preaching yesterday. I pray God to bless it to the hearts of His people.

8th December. – In the evening I preached to a large congregation, a great many strangers being present. I felt the Spirit of the Lord was upon me. The congregation at times was visibly affected. I earnestly pray that the results of last Sunday's exertions may shortly manifest themselves.

[314]

These hopes were not disappointed. W. J. Palamountain says that both Kangaroo Flat, and the adjoining circuit of Forest Street, were 'visited by a very gracious outpouring of the Holy Spirit' with some 250 persons added to the membership of the church in two months. Edgar recorded his 'thankfulness to God for such a wonderful manifestation of His power'.

Edgar's next circuit was at Inglewood where he saw fruitfulness under the preaching – 'here and there our hearts are cheered by the presence and power of the Holy Spirit' – but no extensive work. He knew the blessing was sovereignly given. On moving on again, first to Bendigo and then to Ballarat, there were further times of more general awakening. In the latter place, especially, he was supported by godly Cornish immigrants. Speaking of the outlook which prevailed among these people Edgar's biographer, who represented the view of a later period, writes:

'It was the fashion in those days to look for revivals of religion – times when conversions should take place in great numbers. Perhaps they erred somewhat in not expecting these conversions to take place as the normal result of the preaching of the Gospel.[1] But whether that be so or not, they did expect unusual and even extraordinary manifestations of the saving power of God.

'Such revivals have occurred at times without any special preparation being made for them by the church. They have come as a great rain upon the thirsty land, at the breaking up of the spiritual drought'.

At one Quarterly Meeting it was reported that 'The circuit had been favoured by a work of grace and that two hundred and twenty-five persons had professed conversion'. At another Quarterly meeting thanksgiving was offered to God for the revival, and it was reported that two hundred and ten persons had been received on trial for church membership. Mid-week preaching services multiplied and such was the spiritual hunger that we read: 'It would be impossible to describe the interest taken in these meetings. They were held for the most part in the winter, but neither cold nor rain nor bad roads could keep people away. In the mining places they would thread their way along tracks that wound in and out among the diggers' holes, carrying lanterns to guide them, and they came night after night, drawn by a great

---

[1]We have seen no evidence to justify this opinion.

spiritual magnetism that nothing could resist. It was a gracious visitation from on High'.

During this same period, on December 12, 1882, a mining disaster occurred at Creswick, about twelve miles from Ballarat. Twenty-two men died. Others who survived spoke of the sense of God's presence and help. Entombed men had sung hymns and prayed together as they waited for help in the darkness. Others had scratched messages on billy cans. One such message was the line of a hymn, intended to comfort relatives, 'There's a land that is fairer than day'. Edgar preached at the mine itself as multitudes waited in suspense for news, and again to some four thousand people in the Alfred Hall in Ballarat on the following Sunday afternoon when his text was, 'For here we have no continuing city'.

From Ballarat Edgar went to Port Melbourne (1884–1887) but it is not until he went to Geelong West in 1887 that his biography again speaks of revival. This was connected with special evangelistic services but it is apparent that no one thought that such services could induce revival: 'There was an understanding among the circuit leaders that whenever there were evidences that the Holy Spirit was working, the ministers should follow up the work and arrange for special evangelistic services . . . It was always a settled conviction of A. R. Edgar's to follow and not to precede the operations of the Holy Spirit; not to decide upon a particular time to conduct a mission, but to pray and work and look for "the set time to favour Zion", and then to spend himself, so as to secure the success which under the blessing of God inevitably followed'.

Speaking of the effects of revival in Geelong, Edgar's biographer records:

'Drunkards were reclaimed, unhappy hearts and homes were changed, prodigals returned to the father's home. Sleeping Christians were awakened, careless and indifferent sinners were aroused and convicted of their sin. Numbers who were outside the fellowship of the Church were brought into it, and inactive members became "zealous of good works".

'The result of all this gracious ingathering was that the churches became crowded with worshippers, and all manner of beneficent activities were carried on by people whose hearts were warmed with love for God and man.

'There was a great revival, too, in Christian fellowship. "Classes", as they are called in Methodism, were renewed or formed. In these circles of believing men and women, which met weekly for fellowship, there was the glow of religious experience that each shared with the other, while members were instructed and edified by the leader. They became centres of power and usefulness'.

In 1893 Edgar's work both at Geelong and as an ordinary circuit preacher was concluded as he was appointed to the work of founding the Central Mission at Wesley Church, Melbourne. Palamountain considered this a fitting point in Edgar's biography to make 'some special reference to the subject of revivals'. He was writing in 1933 when such periods were no longer known in the churches and he obviously felt that some explanation of that fact was required. He writes:

'A. R. Edgar's record of soul-saving work reads like a romance, and we are naturally led to ask why, at this particular period, there should have been so much of this kind of work done, and why there should not be a continuance of it. We have been recording revivals with which he was more immediately connected, but he was not alone in successful evangelistic effort; there were many others who, if successful in a lesser degree, were nevertheless true evangelists.

'Some of these revivals broke out in connection with the ordinary church worship. In August, 1875, the Rev. E. I. Watkin preached in the Brown Hill Church in the Ballarat East Circuit from the text, "And they told him that Jesus of Nazareth passeth by". A work of God commenced that night that continued for weeks, when it spread to other places, and hundreds were converted to God. In Geelong, during the ministry of the Rev. J. D. Dodgson, a mighty revival also took place. . . .

'It was a type of evangelism that seemed to run its course and cease to be.

'There was another factor that helped very largely, and this was the hunger for the souls of men that was felt by many Christian people. There was what was called "a yearning for souls", a great desire that others should share in the rich spiritual experience.

'There was also the sense of great responsibility for others which was called "the burden of souls". Souls were in peril, souls might be lost, and men longed, as A. R. Edgar wrote in his last letter to Wesley Church congregation –

> With groans, entreaties, tears to save,
> And snatch them from a gaping grave.

[317]

'One thinks also of the spirit of expectancy that was abroad, when preachers expected results, and were disappointed at the close of their labours on the Lord's day if there were none. They prayed for results, they preached for results, and they expected results. The kind of texts that were chosen and the type of sermons that were preached were for results. They were sermons that had appeal in them, followed by the after-meeting, when "seekers" were encouraged to put their trust in Christ alone.

'All these things have to be considered in any attempt to account for a revival movement that gathered such force and then subsided'.

While these comments are good they only describe symptoms of the difference between the 1880's and the 1930's and do not touch upon the cause. The cause was a withdrawal of the power of the Holy Spirit from the churches as a result of a growing unbelief in the Word of God and a consequent lowering of standards of church membership. The church was less spiritual and thus the experimental nature of vital Christianity, as formerly exemplified by the Methodist emphasis upon class and prayer-meetings, largely passed away. Prayer that 'a Pentecostal baptism of the Spirit may be granted to our churches'[1] was no longer heard and preaching became increasingly indefinite. Giving warning of this in 1901, when he was president of the Methodist Conference, Edgar said:

'Jesus did not speak as the scribes, but as one having authority. These scribes boasted of their antiquity as a class, and based their authority on that ground, and there are in many places men who strive to base their authority on ecclesiastical antiquity . . . To you, my young brethren, men will come who will deny the validity of your orders, but by the power of the Holy Spirit you will so preach Christ that the people will receive it with gladness of heart . . .

'One of the most striking features of the present day – so the press is reiterating – is the drifting away from dogmatic preaching. It is argued that if you preach dogmatic theology the people will turn from you. I assure you that I do not believe this, for I am convinced that the heart of humanity wants something definite. We must not misunderstand the boldness and directness of that firm declaration of Christ, "He that believeth on the Son hath

[1] The words formed part of a resolution passed when Edgar was president of the Methodist Conference in 1901.

everlasting life; and he that believeth not the Son shall not see life; but the wrath of God abideth on him" (John 3:36)'.

After twenty-one years of faithful work at Wesley Church and Mission, Melbourne, Edgar's health gave way in 1912 and he died two years later. His biographer's description of his preaching says much on the kind of man that he was:

'The great truths of the Gospel were eternal facts, and this he endeavoured to make people believe. They were not fictions, but certainties.

'His theology was definite; it even included the doctrine of hell; and his theology influenced his preaching. He does not seem to have been moved by the currents of thought in his time. If there was a wooing note in his preaching there was also the note of warning. The doom of sin was a dreadful one, and there was no hope held out for the finally impenitent sinner beyond. If the consequences of sin were terrible the work of Jesus Christ was sufficient to counteract all those consequences, and to save to the uttermost. He was a persuasive preacher. He "besought men and women to be reconciled to God". "Knowing the terror of the Lord, he persuaded men". It was much the same with Mr. Edgar. No one who ever heard him say, "Oh, my dear friends", could ever forget the yearning persuasiveness of his tones. Who will ever forget the earnestness amounting almost to agony that was depicted on his face as he pleaded with men and women to come to Jesus! Yet he did not win his victories without blood. His sermons were thoughtful and his preparation had to be thorough, as he could not make use of notes in the pulpit owing to defective sight. Behind everything else there was the Divine unction. He preached the Gospel "with the Holy Ghost sent down from heaven". He was in every sense a great preacher, and he was a man of God.'

18

HOW CHRISTIANS DIE

A Wreck

Many temporal difficulties attended the Australian colonists of the last century. Infant mortality and the death of mothers after childbirth were not uncommon, nor was loss of life at sea. In the life of Daniel James Draper, whose name has been often quoted in these pages as an eminent Methodist minister, these afflictions were all combined. After less than two years in Australia, when serving the Parramatta circuit, he lost his wife and their second child in January 1838.

Draper, with his second wife, made a first visit home to England in 1865. In 1866 they were lost with over 240 others when the steamship in which they were returning to Australia foundered in the Bay of Biscay. Wesleyan churches throughout Australia mourned their loss, and 3000 attended a memorial service in Wesley Church, Melbourne, when the Rev. J. Eggleston preached from Psalm 39:9, 'I was dumb; I opened not my mouth'.

The Christian name of the first Mrs. Draper does not appear to be recorded in the *Life of D. J. Draper* by his friend, John C. Symons, from which source these extracts are taken.

I

Mrs. Draper's Death at Parramatta

'*January 3rd*, [*1838*]. My dear wife still very ill. Prevented visiting Liverpool as usual, by the rain, and Mrs. Draper's illness.'

The illness by which Mrs. Draper was attacked proved fatal. For a month she fluctuated between hope and fear. February 3rd she was prematurely delivered of a son. Then some hope of recovery appeared, but only to be speedily disappointed. It was a period of great anxiety and trial to her husband. His journal shows how firm his faith and how great his consolations. One day he writes, 'I trust the Lord will enable me, under the affliction which He has been pleased to lay upon my dear wife, to submit myself unto Him who doeth all things well.' At another time: 'What a mercy that the Lord is the source of all temporal and spiritual good; and while He sees fit to afflict, affords grace to support the mind under the trial, and fulfils the promise, "As thy day so shall thy strength be". Thank God, I feel the consolation of the gospel under the severe trial which the Lord has permitted to visit me, and am enabled to resign myself, my all, into His hands.'

On February 10th the infant, who had been baptized Josiah, 'fell asleep'. He was buried on the 11th, 'in the vault which contains the dust of Mr. Leigh and a child of the Rev. N. Turner's; thence shall they rise together on the resurrection morn, blooming with immortality.'

Mrs. Draper was sinking rapidly. Medical skill was exercised in vain; on the 15th it was evident that her case was hopeless. Crushed and almost heart-broken, Mr. Draper writes:– 'What a mercy, that under her heavy affliction she possesses peace with God, peace with her own conscience, and a bright hope of a glorious immortality. Her faith is strong, her mind serene, and her prospects for eternity bright and blooming. Her strength is sinking fast, and soon, in all human probability, I shall be left in the world to mourn without that hand which has, since it became mine, never ceased to minister to my comfort, – that heart, the pulse of which beats only for God and me. How desolate the prospect. Blessed be God He does mercifully support my mind; and the happiness experienced by my dear wife in the prospect of eternity, tends very much to allay my grief and keep me from sinking.'

The record in his journal of the 16th is so touching, and describes a death-bed of so much peace and joy, that I offer no apology for its length:–

'*Feb. 16th*. This morning, at six o'clock, I was summoned into the chamber of my dear wife. The hand of death was evidently upon her. On my entrance, she threw her arms – cold and emaciated – round my neck, and expressed the conviction that in a few hours she should be in eternity. I spoke to her respecting her spiritual state and prospects; on which she declared her state to be one of settled peace. "Christ," said she, "is precious – I feel Him to be so. I am a sinner, but blessed be God, I know the blood of Jesus Christ cleanseth from all sin, and it hath cleansed me." She continued, "God hath dwelt very graciously with me in my affliction, and I know He will not leave me in the trying hour." She then spoke of the dear boy, and solemnly gave him up to me, saying, "The Lord will provide"; and requested me never to allow him to be from under my own care whilst practicable. As the morning advanced her strength continued to decline, but her confidence in her Redeemer became stronger. She frequently declared that "Jesus was precious". About noon she expressed a wish to see the dear child, on which he was immediately sent for. The conflict was evidently severe; but the *Christian* rose superior to the *mother*. Kissing him several times, she begged a blessing on him at the hands of God, and gave him up to me. Never shall I forget that scene whilst memory holds its seat. May the Angel of the Covenant bless the dear child, and lead him through the vale of tears to that heaven which his sainted mother has now gained! Shortly after this she informed me that she had been enabled to give up every earthly object, and asked me if I was able to resign her up to God. On my informing her (after she had inquired thrice as above) that through the mercy of God I felt resigned to His will, and was enabled to give her up to Him, she said, "That is all," and from that moment I believe lost sight entirely of earthly things. Her mind continued stayed on God and in perfect peace during the afternoon. She observed on one occasion, "I have not that rapturous joy which some have possessed in their last moments, but I have peace – solid peace. Jesus is indeed precious." On my repeating those lines:–

> Jesus can make a dying bed
> More soft than downy pillows are;

she said, "Yes; I feel He does so. He graciously supports me. I shall soon be

> With God eternally shut in."

On my asking her if she regretted leaving her dear mother and sisters and brothers at home, and coming to this colony with me, she answered, "*No*; I only regret I have not been more faithful and more useful. Oh," said she, "if I had strength I would exhort all persons to seek religion, I *feel* its value." On my inquiring if she wished to communicate any thing in particular to her dear relatives at home, she said, "Tell them especially I present them my dying love, and urge them to meet me before the throne of God." As the evening advanced she became very restless, and frequently wandered in her mind; but during lucid intervals she constantly expressed her state as being one of perfect peace. At nine o'clock her change appeared to be rapidly approaching; she ceased to speak coherently, but did not appear to suffer much pain; and at twenty minutes before ten o'clock she entered into the joy of her Lord.'

2

Daniel Draper's Last Prayer Meeting

On January 5th [1866] our friends embarked at Plymouth, and about midnight the *London* set sail. There was at this time nothing to indicate the severe weather which so soon came on; the barometer was unsteady, but not low. It was almost calm when the ship started; and on Saturday the weather was comparatively quiet, and the ship steamed along against a head sea. On Sunday, 7th, the wind freshened somewhat; but it did not prevent Divine service from bing conducted in the saloon. Sunday night it blew a strong gale, with heavy squalls and a high sea; still there was nothing to cause apprehension. Monday, 8th, the sea was so heavy that the engines were stopped, and the ship was put under easy canvas. About mid-day the wind lessened, and steam was again used. Tuesday morning, the 19th, the wind had greatly increased, and, together with the tremendous sea, carried away the flying jib-boom, fore-topmast, topgallant mast, and royal mast. So violent had the gale become that all the wreck could not be cleared, and the spars swung to and fro, doing much damage. Up to this time there was no cause for alarm. The ship was new, tight, and strong, and the loss of a few spars was a matter of very small importance. But on Tuesday afternoon the wind increased to a hurricane, with fearful cross seas, which often broke over the ship, and carried away the port life-boat, besides doing other serious damage. At 3 p.m. of the 10th, the ship was put about, under full steam for Plymouth. She immediately began to ship 'green seas over all', as the nautical phrase is, which swept her decks, carried away the starboard life-boat, and destroyed one of the cutters.

At half-past ten o'clock on Wednesday night, a 'big sea', as described by some, or a 'mountain of water', by others, broke on board, swept away the main engine-room skylight, filled the engine-room, and in *three minutes* extinguished the engine fires. The sea which destroyed the skylight washed two men (a sailor and a passenger) into the engine-room. Efforts were instantly made to repair the broken hatchway; but this was futile. Sails, mattresses, tarpaulings, spars, all available means, were used to stop the opening in the deck, and prevent the water from rushing into the ship; but all without avail. Nor could they succeed in lessening the water, although men were baling with buckets; the pumps and 'donkey engine' were at work even when the ship went down. But all was in vain; for the terrific cross seas of the awful Bay of Biscay dashed over the doomed vessel, which, from the stoppage of the engines had become unmanageable, and was as a mere log at the mercy of the waves. Faster than man could repair, his work was undone by the force of the gigantic waves which deluged her decks. Could the hatchway have been secured there was still hope; so long as it remained a gaping rent all was hopeless. Long and gallantly was the struggle continued between man and the furious elements; and at last, when the issue was no longer doubtful, Captain Martin said to his men, 'Boys, you may say your prayers.' All earthly hope was gone, and unless winds and waves were hushed and stilled by the power or word of their Creator, it was a mere question of time as to when the *London* should go down.

But the gale increased in fury; wind and waves combined to wreak their vengeance upon the helpless bark. As darkness closed in on that Wednesday night, all on board regarded it as the prelude to the deeper darkness of the wild waves under which, in a few hours, they should be engulfed.

At midnight Mr. Draper commenced that memorable prayer-meeting which lasted till the ship sank on the next day at two o'clock. With one impulse the passengers and crew (all of the latter not on duty) gathered in the saloon. Distinction of class was forgotten. Who shall depict the scene then presented! One of the rescued tells that there were no cries or shrieking of men or women, no frantic behaviour. Mothers were weeping bitterly over their little ones, and the children strangely and pitifully inquiring the cause of such tears. Friends were taking leave of their friends, as on the eve of some long journey. The composure of the doomed ones was all but incredible.

[327]

In the midst of these heart-stricken people, Mr. Draper held a 'general prayer-meeting', and in the intervals of prayer earnestly besought the people to come to Christ for salvation. Many brought their Bibles, and, crouching down, read and searched them with eagerness. Captain Martin, himself a God-fearing man, would occasionally join the praying ones for a few minutes; but his duty kept him to the deck.

Thursday, the 10th, dawned; but it brought no ray of hope to the perishing ones. Hope there had been none before; but now the captain, 'in answer to a universal appeal', calmly told them that all hope was over. There was no wild outburst of grief at this confirmation of their worst fears; but amid the solemn silence which reigned, – silence the more solemn and impressive because of the rage and fury of the tempest around, – Mr. Draper stood up, the tears streaming down his face, but with a firm clear voice, said: 'The captain tells us there is no hope; that we must all perish. But I tell you there is hope, hope for *all*. Although we must all die, and shall never again see land, *we may all make the port of heaven*.' We know not all the words of warning and entreaty which our brother would use during those last four hours, but the testimony of the survivors is unanimous, that from the prayer-meeting at midnight till the boat left, he was incessant in his prayers, warnings, and invitations. Of the former it is remembered that he often exclaimed: 'O God! may those that are not converted be converted now; hundreds of them!' That among his last-heard words were: 'In a few moments we must all appear before our Great Judge. Let us prepare to meet Him.'

A few minutes before the ship went down, one who was saved saw Mr. Draper, 'his eyes filled with tears, which streamed down his face, and heard him with the *clear distinct voice* of a man *calm and collected*, exhorting all to come to Christ'.

The last man who left the ship was asked, 'What was the last you heard or saw them doing on board?' His reply was: 'The last I heard was this: they were singing,

Rock of ages cleft for me.'

And so he died like a real Methodist preacher; nay, like a true Christian man, for Christianity is above Methodism; illustrating the words of the Methodist hymn which he loved so well, and sung so often with so much feeling:

[328]

How Christians Die

Happy if with my latest breath,
  I may but gasp His name;
Preach Him to all, and cry in death,
  Behold, behold the Lamb.

19

SOME LESSONS FOR TODAY

Australian Trees

Some Lessons for Today

A park which one may visit today in North Parramatta gives scarcely any suggestion of what it once was. A few headstones, including one which marked the grave of James Watsford, now removed to a corner, are the only reminders that this is the resting place of large numbers of Christians. As far as its present appearance is concerned, the old Methodist graveyard has been reclaimed for other purposes and is no more.

Until recent days a plaque on a monument at Mount York, on the western side of the Blue Mountains, used to record that it marked the original road first used by James Watsford's coaches to Bathurst in 1832. Watsford's success over that hazardous track earned the inscription, 'Not of an age but for ever'. Today vandals have ripped and removed the bronze plaque from this monument and left no message for posterity.

There are other means, besides bulldozing and vandalism, with which to obliterate history. One is simply for books and records to be laid aside for so long that their very existence is forgotten. In these pages we have given a selection from a considerable number of older books of which scarcely one is in print at the time of writing. The Christian past of Australia has largely vanished out of sight. Not surprisingly, many have drawn the conclusion that the country has no Christian history of which it is worth speaking. Reflecting upon this attitude, as it currently exists in University studies, J. D. Bollen has written:

What is most intellectually dismaying within the profession is the general unthinking assumption that Australian history is perfectly understandable without reference to religion which is seen . . . as something separate from and marginal to Australian history's real concerns . . .[1]

[1] Australian Religious History, *The Journal of Religious History*, vol. 11, no. 1, 1980, p. 28.

In other words, the popular assumption is that Christianity has never played any larger role in the life of the nation than it does today. And what is still more significant is that this attitude to Australian Christian history is prevalent in the Australian churches themselves. Few church members would have any idea how to answer the question, 'What does Australia owe to Christianity?' That it was Christians who established schools and an honest press, Christians who led the way in fighting monopolies and in securing individual rights and representation, Christians who constituted a unity out of which a nation could grow – all these and similar facts are virtually erased from 'the history of Australia' presented by a modern secularism. Such has been the loss of Christian leadership in the print media that the churches are not even aware of the existence of the literature which would tell a different story. With little or no access to older books and papers which would be both an inspiration and a standard for self-critical reflection, Christians have instead been led to believe that a re-examination of the past can be no aid to the recovery of Christianity today. Many have been conditioned to think that whatever Australia's religious past, it can only stand for 'traditionalism' and it is at the door of traditionalism that so much of the blame for contemporary Christian failure is laid. The new, not the old, is supposed to be the answer to present needs.

If there is one thing, however, which the Bible makes clear it is that generally the church does not move smoothly forward and upward from one generation to the next. There is no such thing as natural progress in spiritual things. New generations may witness sad decline in the cause of God. The church may make such a detour from the right way – as Israel in the wilderness – that the voice of faithful teachers has to summon her to 'ask for the old paths, where is the good way' (Jer. 6:16). This is not to say that any age of church history is to be treated as normative, but the Bible does hold up particular periods as times when there was marked spiritual blessing, and it leads us to believe that the *principles* to which the church was more largely faithful in those periods have abiding importance.[1] The rediscovery of history can, therefore, be of immense importance. The way *forward* for a declining church is to 'Remember therefore from whence thou art fallen' (Rev. 2:5).

[1] *e.g.*, Psalm 44:1; Jeremiah 2:1–3; Hosea 13:1.

Some Lessons for Today

The principles which the Bible so clearly connects with spiritual prosperity have appeared repeatedly in the preceding pages, and they show that when the priorities of the church are the priorities of the New Testament her witness will not be unheeded by the world. The apostolic first principle remains the same: it is that Scripture gives us a clear and definite message with respect to man's need and to the nature of the salvation which is in Jesus Christ (1 Cor. 15:3–4). The church exists to proclaim a message which has been 'delivered' to her. Those who built the church in Australia had no doubt about this fact. They could say with Paul, 'I delivered unto you first of all that which I also received, how that Christ died for our sins according to the scriptures . . .'. Faced with opposition from without, and differing sometimes among themselves in their understanding of certain parts of Scripture, these men (and the no less heroic women who supported them) were one in believing that man is by nature lost, that he is under the just condemnation of God, and yet that he may be the receiver of new and eternal life through faith in Christ crucified. Anglican, Methodist, Presbyterian, Baptist and others were united in this first principle. All believed that man had to be converted and that he must hear and believe the truth in order to be saved. In other words, they regarded the gospel as a divine message of stupendous consequence and they viewed whatever hardships they might endure in making it known as trivial compared with the joy and peace which it gave to them and which it offered to all. The language of the Methodist missionaries, Hurst and Tuckfield, wandering in the bush of Victoria in 1839, without food or fire, is representative of that whole outlook:

Our assurance of the Divine favour was clear, and our hope of heaven bright and exhilarating. We did not regret having left friends and home to preach among the Gentiles the unsearchable riches of Christ, and were content to go at once to our reward in glory, if such should be the will of our heavenly Father.[1]

In the later nineteenth century this spirit began to decline in the churches, and the decline was contemporary with the passing of emphasis upon this first principle. Doubt gained entrance into the churches over whether there are any *definite truths* which have been

[1]Robert Young, *The Southern World*, p. 401.

[335]

received from God and which sinners must believe in order to be saved. What an earlier generation would have condemned as error now came to be tolerated alongside truth. But according to the New Testament, error is a cancer which destroys spiritual life (2 Tim. 2:17). Hitherto Australian Christian life had been characterized by definite commitment to Scripture as the Word of God. Disbelief in the Bible was seen as the equivalent to disobedience to God himself. William Cowper, first chaplain at St. Phillip's, Sydney, recorded his shock in May, 1831, at the teaching of a newcomer to the diocese: 'A young chaplain, lately arrived, preached that St. Paul's Epistles do not apply to us Christians, etc., that virtue is our only guide to heaven.' Such preaching, Cowper asserted, was not that of a man 'inwardly moved by the Holy Ghost'.[1] Henry Bobart was Marsden's successor at St. John's, Parramatta, and he preached the same message as the first generation. His gravestone today bears a text which summarizes the emphasis which he had received, 'Hold fast the form of sound words, which thou hast heard of me, in faith and love which is in Christ Jesus' (2 Tim. 1:13). Against his wife's name on the same stone are the words, 'She died in Faith'.

By the late nineteenth and the early twentieth century a great change was taking place with regard to the necessity of faith in the 'sound words' of Scripture. Australia imported from Europe the new 'understanding' of Scripture – the teaching which said that the Bible could only partially be a rule of faith, for in some parts, at least, it was fallible and erroneous. Yet this teaching, it was asserted, was no cause for alarm in the churches because 'experience of the living Christ is not dependent upon a book'.[2] And it was further promised that if the churches went forward in partnership with 'modern scholarship' they would achieve far greater credibility and influence in the world than they had ever possessed before. An older generation, some of whom have been quoted in these pages, viewed this claim with alarm. They saw that

---

[1] *Autobiography and Reminiscences*, W. MacQuarie Cowper, p. 80.

[2] The opinion that man must be the judge of Scripture is, of course, a denial of the biblical teaching on the darkness and corruption of the mind of fallen man. Confidence in human reason is impossible when sin is taken seriously. If man could do what the Higher Criticism claimed then it was not *salvation* which he needed from Christ but only a good ethical example. The plausible idea of not a book but 'the living Christ' meant, in truth, a denial of the gospel.

it could do nothing but introduce a new age of unbelief. John Watsford, for example, speaking of things 'that will, if allowed to continue and grow, one day rob us of our power and glory as a Church', wrote near the end of his life:

Our theology, so scriptural and clear, we have firmly held for many years. Whatever agitation there has been at any time in our Church, it has not been about our creed . . . For years scarcely a whisper was heard of any weakness here. From first to last our ministers were believed to be sound in faith. But is it so to-day? I fear not. the question we ask every year of every minister is, 'Does he believe and preach our doctrines?'. It is not enough that he preach them: he must believe them . . .[1]

Among the biblical doctrines now quietly being set on one side Watsford instanced the eternal punishment of the wicked. He did not live to see the full consequences of what he had feared. Dr. W. G. Torr (who studied theology in Oxford and was a close friend of the liberal Arthur S. Peake) became a leading Methodist teacher in Australia. It was he who pressed for the adoption of Peake's book, *A Commentary on the Bible*, 1919, as a text for all probationers preparing for the ministry. The issue was debated at the General Conference of Australian Methodism in 1920 and again in 1923. In the latter year Peake's critical work was adopted, and in a letter to Peake the Conference described its decision as 'a vote for truth and thousands will thank God'. Dr. W. H. Fitchett of Melbourne was one of the few who mourned. For him the decision meant 'a tattered Bible and a mutilated Christ'.[2]

What happened in Methodism was being paralleled in all the main Protestant denominations. Resistance to the new 'scholarship' from Europe was fragmentary and no denomination took a stand against it for long. Significantly in this connection, Australia had never known a major theological controversy (such as had occurred in Europe at the time of the Reformation) and the catholicity which shunned contention among brethren in the earlier period of Australian Christian history now turned into a willingness to live with all 'opinions'. In 1852 John West (a Congregational minister) wrote of 'the liberality of Australians' as something observed 'by every stranger', and he noted that it was a

[1]*Glorious Gospel Triumphs*, p. 322.
[2]*This Side of Heaven*, Arnold Hunt, p. 264.

liberality impatient with 'religious antipathies'. 'Bigotry assumes the character of ill temper and puffing'.[1] These words, however, were written at a time when no one dreamed of *churches* denying fundamentals of the faith. But the commendable catholicity of one generation became a lukewarmness over truth in the next.

Perhaps it was among the Presbyterians, who in early years were ready to divide their churches rather than to sacrifice any truth, that the Higher Criticism would have seemed least likely to succeed. Certainly in the 1870's there were warnings enough against it. Yet within fifty years of that date the Australian Presbyterian Church had also largely abandoned its first principles. Her best-known Professor of Theology, Samuel Angus, an Ulster Scot, who taught in Sydney from 1915 to 1943, denied the foundations upon which all the Presbyterian churches had been built. 'Jesus,' he said, 'had not the slightest interest in what men were to believe, and he never required any intellectual creed.' The message of the cross – Christ suffering judgment in the sinner's place – he declared to be 'unethical'. Christ's death was a sacrifice but not a sacrifice for sin. Angus preached the dawning of a new age of Christian charity and ecumenicity: 'I would like,' he declared, 'to unite all orthodox and heretics, traditionalists and modernists in His blessed service.'[2] When 'The Angus Case' was debated repeatedly in the General Assembly in the early 1930's it ended in a vote for 'toleration' and in a Judicial Commission which called the Church to work and pray 'for unity'.

Such was the abandonment of first principles and the respectability of unbelief in the Church. By this time, Angus' principles were the standard outlook in almost all theological training in Australia[3] and the inevitable result was that the churches lost any

[1]*The History of Tasmania*, pp. 528–29.

[2]'Dr. Angus and Modern Theology', W. R. McEwen in *Our Banner*, June 15, 1933. The antipathy of Angus to the theology of his own denomination was especially marked. He could say, 'We Presbyterians know the love of God not through our confessional knowledge, but in spite of it' (*Truth and Tradition*, 1934, p. 51). Angus proposed 'Christian' morality in the place of Christian supernaturalism but it was not the morality of the Bible. Enoch Powell has recently written: 'Sammy Angus, the theologian, was another mentor. It was in Sydney in his company I made the discovery that, if sufficiently inebriated, I could carry on any conversation I wished in Greek iambic verses' (*Sydney Morning Herald*, July 11, 1987, p. 44).

[3]Moore College, in the Diocese of Sydney, was the notable exception.

sense of an authoritative message which could be preached with certainty. The Methodist Church became one of the saddest examples. Once so strong in her convictions, at her General Conference of 1972 she could not even make a pronouncement on homosexuality and lesbianism apart from saying that it was up to the individual Christian to decide 'whether or not such relationships are worthy for him or her in the light of Christian teaching'. One of her ministers, Dr. Arnold Hunt, comments that 'rigidity had given way to flexibility, and this was why the church, officially at least, could not adopt a socially pragmatic stance on the questions of abortion and homosexuality'.[1]

The fact is that by the second half of the twentieth century the churches were preoccupied with attempting to arrest their declining influence and fearful of putting themselves out of sympathy with the current public opinion. Further, the loss of distinctive doctrinal convictions, instead of being regarded as a loss, now became an argument for 'Christian unity'. In the face of dwindling congregations a merger of the churches seemed a sure way to recover some numerical strength. 'Another factor facilitating a favourable attitude to union among Methodists,' writes Hunt, 'was the decline of the belief in a distinctive Methodist mission and a distinctive Methodist message . . . The ethos of the Methodist Church had changed. Methodist ministers had always done a course in Methodist doctrine, or "Methodist Emphases", but this had become an increasingly minor element in their theological education.' The residual belief that was left, writes the same author, was 'very much the same' as among the Congregationalists and the Presbyterians. Common convictions over biblical truth were not the driving force behind the ecumenical Uniting Church formed out of this amalgam in 1977. 'Union took place in a time of growing indifference, if not hostility, to Christianity in an increasingly secular society. There was, as a result, an inchoate, undeveloped feeling – often not clearly articulated – that union would result in church growth.'[2]

It is hard to think of any attitude further removed from the first principle of all the pioneer churches of this land.

We must turn to a second principle which has also been equally evident in the preceding pages. The first Australian Christians did

[1] *This Side of Heaven*, p. 399.
[2] *Ibid.*, p. 426.

not stop at asserting the necessity of biblical truth. They believed, as a second principle, that for the Christian faith to win sway in the world it had to be accompanied by supernatural power – power exhibited both in the delivery of the message and in the life of the Church. With regard to the source of this power, they held no special theories and they advanced no particular 'methods' by which it might be secured. It is, indeed, demonstrable that when the churches became 'method-orientated' in their concern for success – as happened towards the end of the last century – the era of their greatest spiritual usefulness was already passed. With the book of 'The Acts of the Apostles' as their model, the earlier generation believed that power is the consequence of real communion with God. And, more particularly, they believed that God may give an abundant anointing of the Holy Spirit so that in an observable way Christians are 'filled with the Holy Ghost'. It was in this sense that they understood the meaning of revival. God is pleased at times, they held, to give such an enduement of His Spirit to many Christians at once that the effect on Christian life and testimony again resembles the effect seen in apostolic times. In the words of Jonathan Edwards:

From the fall of man, to our day, the work of redemption in its effect has mainly been carried on by remarkable communications of the Spirit of God. Though there be a more constant influence of the Spirit attending his ordinances, yet the way in which the greatest things have been done has been by remarkable effusions, at special seasons of mercy.[1]

Today there is a general absence of interest in the whole subject of revival and part of the reason is that the very word has lost its once clearly-understood meaning. When modern writers on Christianity comment on revivals, as they find reference to them in history, they generally interpret them as times of religious fervour and excitement, induced perhaps by an evangelistic campaign or by the volatile temperament of a particular ethnic group.[2] If such

[1]*The Works of Jonathan Edwards*, Banner of Truth Trust, vol. 1, 1974, p. 539. For the same emphasis see John Wesley's sermon 'Scriptural Christianity', on Acts 4:31. Calvinists and Arminians were both agreed in this view of revival and Australian Methodists made frequent use of Edwards' writings. For the best contemporary exposition of the subject see D. M. Lloyd-Jones' *Revival*, 1986.

[2]Cornishmen have been singled out in Australia in connection with revivals

is 'revival', they argue, then it cannot be a primary need for the church today because Christianity is not 'emotionalism'.

The churches themselves have been partly responsible for this modern change of view with respect to revival. To call preachers 'revivalists', and to give the impression that revivals are events which can be arranged, as too many have done, is to direct attention *away* from the biblical teaching. Pentecost was not 'arranged'. It was not an ephemeral period of high emotion. It was not an evangelistic campaign. Rather it was an abundant giving of the Holy Spirit, imparting vigour, boldness and authority to the church and bringing conviction and conversion to the world. Revivals of this kind are turning-points in history; they show themselves in their moral effects and in the changed standards which become established in whole communities. True revivals make God himself a conscious reality so that again it may be said, 'fear came upon every soul' (Acts 2:43).

The earlier generation of Australian Christians understood this, in part, because they lived much nearer than we do to an era of revivals. From the third decade of the eighteenth century, and for the hundred years following, many parts of the British Isles saw times when the Spirit of God was manifestly at work. Australia's first preachers came from this background as William MacQuarie Cowper says in the opening words of his *Autobiography and Reminiscences*:

It is an interesting fact, that the planting of Christianity in Australia was one of the fruits of that Evangelical revival which God vouchsafed to the Church of England in the eighteenth century. The first four Chaplains sent from England to minister in this Colony were

---

but, as one Cornish writer says: 'I am quite satisfied that neither Cornish nor any other people could produce revivals without the power of the Spirit, for they would never be without them if they could raise them at pleasure. But, as a fact, it is well known that revivals begin and continue for a time, and that they cease as mysteriously as they begin' (W. Haslam, *From Death into Life: Or, Twenty Years of My Ministry*, 1894, pp. 70–71). True revivals know no racial barriers and, last century, the same power was seen in the Pacific as in Australia. What happened in Tonga, for instance, in 1834, is spoken of as 'unquestionably one of the most extensive revivals of religion since Pentecost' (*The Pioneer Missionary Life of Nathaniel Turner*, J. G. Turner, 1872, p. 289).

children of that revival; men firmly rooted in its principles, animated by its spirit, and living witnesses in their lives to the power of those truths by which it was distinguished.

Cowper is referring, of course, to Johnson, Marsden, Cartwright and his own father, but the same fact is noteworthy of many others for it was not only the Church of England that had been stirred since the days of the Wesleys and Whitefield. All the pioneer churches in Australia, along with the parallel missions in the South Pacific, were, in a sense, the consequence of revival in the northern hemisphere. It is true that some of the clergy and ministers who arrived on these shores – such persons as the 'young chaplain' mentioned by Cowper in 1831 – had no sympathy with this outlook, but these men achieved virtually nothing. They built no congregations. They compromised with a worldly society, finding themselves helpless to work for its transformation. The evangelical Christians who did take on the combat involved in establishing the gospel in a penal colony, and in the cannibal islands of the South Seas, were all men who *believed* in the Holy Spirit, and no measure of opposition, no period of delay, could move them from the fundamental conviction that He could change the moral desert to which they had been brought.

This second principle concerning the need for a living, powerful Christianity had vast implications as the preceding pages reveal.

It led to an insistence upon the place of prayer in the life of the church. At almost every point in the early records – whether at 'the Rocks' in the days of Leigh, in the drawing room of Frederic and Jane Barker, in the pioneer Presbyterian churches of the Hunter and Shoalhaven Rivers, or in the Methodist Chapel at Parramatta in the youth of James Watsford – prayer meetings are the ever-recurring subject. And if the Methodists saw the most notable success in terms of the numbers of conversions, it is noteworthy how determined they were to allow nothing to take the place of prayer. The diary of Ralph Mansfield, written in Tasmania ('the general receptacle for the worst characters in the world') in 1824, is typical in the way it records a decision following a 'serious conversation on the means of promoting a revival of the work of God'. It reads: 'We solemnly engage to give

ourselves afresh to God . . . We resolve to make special intercession with God for the outpouring of His Holy Spirit on
ourselves. . . .'[1]

Numerous examples of the results of such praying have already
been recorded in these pages. As one final instance of the same
thing, we would mention a revival in the Bathurst Circuit of New
South Wales early in 1858. It began following a decision to appoint
a day 'for special fasting and prayer, especially for the conversion
of the young'. When that day came, writes Joseph Oram:

Public Prayer Meetings were held during the day in most of the places
in the Circuit, which were well attended by the Members of the
Church and by others, and all seemed to come impressed with the
solemnity and importance of the occasion. At Bathurst, the School
Room at 8 o'clock in the Morning and at 1 o'clock in the Afternoon
was filled, and in the Evening it was crowded; and I shall not soon
forget the sense of the Divine presence and holy awe which evidently
prevailed in the minds of all present, the influence of the Holy Spirit
seemed to descend, and distil upon the people like 'the small rain
upon the tender herb'. A gracious power was then obtained from
heaven, which in a short time resulted in the addition of nearly a
hundred persons to the Church.[2]

It was not without reason that the next year a writer, looking
back on the lessons of Methodist history in Australia, could say:
'Our church started into being and was fostered and enlarged in
the midst of amazing difficulties. Fasting and prayer were
constantly used by the early Methodists and followed by outpourings of the Holy Spirit.'[3]

At the same time it would be a great mistake to suppose that
these men and women saw prayer simply as a means to obtain
blessing from God. On the contrary, prayer itself is God-given. A
true exercise of heart in prayer is the work of the Spirit of God
and, therefore, when the ageing representatives of the older
outlook saw a growing neglect of prayer it was to them a sure sign
of far-reaching spiritual change in the churches. John Watsford
wrote:

[1]*A Chronicle of Methodism in Van Diemen's Land*, R. D. Pretyman, 1970,
p. 52.
[2]*The Christian Advocate and Wesleyan Record*, vol. 1, 1858–59, p. 4.
[3]*Ibid.*, Dec. 21, 1858.

The desire to-day seems to be for less prayer and exposition of the word of God, and for more amusement, more entertainments in the church. Look at our Monday evening prayer meetings, and our week evening services! In most places very few attend; in some these meetings have had to be given up altogether. Let it be announced that an entertainment will be given, and people will flock to it; but to the call to prayer there will be little or no response. If it be true that the Monday evening prayer-meeting is the barometer of the Church's piety, then we need to be humbled and alarmed.[1]

William George Taylor outlived Watsford and spoke still more strongly:

I have often ventured the remark, which I again repeat, that let the class and the prayer-meeting die out of this Central Methodist Mission, as, unfortunately, they have died out of not a few of our churches, and you may substitute what else in all this wide world you please, 'Ichabod' will soon be found written upon its doorposts. We may go on feeding the hungry, caring for the outcast; we may educate our young men, and seek to interest our young maidens; we may multiply our guilds and bands; we may attract crowds by startling preaching, and give them the very best of music; we may do all this, and more – and yet, if the Holy Spirit of God is not honoured, it will all amount to little more than 'sounding brass or a clanging cymbal'.[2]

These men thus saw that a very great deal is involved in the preservation of vital Christianity. Essential as prayer is, it alone is not the answer for the Holy Spirit himself is needed, and if He is not honoured and His presence prized all else will fail. This leads back to the first principle: if the church is untrue to the Bible, if she no longer declares with Christ, 'thy word is truth' (John 17:17), nor takes 'the sword of the Spirit which is the word of God' (Eph. 6:17), then it is certain that the Spirit of truth will not set His seal upon her falsehood. Hesitation and uncertainty will replace power and light as preachers can no more say, 'I believed, therefore have I spoken' (Psa. 116:10). But this principle of the church's need of divine aid for all effective testimony also involves practical Christian holiness. The Holy Spirit is grieved and quenched by all forms of disobedience. In the midst of self-denial and the persecution of a hostile world, the early church could say, 'We are

[1]*Glorious Gospel Triumphs*, p. 321.
[2]*The Life-story of an Australian Evangelist*, p. 143.

his witnesses . . . and so is also the Holy Ghost, whom God hath given to them that obey him' (Acts 5:32).

The Christians from whose writings we have drawn in this book well understood the reason why the New Testament places more emphasis upon the church's character and walk than upon her outreach into society. They knew that real usefulness in the world is the *consequence* of an inner life and that only when her life is right will the church fulfill her calling. In a sense, they saw that the church is most evangelistic when she is least concerned about impressing the world or with adding to her numbers. The first need is always to be faithful to Christ, and when this motive is uppermost, Christians, far from being anxious to hurry the world into the church, will be concerned, chiefly, that the church faithfully represents Him. In the light of the New Testament teaching, it should not be a surprise that the Methodists, who were so owned of God in evangelism, were also so conspicuous for their demanding standards for church membership. In the words of their 1863 Annual Conference, next to 'the presentation of the sublime and saving doctrines of the gospel', they put 'enforcing that godly discipline by which the efficiency of the Church is conserved'. They knew that only as the church stands apart and enjoys her true life will she see that same life imparted to others. Thus Luke says of the churches of Judea, Galilee and Samaria, that it was *when* they were 'walking in the fear of the Lord and in the comfort of the Holy Ghost' that they 'were multiplied' (Acts 9:31).

To ignore this principle and to abandon church discipline is to make spiritual decline a certainty. Yet, when Watsford and others warned that 'the growing worldliness of the Church is a great hindrance to our success', they were unheard. People had ceased to believe that 'a revival of holiness in the Church means an awakening among the unsaved'.[1] Watsford was not teaching that holiness *produces* revival. But he was affirming that a church unconcerned about holiness of life is blind to her greatest need:

The Churches need the Pentecostal baptism: then we shall have the Pentecost, holy living, simplicity, power, success, and, perhaps,

[1]*Glorious Gospel Triumphs*, p. 321, p. 160.

[345]

persecution. May our day of Pentecost soon fully come on all Australia![1]

In conclusion, it may be said that the lessons of this book refute an assumption which is all too prevalent in the contemporary church, namely, the idea that the cause of the modern decline in Christian influence is to be found in the secular world around us and not in the church herself. The whole priority of attention in the churches for many years upon programmes for outreach and for achieving modernity in worship ('remove old versions of everything to bridge the communication gap with the present age') has been based upon this assumption. But it is false. Let the contemporary church be compared seriously with 'The Acts of the Apostles' and what stands out is not the difference between the first century and the twentieth but the difference between the *church* then and now. An understanding of the supernatural has already been abandoned when we begin to explain the hindrances to Christian success in terms of the problems of our age. The churches of Australia would never have come into existence if Christians had thought in that way two centuries ago. As an older writer says, 'It is one of Satan's deep devices to call off the attention of the church from its own state, to the condition of the world without and around her'.[2]

For the recovery of the church we have to deal with God himself and to plead with Habakkuk, 'O Lord revive thy work in the midst of the years, in the midst of the years make known; in wrath remember mercy'. The testimony of history will help us to do so as it helped that prophet and countless others since his day. All that God has done in grace and power in any age or land He can do again. By painful chastening the churches of this century are being taught what Frederic Barker asserted over a hundred years ago: 'What we want is not so much fresh organization, but new life, the life which the Spirit of God imparts, the life by which a church becomes a light and a power in the world'.[3] When a repentant church turns to God, and pleads with Him to work, another new

---

[1]*Ibid.*, p. 280, see also p. 286 where he argues that such a 'baptism' would meet all the church's need for men and money. 'We have too little of God, and faith in Him, in our money arrangements.'

[2]*Primitive Piety Revived*, H. C. Fish, 1855, p. 93 (reprinted 1987).

[3]*Hewn From the Rock*, Marcus Loane, p. 89.

era will be at hand. Peter Dodds McCormick, a Presbyterian author and composer, taught Australia to sing, 'Advance Australia Fair'. For those words to be fulfilled we need first the words of another Australian Christian and Presbyterian, Ernest Northcroft Merrington, who wrote:

> God of Eternity, Lord of the Ages,
> Father and Spirit and Saviour of men!
> Thine is the glory of time's numbered pages;
> Thine is the power to revive us again.
>
> Pardon our sinfulness, God of all pity,
> Call to remembrance Thy mercies of old;
> Strengthen Thy Church to abide as a city
> Set on a hill for a light to Thy fold.
>
> Head of the Church on earth, risen, ascended!
> Thine is the honour that dwells in this place:
> As Thou hast blessed us through years that have ended,
> Still lift upon us the light of Thy face.[1]

[1] *The Church Hymnary*, Revised Edition, 1927, hymn 642.

GENERAL INDEX

(Followed by an index of authors and titles)

AUTHOR AND TITLE INDEX

[355]

Lloyd-Jones, D. M., *Revival*, 1986: 340
Lloyd-Jones, D. M., *Preaching and Preachers*, 1971: 136
Loane, Marcus, *Hewn From The Rock*, 1976: 218, 346
Loane, Marcus, *A Centenary History of Moore College*, 1955: 246
McCheyne, R. M., *Memoir and Remains*, 1844: 230
MacDonald, Aeneas, *One Hundred Years of Presbyterianism in Victoria*, 1937:
    160
McEwen, W. R., *Our Banner*, 'Dr. Angus and Modern Theology', 1933: 338
Macintosh, Neil K., *Richard Johnson, Chaplain to the Colony of New South
    Wales*, 1978: 3
Mackaness, George, *The Life of Vice-Admiral William Bligh*, 1951: 35
Mackaness, George, *Some Letters of Rev. Richard Johnson*, 1954: 9
Mackray, Archibald N., *Revivals of Religion*, Their Place and Power in the
    Christian Church, 1871: 267
McPheat, W. Scott, *John Flynn, Apostle to the Inland*, 1963: 179
Manley, K. R. and Petras, M., *The First Australian Baptists*, 1981: 115
Marsden, J. B., *Memoirs of the Life and Labours of the Rev. Samuel Marsden*,
    c.1858: 33
Palamountain, W. J., A. R. Edgar: *A Methodist Greatheart*, 1933: 311
Peake, Arthur S., *A Commentary on the Bible*, 1919: 337
Pretyman, R. D., *A Chronicle of Methodism in Van Diemen's Land*, 1970: 343
Prior, A. C., *Some Fell on Good Ground*, A history of the beginnings and
    development of the Baptist Church in New South Wales, 1831–1965: 115
Ramsden, Eric, *Marsden and the Missions, Prelude to Waitangi*, 1936: 37
Reeson, Margaret, *Currency Lass*, 1985: 51
Reid, George R. S., *The History of Ebenezer*, booklet, seventh edition 1977:
    119
Roe, Michael, *Quest for Authority in Eastern Australia*, 1835–1851: 116
Ross, C. Stuart, *Colonization and Church Work in Victoria*, 1891: 135, 160
Slessor, Kenneth, *Selected Poems*, 1977: 32
Smeaton, George, *The Doctrine of the Holy Spirit* (1882), 1958: 313
Smith, F. B., *Religion and Free Thought in Melbourne, 1870–1890*, 1960:
    xiii
Strachan, Alexander, *Remarkable Incidents in the Life of the Rev. Samuel
    Leigh, Missionary to the Settlers and Savages of Australia and New Zealand*,
    2nd edition, 1855: 52
Symons, John C., *Life of Daniel J. Draper*, 1870: 136, 291, 322
Taylor, William, *The Life Story of an Australian Evangelist*, 1920: 292, 344
Taylor, William George, *Pathfinders of the Great South Land*, 1927(?): xiv, xv
The Christian Advocate and Wesleyan Record, 1858–59: 86, 273ff., 291, 343
The Presbyterian, 1872: 267ff.
Turner, J. G., *The Pioneer Missionary: Life of the Rev. Nathaniel Turner*, 1872:
    142–43, 341
Watsford, John, *Glorious Gospel Triumphs, As Seen in my Life and Work*, 1900:
    141ff. 337, 344, 345, 346
West, John, *The History of Tasmania*, 1852: vi, 131, 338
Wilkin, F. J., *Baptists in Victoria, Our First Century*, 1939: 134
Willoughby, Howard, *Australian Pictures*, 1886: 283